Endorsements

"*The Good Doctor Is Naked* is a deeply moving account of someone coming to terms with a painful and burdensome past. It will be a help to many who have found it difficult to forgive themselves and who carry a debilitating burden."

—Archbishop Desmond Tutu, religious leader and Nobel laureate

"You write in your own true voice, and your insights into the problem of the dysfunctional family with its closely kept secrets I should think would prove helpful to many people. You have told your story honestly, convincingly, and skillfully."

—Frederick Buechner, teacher, clergyman, and novelist

"Bob Barnes is that rare physician who combines the best of science and religion, head and heart. The touching stories of this book, baring life and death, body and soul, bestow profound consolation."

—Neil J. Elgee, M.D., Clinical Professor Emeritus, University of Washington School of Medicine

"Barnes's writing is deeply personal, yet it speaks more widely to the psychological impact of the Depression. *The Good Doctor Is Naked* bears the unique force of memoir and autobiography—writing that can be transformative for both author and reader."

—Prof. Richard Dunn, Chair, Department of English, University of Washington

The Good Doctor Is Naked

The Good Doctor Is Naked

◆

Finding the Human Beneath My Mask

Robert Hardy Barnes, MD

iUniverse, Inc.
New York Lincoln Shanghai

The Good Doctor Is Naked
Finding the Human Beneath My Mask

iUniverse, Inc.

For information address:
iUniverse, Inc.
2021 Pine Lake Road, Suite 100
Lincoln, NE 68512
www.iuniverse.com

ISBN: 0-595-31575-5

Printed in the United States of America

To June, my wife. She saved my life. Without her, there would be no book.

To David Paul, Ph.D., my dear friend, writing coach, and editor.

To Delmas Luedke, Director, Clinical Pastoral Education, Swedish Hospital, Seattle. He took my hand and walked with me.

To my daughters Julie, Debbie, and Tucker, and their husbands, Bob and Buster. I've learned so much from them.

To my grandchildren, Kerry, Courtney, Sara, and Andrew, who carry our hopes forward.

To Robert Barnes Link, M.D., my nephew, whom I love.

Contents

Acknowledgments

I gratefully acknowledge the help, support, and comfort of the following individuals and organizations:

Richard Hugo House in Seattle and, especially, its Director, Frances McCue, always my advocate

Henriette Anne Klauser, Ph.D., author, who stimulated both my right and left brain

Lois Fein, teacher, who never ceased to inspire me

Barbara Huston, who made my day when she told me she found God in six chapters of this book

Molly Purrington of the English Department, University of Washington, an inspiring friend

Rosemary T. VanArsdel, Ph.D., Distinguished Professor of English, Emerita, University of Puget Sound, who, as an editor and dear friend, urged me on

Professor Richard Dunn, chair of the University of Washington's English Department, whose enthusiasm for my work is gratifying

Edward K. Rynearson, M.D., psychiatrist and founder of the Support Project for Unnatural Dying, my friend

The Rev. Dr. Herbert Anderson, the loving priest who heals

King County Medical Society, Seattle, who provided me with a wonderful writing space

St. Mark's Cathedral, Seattle, the setting for a number of my stories

Tom Hart, Ph.D., S.J., Jesuit priest and friend, who has me figured out

Candace Jorgensen, for her skilled work in file preparation

Introduction

In my dream, the other person's face is covered by a mask. I cannot stop myself from reaching out to peel it off. My hand thrusts forward and my fingers dig into it just in front of the ears. The mask is a brilliant sky-blue and thin like latex, and it resists my pulling. I tug and tug, but the mask only grows thicker and turns blood red. I pull with all my might, and the mask swells until it fills the entire space we occupy, this unknown person and I. On the floor beside me is a hammer. I pick it up and strike the mask, but the mask grows even larger and steam pours out of its nostrils. I strike it again and again, harder each time, but it has an unearthly strength and does not break. It engulfs me, I am suffocating, I am dying. There is a mirror to my right, on a stand, and in the glass, my own face, covered by a blood-red mask. Two frightened strangers, separated by our masks.

We all wear masks. We all wear costumes. Our costumes tell who we mean to be, but not necessarily who we are. I, for example, wore the white coat of a doctor for decades. A great many people knew me only in the role of the doctor, the authority figure, and did not realize that beneath the white coat breathed an ordinary man who had weaknesses and vulnerabilities just like many of his patients.

This book is my personal story about growing up with a secret, hiding my core identity behind the mask of a successful career, and struggling through depression. But its message is not only about me. It is about how to recognize the metaphorical costumes and masks that we are all tempted to hide behind. It is about understanding that we can be crippled emotionally if we allow our fears and insecurities to lead us on a false journey, forever seeking something that will not fulfill us. It is about facing ourselves in that frightening mirror, and then telling our story to others, as a way of opening up our full potential for finding peace in our lives.

PART I
The Clothing of Childhood

1

The Little Boy in the Blue Suit

The day my father shot himself, the school bell rang at 3:00 p.m. as it always did, and there was a mad rush of children down the hall and out the door. On the playground, I jumped hopscotch on chalked squares, then crossed the street to the little store, where I bought three spearmint gumdrops. I ate one and put the other two in my pocket.

It was a clear, crisp February day in Richmond, Virginia. The sun shone with winter paleness, and the maple trees lining the streets had no leaves. I was ten years old and I walked the five blocks home by myself past a grocery store, a pharmacy that smelled like iodine, and a beauty parlor. I crossed Stewart Avenue, Park Avenue, and Monument Avenue. When I turned the corner into Grace Street, I saw cars parked along the block, many more than usual. Across the street, four houses down, the shades were drawn in the bedroom window above our porch.

I climbed the front steps, pushed the door open, and yelled, "Mom!" My mother's voice, from upstairs, didn't sound the way it usually did. "Is that you, Bobby?"

I bounded upstairs and into my parents' bedroom, where my mother was lying on a chaise longue, in a pink bathrobe with a blanket over her legs. She was crying, and a woman I didn't know was with her. I had never seen my mother lying on a chaise longue crying with a stranger in the house in the middle of the afternoon, and I felt scared.

I remember vividly how the room looked at that moment, as the stranger raised the shades and opened one window a crack. The sun shone in, and the sheer curtains blew out over the radiator. There was another radiator under a second window behind the chaise where Mother lay. The hardwood floor was exposed, except for a round, pink throw rug in the middle of the room. My parents' double bed, a mahogany wood four-poster, was made up with a white, tufted bedspread. At the end of the bed was a white wicker chair with a flowered pillow on the seat. Across from the window was a chiffonier where my dad kept his socks, handkerchiefs, underwear, and cufflinks. He kept his suits and shoes in a hall closet just outside the bedroom door.

Mother held her arms out and motioned me to come over. She hugged me and said, "Your father is very sick. He is in the hospital. We don't know what is the matter yet. You can go eat and play."

That sounded like a good idea. I left my mother's arms and walked down the hall to my room. I changed clothes, got out my roller skates, and ran down the stairs. Outside, I tightened one skate wheel with a key and set off down the walk. Soon I was joined by Tito and Robert, who lived across the street. Before long, several other boys joined us and we played an exuberant game of street hockey. We had a great time, skating and yelling and smacking the puck with the stick. Whatever was wrong back home, I put it out of my mind.

The next thing I remember was being down on my knees back in the house with Sally Moore, my sister, who was eighteen months older and shared my bedroom. We had our ear up against the door that connected our room with our parents' bedroom, where Mother was talking with Uncle Joe and Sister, my aunt (we called her that because she was my mother's sister). They had come in from North Carolina. Mother was crying and blowing her nose and breathing heavily. We could not hear exactly what they were saying. We were afraid they would find us eavesdropping.

Mother sent me to stay for a day or two with neighbors who lived several blocks away. She sent Sally Moore to another neighbor. I knew deep down something terrible was going on. I could tell because no one talked about my dad and everyone tried to act like everything was normal.

When I got back home, Mother was lying on the chaise longue again, still weeping, her face covered with Pond's cold cream. (Ever since, I have hated the smell of Pond's cold cream.) She looked terrible—like a witch, I thought. I don't know where my sister was, but Mother had me sit down on the end of the chaise and told me Dad was dead. I cannot remember her exact words. I felt as though I was in a dark passageway, unsure of who was with me or what exactly was happening around me. Nobody I knew had ever died, and it never occurred to me that my father, or anyone else, would kill himself.

The funeral was held in the parlor of our house. I had on my best clothes—blue short pants, blue jacket, dark stockings up to my knees, white shirt, and a narrow red bow tie. I slid down the banister to the hallway where family, neighbors, and friends were gathered in their dark blue suits and black dresses and veils. A tall man scolded me for sliding down the banister. I didn't know how to behave at a funeral, and I didn't understand adults crying and whispering and acting in strange ways.

Mother was dressed in black, and Dad was lying in a casket on a gurney in front of the fireplace. I was the smallest person there, and the casket seemed way up in the air. I had never seen a casket before, or a dead person. The lid was open at the head, and from my low angle, I could barely see over the edge of the casket. I saw a little bit of Dad's face in profile, his nose and his right eye, which was closed, and the top of his head. His skin was all waxy. This is the eternal image I have of him, an image that never fails to make me feel ten years old, confused, and diminished.

They closed the casket, pushed it out the door, carried it down the front steps, and maneuvered it into the funeral car. My sister and I each held one of Mother's hands as we walked down the steps to the curb, where a black, shiny car waited for us, bigger even than my dad's Pierce Arrow, behind the hearse and in front of a line of other cars. I glanced up and down the street, hoping none of my friends were watching. A uniformed chauffeur held the back door open as the three of us stepped across the running board and got in. I could see tears under Mother's veil. The ride out to the cemetery was uncomfortable, quiet, strange, smothering. None of us made a sound, except that Mother sobbed occasionally and squeezed my hand.

I still wasn't quite sure what all this was about. I didn't know you put a dead person in the ground. I did understand that Dad had gone away, to heaven or somewhere. He sometimes took trips on business, but this time

I had a pretty good sense that he would not be coming home. He was closed up in that box, after all.

We drove very slowly, a long way, across town and over a bridge. Finally, we passed through a stone archway, and I had my first view of the cemetery with its narrow roadways lined by massive oak trees. Tombstones were everywhere across the landscape, and flowers were blooming. Later I learned that this cemetery was the resting place of the President of the Confederacy, along with many other Southern Civil War heroes.

We parked near a hole in the ground with the dirt piled on one side. Car doors opened and people gathered around the hole, no laughter, no chitchat. I certainly wasn't going to open my mouth. I don't remember a minister or anyone in a black cassock; don't remember what words were spoken, if any. I only remember some strong men lowering the casket into the ground and I knew Dad was in it. I could still picture the waxy right side of his face.

Afterward, people came back home with us for coffee and cookies, and at last, they talked. They talked a lot. I still hadn't shed a single tear.

A day or two later, Mother sat down with me up in her bedroom. She told me Dad had killed himself with a pistol, stuck it in his mouth and pulled the trigger. I did not ask her any questions, such as why he did it or whether it hurt. I eventually learned from Sally Moore that Mother had told her on the day Dad died.

Mother told me, "Never tell anyone your dad committed suicide—not your friends at school, not anybody, because they might not understand and they might reject you."

I remember Dad as a well-dressed, dapper gentleman, a businessman. His father was the same. Grandfather wore a cutaway jacket to work, my dad a conservative, well-fitted suit. They both wore vests, along with the high, white, starched collar typical of the time, the kind that fastened to the shirt with a gold stud. Dad had a gold watch chain across his vest.

He was a man of moderate height, with a high forehead, neatly cut hair, and short sideburns. I used to go to the barbershop with him. It felt good being there, and even today I love the smells of a barbershop, shaving cream and after-shave lotion, and I see the image of Dad sitting in the chair with the barber working on his hair and the shoeshine boy polishing his shoes.

Dad drove a light tan Pierce Arrow with a matching canvas top and celluloid windows. The spare tire was mounted on the rear. We used to take Sunday afternoon rides, all of us decked out in our Sunday best. I wore a round leather sailor hat, brown with a little black bow on one side. One time when I was five or six, I sailed my hat out the back of the car into the road. Dad slammed on the brakes and stomped back to fetch the cap as I watched through the rear window. I didn't do that again.

These outings usually led us to my grandparents' home, despite the fact that Mother didn't enjoy Sunday with the in-laws. She and Dad often argued about his parents on the way there. I, however, loved them. Grandfather took me upstairs to his bedroom, where he had a glass jar filled with candy canes. For dinner, there was southern fried chicken and chocolate cake and ice cream. Mother told me not to kiss my grandmother because she'd had tuberculosis when she was younger.

Dad smoked a cigar, and to this day, I love the smell of a good cigar. When I took up golf years later, I smoked a cigar and thought of my dad because that is what he did when playing golf. Sometimes he let me caddy for him. If I were not caddying for him, I would spend the time with Mother and my sister, playing in the club's swimming pool. Afterward, we could get fresh-squeezed orange juice at the club restaurant.

I have a photo of Dad before he got married, in top hat and tails, standing by a tree in a garden. He is handsome, with big brown eyes and lovely smooth skin. My aunt, one of his sisters, told me he was quiet, not aggressive. I mention this because, as President of the Barnes Safe and Vault Company, Dad was the front man, the marketing salesman, and I get the impression he may not have been entirely suited for the job. My aunt quipped that his way of initiating a sales pitch was to approach a bank official and say, "You don't want to buy a safe, do you?"

He traveled a great deal on business, and before he married my mother, he wrote her tender, loving letters in a beautiful handwriting. He addressed her as "My dear girl," and told her in the letter how much he loved her and missed her.

One summer while he was still alive, Mother took some classes at William and Mary College in Williamsburg, Virginia, and Sally Moore and I stayed there with her. We rented two rooms in a doctor's house. Dad drove up in the big Pierce Arrow to spend the weekends with us. On Saturday evenings, he gave Sally Moore and me a dime, and the two of us walked downtown to a movie while Dad and Mother played bridge with the doctor and his wife.

I do not recall playing with my dad, wrestling with him, or sitting on his lap. Once he gave me a penny, and I must have grumped about its not being a nickel because he said, "A penny saved is a penny earned." I don't remember much else that quiet man ever said to me. Sometimes I close my eyes and see him sitting in his upholstered chair while Mother fixes dinner. He is reading the paper and smoking a cigar. There is a floor lamp to his left. Even in the evening, reading the paper, he wore one of his high collars.

The Barnes Safe and Vault Company occupied a small office in a glass-front, one story building that needed painting. It was on Main Street in downtown Richmond, about two blocks from the train station. Main Street sloped downhill and had similar storefronts all along.

The office had a dark wooden floor, and a counter out front where they sold locks and spare parts for safes. You could say it was a small store with an office in the rear for my father and a shop for Uncle Elwood, Dad's brother. Bank officers did not come there; my dad went to the bank to do business with them. Large vaults and safes were ordered from the Diebold Safe and Lock Company in Canton, Ohio, and shipped to Virginia by rail.

My grandfather started the business, but by the late 1920s, he had gone into semi-retirement, and my dad became president as well as sales manager. Uncle Elwood, a stocky, strong, plain sort of man, did the maintenance work on the vaults and safes at the banks.

In contrast to Dad and Grandfather, Uncle Elwood wore old work pants with a leather tool holder strapped around his waist. He was better than any thief at opening a safe's door. His hands were dirty and greasy, but he had a big smile. I liked Uncle Elwood, because down at the office he played with me and showed me his tools and what he did with them.

You wouldn't have guessed that Dad and Uncle Elwood were brothers. It seemed the only thing they had in common was that neither of them went to college. Dad visited the president of the bank and invited him to play golf; Uncle Elwood never mingled in high society. My mother would have little to do with Uncle Elwood or Aunt Myrtle. They lived in the wrong part of town; Mother said they were nice, but plain.

One time an important officer of the Diebold Company came to visit Dad and stayed in town for two days. Mother told me I should not mention this man to any of my pals because he was a Yankee and talked funny. She was right about his accent. I wondered why he talked like that, and I was relieved when he left. Like most southerners, my mother had a few biases left over from the Civil War that I later discovered had become a part of me. Children pick up bigotry the way flies stick to flypaper. When my mother used words like Jew, Catholic, Yankee, or colored, she tended to come closer and whisper the words.

One block from Dad's office was the Second Presbyterian Church. That was our church; I went to Sunday school there, and Mother played the organ. She always emphasized the "Second" when talking about her church, because most of the important Richmond Presbyterians went to church there, not to the First Presbyterian Church.

Sometimes after church, Dad and I would walk to the office and he would check mail or make a phone call. He didn't think much of church. He said the ushers took up the collection on Sunday and cheated in business transactions on Monday.

My dad died on February 17, 1930. He was 47 years old. He was not alone in the way he died, for he died amid an epidemic of suicides brought on by a nationwide financial crisis.

Following the economic recovery after World War I, the 1920s were a hilarious, dancing, get-rich time. A businessman who opened a new factory was canonized almost as if he had built a cathedral. Consumerism was at its height, and new banks dotted the nation, each eager to lend money. The stock market kept rising year after year, as if there were no ceiling to the value of stocks. Buying on the margin was the way to go. The buyer invested 25 percent of the stock's cost, signing a note for the balance or pledging any stocks he owned for security. The stockbroker in turn borrowed the 75 percent owed from the bank. Stocks became greatly overvalued. On Tuesday, October 29, 1929, the market collapsed. The American way of high-risk investing went bust. Millions of businesses failed, and the Great Depression began.

It was no time to sell vaults and safes to banks, which were collapsing. Except for some maintenance on safes and vaults that had already been sold, my dad's business, too, went under. It was not quite four months after the stock market crash that Dad took his life. The newspaper column announcing his death did not mention how he died. I suspect that everyone instinctively knew the underlying cause.

It was a time when people jumped out of windows, sat in cars with the exhaust pipe exhaling its poison, and blew out their brains with guns. By 1932, the suicide rate in America rose so high that it upset the insurance companies' actuarial tables. The number of concealed suicides was perhaps two or three times as high. The loss of life by self-imposed violent death is a monstrous price to pay, especially when it is precipitated by the loss of money.

◆   ◆   ◆

As a little boy, my mother gave me a small bouquet or a pot of flowers to put on my fathers grave. I rode the streetcar alone. It was a long way, across that bridge over the James River. I stepped off the bus and passed through the same stone archway, and wandered along the narrow, winding asphalt lanes until at last I found the Barnes plot. It was frightening to be there alone, and I hurriedly put the flowers on the grave and dashed out of the cemetery.

Years later I became more and more aware how devastating it was to me as a little boy to lose my father in such a tragic manner. The death of a parent under any circumstances is earth shaking, but adding to that the burden of shame, secrecy, and a deep sense of abandonment can shatter a child's self-image and steal the freedom and joy of his childhood.

Following such wounds, a child's need for love and approval are tremendous. Unfortunately, my mother could not give them to me. My dad's death left her so distraught she could not function with any sense of peace. Mother worked hard to support us; she fed, clothed, and housed my sister and me. Her soul was not mated with ours—or, it seemed, with anyone's. Bereft of the man she had loved, the man who had given her identity, Mother was caught in a never-ending depression.

Shameful secrets do not bond family members together; they separate them. My father's suicide was a shameful secret, a secret the family kept buried in the closet. My dad might as well have died of syphilis or leprosy, the kind of diseases considered taboo. The awareness of this secret made us all cautious, nervous about revealing ourselves, afraid of intimacy even with each other.

For decades, I kept my mother's commandment—I never told anyone the family secret, not even, later, my wife. I lied when I applied for life insurance and had to give information about the cause of my father's death. I would have lied about it if I had been President of the United States (God forbid) and I was being interrogated by the Supreme Court. When Mother said, "don't say anything", I shut the lid tight. When I left my native Virginia as a young man and moved to Seattle, about as far as you can go and remain in the United States, one of my motives—a hidden, secret motive—was to live in a place where no one had ever heard about my father's death. In Seattle, my secret would be more secure.

Mother's depression meant that, growing up, I had to fend for myself emotionally. My pathway to self-esteem became perfectionism in schoolwork and activities in the Boy Scouts. I was a model student, and I became an Eagle Scout at age thirteen, the youngest on record at the time. *The Richmond Times Dispatch* ran a picture of me in my uniform, displaying the mass of merit badges I had won in such a short time.

In truth, it was not for the joy of being a good student that I worked hard. I wasn't excited about the Scout program, learning to identify birds and trees and to survive in the woods. I wanted the praise of winning the merit badges, and I wanted to have more of them than anyone else. The merit badges became a kind of mask I wore to cover my real self—the first of many masks I would wear in my lifetime.

My father's suicide and the family secret surrounding it was a burden made heavier by the fear that the secret might leak out and something awful would happen to me. I might become "nobody." I was certain that anyone could look at me and tell there was something strange inside me, unlike anybody else. The mask was aimed at covering it up. The result is poor self-image, not being our true selves. Stuffing secrets deep inside can destroy the soul and even result in sickness, depression, or premature death. Sometimes the false journey drives us to become seekers, hoping to find happiness, freedom, and peace. The grass is greener on the other side of the road.

2

Uncle Joe

Mother took me to stay with Uncle Joe and her sister, my aunt, for the summer after my dad died. They lived in Maxton, North Carolina. Mother, Sally Moore and I traveled the hundred and fifty miles by train. It was an overnight trip from Richmond, and sleeping in a berth in a Pullman car was so special that I visualize it as fairyland. The train stopped at many small towns along the way. My sister and I raised the shade a few inches and watched the boarding of new passengers waving goodbye to friends, family and tipping porters. The stops were short. As soon as we heard the whistle blow and the sound of wheels chugging we lowered the shade and fell asleep until the next stop. Two days later, Mother and my sister returned to Richmond.

Maxton was a little town, with a population of about 1500. There was one main residential street lined by large, colonial homes painted white, with front porches extending the length of the house. On some of the bigger houses, the porch was curved outward like a bay window, seeming to wrap the entire front of the house. My uncle's house was one story, with a peaked roof, a large window on each side of the entrance and a swing at one end. Just inside was a large living room on the left; to the right were an upright piano and a door into a bedroom. In the floor of the wide hallway leading to the rear of the house was a grate through which the furnace blew hot air upward to heat the house. The country kitchen at the back had a large wood stove, which immediately caught my eye because at home we had a small gas stove that wasn't nearly as impressive. Sister made fresh bread daily, and the smell gave me a sense of being in a happy, secure, and caring home.

Every morning Sister went out to the garden and brought in a rosebud to pin on the lapel of the doctor as he left for the office. When the phone rang, she answered, "I will get the Doctor." I remembered this later when I was practicing medicine, and when the phone rang, my children answered and said, "I will call Dad" and my wife said, "I will call Bob."

I have many wonderful images and stories of Uncle Joe. On Sundays, he wore a white linen suit with the rosebud neatly tucked in his lapel buttonhole. His reddish hair, flushed face, and strong, stocky body created a striking picture. We walked together, he holding my hand, Sister the other, as we went across the street to the Presbyterian Church. I was proud and comfortable to have them hold my hand and introduce me to the preacher and to their friends. I had never experienced such belonging or love. The place I had left behind was different, heavy and without joy. I have often thought that Uncle Joe was sent by the Holy Spirit to hold my hand during that time just after I lost my dad.

Those summer Sundays in North Carolina were hot and humid—days when the churchgoers quietly fanned themselves. When they stood up to sing, the men's shirts were wet and the ladies reached around and pulled their cotton dresses away from their damp bottoms. After church, we went back to the house, sometimes with the preacher and his wife as guests, and we sat down to southern fried chicken, hot biscuits, mashed potatoes, and chocolate cake and ice cream.

Sunday afternoon in the heat of the summer is a quiet time. The street is deserted, the leaves of the maple trees still. Everyone has eaten a big, middle-of-the-day meal and is now napping or quietly sitting in the cool of the house.

One Sunday afternoon was different, however. Uncle Joe took me on my first home call, along with his dog Spot. We rode in his two-door, black, T-model Ford. The metal door handle was fiercely hot, and Uncle Joe laughed when I jerked my hand away from it with a loud "Ow!" He opened the door for me and when I sat down, I popped right back up because the seat was hot on my bare legs. Uncle Joe pulled an old towel out from behind the seat and stuck it under me. Spot stretched out behind the seat, and off we drove. I sat next to Uncle Joe, feeling like a big shot.

Uncle Joe's black doctor bag sat on the floor in front of my feet. There was a shotgun on the floor behind us.

We passed large, green lawns shaded by maple trees, and I envied the grass being sprayed with cool water. No one sat on any of the porches. There was an occasional dog curled up in the shade of a house, or a horse drinking water out of a trough. Otherwise, there was nothing. I could hear Spot panting and the sound of the car's motor, but that was all.

Quickly we reached the outskirts of town and the maple trees stopped. Extending to the horizon were rows of scrubby cotton bushes with soft, white cotton bolls filling the green seed pods, each bush one or two feet tall. There were no trees, no lakes, no rivers, nothing except the cotton bushes, interrupted here and there by a distant farmhouse that looked like a black square with a short smokestack sticking up skyward. There was no smoke, but dust swirled up from the dry earth when a blessed little breeze stirred itself. I had seen pictures of cotton fields but I had never seen one. The air above the fields shimmered in the heat, and every so often I saw a group of black people bending over, pulling cotton bolls off the stems and stuffing them into large potato sacks.

Narrow dirt roads branched off the main road and wound their way through the cotton fields to the farmhouses. We turned and took one of these. The ride was bumpy, and cotton bolls scratched noisily against the door. Dust swirled behind us and obscured the view through the rear window. Inside the car, it got hotter and hotter because Uncle Joe had closed the windows to keep out the dirt. My tongue felt dry and when I opened the window to spit, it came out brown. There was no relief from the sun, no beckoning shade trees in any direction. I thought to myself that it was not easy making a home call.

We approached a shack that was surrounded by hard, packed clay. There was a cow out to pasture behind the house. The shack was the color of an old ship, wrecked and abandoned on a beach. The wooden planks had turned silvery gray; they were warped, and nails protruded from them. The windows on each side of the door sagged, and the broken panes were plugged with yellow newspaper. The corrugated metal roof had rusted, and the bricks of the chimney on the side of the shack were crumbling.

There was an outhouse close by. Everything seemed worn out and tired, like a malnourished old man, slumped over on a sidewalk in the heat.

We pulled up in front of a small porch with a swing. Spot jumped over me and out the door as if he knew the place, and he began sniffing around the shack. Uncle Joe asked me to carry his black doctor bag for him. I felt like a king strutting up to the shack beside my uncle, The Doctor. The two steps up to the door slanted to one side, the support having given way.

A muscular colored man pushed open the screen door and said in a friendly voice, "Glad to see you, Dr. MacClelland. Who's your boy here?"

Uncle Joe, with a big smile, introduced me as his nephew, and I shook the man's hand. We followed him into the cabin. It took me time to adjust, because the windows were covered with dust and it seemed dark after the overwhelming brightness of the sun. There was only one room, close and hot and filled with body odors. As my eyes adjusted, I could see the mother lying in a bed off to the left, covered by grayed sheets and a thin blanket with a hole in it. She smiled pleasantly, beautiful teeth shining. There was a small, potbelly stove and, to the right, a cot on which a small, diapered baby lay. I noticed immediately that the baby had a gauze bandage around her abdomen and there was a lump sticking up about where the baby's navel was. Standing in a corner were two other children, about three and five years old. They watched everything closely but said nothing. The girl had her hair in pigtails and her thumb in her mouth.

Uncle Joe had delivered the baby one week before, and now he asked how the baby and mother were doing. He leaned over to me and whispered in my ear, "Bobby, I'm going to take the bandage off the baby. Don't say anything, and I will tell you about what you see later."

He bent over the baby and quickly removed the bandage, revealing what the lump was. Lo and behold, it was a small dead turtle. Uncle Joe held it up and showed it to me. Then he carefully replaced the turtle on the baby's navel and put clean gauze around her abdomen. He asked me to look the other way while he examined the mother. Afterward, we stayed there for a while as he talked and laughed with the family. He assured them that mother and baby were fine. Eventually we hopped back in the Ford, along with Spot, and took off.

As soon as we were down the road apiece, Uncle Joe turned to me and asked, "What did you think about that turtle?"

I remember asking, "How did it get there?"

He said colored people believed that if a baby was born with yellow eyes, now called jaundice, putting a small turtle on the navel made the jaundice go away. He said it was something they felt very strongly about, even though the jaundice would have cleared by itself without the turtle.

Uncle Joe and I had a riotous time returning home. We laughed about the turtle, and Uncle Joe told me more stories about patients. We headed back by a different route that circled around and took us into the opposite end of town from the way we went out. On the main road, Uncle Joe let his foot get heavier on the accelerator; the T-model rattled along and the cotton fields raced by on either side of us. Spot held his head up high, watching the road and barking whenever he saw a bird or another car passed going in the opposite direction. Uncle Joe seemed to know each driver, waving and smiling broadly at them all.

Suddenly, Uncle Joe pulled over to the roadside and we got out. He reached behind the seat, grabbed the shotgun, and fired at some birds sitting on a telephone wire. Spot went crazy, flinging his tail in all directions and bouncing up and down. It was the first time I had seen anyone shoot a shotgun. When I told the story in town about Uncle Joe shooting at sitting birds, I got the message that only Uncle Joe, whom everybody loved, could get away with that. However, I thought it was a bang, so to speak. I don't recall him hitting anything, but Spot and I both acted as if we had been goosed. Back in the car, Uncle Joe laughed as if he was having the time of his life. I believe he was.

After Uncle Joe had his fun, we took off again. Soon we came to a small store on the side of the road, with a wooden sign hanging from a rod: "MacQueen's Grocery." It seemed everyone in that part of North Carolina had "Mac" in front of the last name—MacClellan, MacQueen, McCowan, and so on. Later I came to suspect that the name of the town Maxton came straight from Scotland, like the other Macs.

A brown awning, sporting a few holes from long use, shaded the entry of MacQueen's Grocery. Uncle Joe and I went in, leaving Spot in the car with the windows down. There were two or three other cars there, all of them black T-models just like Uncle Joe's. The clerk greeted the doctor by name, and Uncle Joe introduced me.

Hanging from the ceiling was a fan with four blades, circulating cool air over the scales in the meat and cheese section. There were fresh vegetables displayed on a stand, and potatoes piled up next to fresh corn, tomatoes, cucumbers, and watermelon. The shelves were filled with canned vegetables and fruits, toilet paper, and soap. There was an icebox, and bottles of Coca-Cola and Dr. Pepper displayed on cracked ice. Uncle Joe asked me which I wanted, and because he chose a Dr. Pepper, I did, too. Near the front of the store was a case that had gum drops, chocolate mints, candy canes, and all sorts of goodies. Uncle Joe asked the shopkeeper to pull the box of chocolate mints out onto the counter. He explained to me that most of the mints had white cream on the inside, but if you picked one with pink cream, you would win a prize. Uncle Joe said I could keep biting into mints until I found a pink one. The fifth one came out pink, and my eyes were bulging when I found I had won a harmonica with a booklet of directions. To this day, I am still playing the harmonica—nothing to brag about, but at least a pretty good rendition of "My Country Tis of Thee" and "Row, Row, Row Your Boat." It was a perfect Sunday afternoon.

I spent no more than three months with him but it was quality time, bonding time, learning time, memories that lasted a life long. He made me feel special. He once asked my mother if he and my aunt could adopt me. I would have jumped at the chance, but Mother said no. Sometimes I wonder how different my life would have been if I had grown up with Uncle Joe and Sister. Perhaps it doesn't matter. The main thing is that those three months with Uncle Joe gave me a glimpse of my future. It was his example that inspired me to become a doctor, his role model that showed me the way.

In those days, a doctor smelled like a doctor. When he delivered babies at home, he poured ether or chloroform onto a gauze mask over the mother's face for anesthesia. He swabbed the skin of a wound or incision with iodine. In addition to these smelly substances, there were bottles of mysterious healing solutions in the doctor's little black bag. Put all of these together in a day's work, and the doctor became a walking pharmaceutical aroma. When Uncle Joe walked into the house, his unique smell announced his presence. I thought it was the most special smell in the world. From then on, I always wanted to smell like that. Later, back home in Richmond, whenever I walked past a drug store the smell reminded me of Uncle Joe and I felt good. Still later, when I became a doctor, I was disappointed that I did not smell like one. The practice of medicine had changed since Uncle Joe's day. Iodine was still available but seldom used any more, and home deliveries were becoming rare; antibiotics and tranquilizers had no doctor smell. I thought about making a solution that smelled like a doctor and spraying it on myself.

As a pre-med student at the Virginia Military Institute, I had a job as assistant trainer for the football team. One fall our team played in my hometown of Richmond, and I sat on the bench, aware that in the stands were some of my friends from both high school and college. When one of the players got hurt, I grabbed the black doctor bag sitting beside me and rushed onto the field. It was the first time I had carried a doctor bag since the house call with Uncle Joe, and his image was in my mind as I trotted out to the injured player. The injury turned out to be a muscle spasm, and before long, the player stood up, stretched his leg, and limped off the field. My friends in the stands gave me a standing ovation, not knowing I had really done nothing.

The stories that Uncle Joe told me, his unique doctor smell, his little black bag, his dog Spot, and his care and enjoyment of his patients have stayed with me all my life. I never forgot the turtle on the black baby's navel. I came to realize that Uncle Joe, in his wisdom, thought it important to honor the myths of the African-American culture. This was a powerful lesson for me, and when I became a doctor, I always took care to honor people's myths and cultural beliefs, as long as they were not harmful. I saw patients with copper bracelets on their wrists for arthritis, and mustard plaster on their chests for pneumonia. Once I even gave a talk holding an Indian medicine stick with reindeer hooves on it, explaining to my audience that belief and hope are powerful medicines.

But the most important gift I got from Uncle Joe was a positive image that I could apply immediately to myself. While my mother grieved her loss, I began to see myself as a doctor like Uncle Joe, and this image persuaded me that everything would be all right. I wanted to smell like him and hoped people would love me just as they loved him, in spite of my secret about my father.

Years later, Uncle Joe developed Parkinson's Disease and was confined to a wheelchair. I was a medical officer in the army when I learned this, and I never saw him again. I have always been sad that I was not with him when he died. I'm left with the wonderful memories I have of him—laughing with me, holding my hand—heaven on earth compared with the misery I faced when I returned home at the end of that summer.

3

The Costume of Misery

At the end of the summer, I found Mother in a miserable state. Her clothes were unclean, and her stockings hung down around her ankles. Sloppy dress at home had become her norm. She wore an old, pink cotton bathrobe with her pink, dirty pajama pants dragging below. She smeared her face with Pond's cold cream and left it on all day. Her hair was thinning, and she hid it under a pink boudoir cap. I still associate the color pink with her—and with her depression.

When Mother had on her pink boudoir cap, I knew she was in no condition to receive visitors or go out in public. If the doorbell rang, she hid behind the hall curtains, peeking through one of the two narrow windows flanking the door to see who was there. Sally Moore and I hardly ever brought anyone home from school. It was just too embarrassing.

I learned later my mother could not collect on my father's life insurance because of his suicide. Mother gave the Pierce Arrow to Uncle Elwood; apparently in payment of some debt my dad owed him. I soon learned the value of a penny. Until I earned enough to buy a bicycle, I walked to school and took the streetcar to go downtown. Mother, when she went out, also rode the streetcar. Sometimes when I was playing in the field across the alley from my house, I saw her get off the streetcar, carrying heavy bags of groceries.

My mother took a business school course and subsequently earned her license to sell life insurance and real estate. She said she would never work in an office as a secretary. In fact, she was remarkably well educated for a woman of her time. She earned advanced degrees from a couple of colleges. She was also an excellent pianist, organist, and soloist in the church choir.

Mother was always in the house after school, but in the evening, she made home calls by appointment to sell insurance. In the morning, she showed houses for sale. She covered up her depression and put on a good appearance for work. I hated to look at her in the house, but was proud to be with her in public. She had excellent taste, did her hair perfectly, using an added hairpiece. People thought she was rich because she was so well "turned out." She bought fashionable clothes on sale and looked good in them.

At home, to make ends meet Mother decided to rent out the four bedrooms upstairs. She put up a sign on the front of the house that said, "Rooms for Rent." I was embarrassed, hoped my friends would not see it. They would think we were poor if we had to rent out rooms. Mother was careful to say she did not run a boarding house, because to her way of thinking, a boarding house was lower than rooms for rent. Therefore, she did not serve meals.

Mother and Sally Moore moved downstairs, and the upstairs linen closet became my room. I loved it. It was the same length as the upstairs bedrooms, only quite narrow, with shelves on both walls where towels and sheets were stored for the roomers' beds. I slept on a cot under the shelves. I liked the clean smell and the quietness of the closet. A window looked out at a brick house next door, only ten feet away. That brick wall had no windows facing me, so I felt I had complete privacy. I had a crystal radio set and strung a wire antenna from my window to a tall, skinny tree outside. It was wonderful to put my earphones on, get in bed, and listen to the Hit Parade and the Amos and Andy show. My crystal radio set took me away, into a dream world where I could imagine myself being someplace wonderful, like the famous ballroom in New York where Tommy Dorsey's orchestra played and elegant dancers glided across the floor.

I used the bathroom that all the roomers used. Every night I listened intently to determine when it was clear, and then I ran down the hall in my underwear and took my turn. I had to be careful to get out quickly so no one complained to my mother that they couldn't get in.

For a while, a young woman who worked downtown lived in the room next to the bathroom. She had dark hair and a voluptuous body, and I thought she was gorgeous. Sometimes I tiptoed down the hall to her door and peeped in through the keyhole. Our alluring tenant was the first woman I ever saw naked. I didn't want to think about what Mother would have done if she caught me.

On Saturdays, it was my duty to clean the bathroom and empty the trashcans in each room. I used Old Dutch Cleanser with a brush in the tub and the toilet. The dark ring around the tub took a lot of scrubbing, and my mind was always on the question of when I could get out of the house and play. We did not recycle trash in those days; we dumped everything in one large barrel. I carried it out the kitchen door to the containers at the back gate near the cobblestone alleyway. The containers were never big enough, and by the end of the week, the trash spilled over. It attracted large rats that made a mess out of the garbage, cigarette stubs, and ashes. It became another one of my tasks to clean up the mess with a shovel and broom.

At night, I banked the coal furnace in the basement, where I could hear the rats running around and sometimes see them. Their beady, black eyes reflected the light bulb hanging by a cord from the ceiling. Mother bought what we called "rat cheese"—cheap cheddar, costing five cents a pound—and I put out traps. I dumped the dead rats in the barrel out at the gate. In the summer, we had cockroaches, large black ones that crackled when you stepped on them and made a mess of black shell and white, creamy ooze on the floor.

But it wasn't all work and no play. Besides street hockey, the kids on my block liked to play in the field across the alleyway from our houses, next to a bookbinding factory that gave off the smell of glue. There were exciting things to do, all to the accompaniment of the bookbinding machines clanking within the factory. We built a tree house—or, I should say, a tree platform—with boards nailed to the tree trunk as a ladder. Near the tree, we dug a deep trench and covered it with wooden planks. We stored rocks in the trench, and I once hid a piggy bank there. We made hockey sticks from saplings that grew there. We bent the sapling over and pined its top to the ground with a rock. Then we built a fire beneath the place where we wanted the curve to be in the hockey stick, and the heat fixed it.

Across the field from the trench near the big tree was another trench. We boys divided up into two groups, one in each trench, and played war. Shielded by trash-can lids that we "borrowed" from all of the houses along the alleyway, our two armies faced each other about forty yards apart, throwing rocks and yelling. I thought it was great to raise my trash can lid in the air and hear a rock bang against it.

The streetcar line ran parallel to our battlefield. One day, Mother got off the streetcar laden with groceries and caught us in battle. She screamed and hollered and stopped the war, much to our disappointment. We played war many times when she wasn't around, and I don't remember anyone ever being injured, no bloody heads or teeth knocked out.

I didn't get in trouble much, but then I also got away with more than my sister. This may have been because I spent a lot of my time outside. In contrast, Sally Moore spent most of her time in the house reading or studying, lying on the floor with her feet up against the wall. From early childhood on, she read the classics—Dickens, Thackeray, Sir Walter Scott. She read *Little Women* and *Little Men* when she was only eight. I can remember Mother yelling at her to get up and do something, go out of the house, or help with the cleaning. Whatever went on between them, it made Sally Moore feel as if she was nothing and that, in Mother's eyes, I could do no wrong. My sister and I were not particularly close, and I didn't realize at the time how much she resented me because Mother treated us differently.

Sally Moore received some financial assistance to attend Collegiate School for Girls, a private school, and she won a scholarship to West-hampton College, which replaced the Women's Institute at the University of Richmond. Later, she earned a Master's degree elsewhere. Still, she never did satisfy Mother. Mother hoped Sally Moore would catch a high-class man and become a society lady like Mother wanted to be. She wouldn't get there by lying on the floor and reading *Lady of the Lake*. She didn't get there by going to private schools, either.

In time, Sally Moore married a Presbyterian clergyman. On the face of it, that should have fitted Mother's plan just fine. However, Albert turned out not to be the *right kind* of Presbyterian clergyman. Mother had in mind a scholarly theologian, or at least a sophisticated, urban minister, a great preacher, who moved in the right social circles. Albert came from Charles Town, West Virginia, from a good family that included a Princeton professor and a distinguished librarian. Albert himself was a modest, quiet man, a good pastor to his congregation, a man loved for his sincerity and integrity. He was twelve years older than Sally Moore. Bald and of a pale complexion, he dressed in simple preacher's clothes—a regular collar, black four-in-hand tie, plain black shoes. In the summertime, he wore a seersucker suit. He recognized the bossy and controlling nature of Mother; she, in turn, considered him plain and far too meek. In short, he didn't measure up to Mother's expectations.

My image of myself as a teenager is that of a skinny guy riding a bicycle to high school, books strapped to a rack behind the seat. I was the same kid riding the streetcar across town to work in a Safeway store after school on Friday and all day Saturday. I hated missing the high-school football games on Fridays, but it was the depth of the Depression and we needed my income. Like other kids, I also sold *Liberty* magazines at five cents per copy, covering my assigned route and carrying a canvas bag inscribed with the word "Liberty" in big letters. Between the Safeway store and selling magazines, I bought my bike, second hand, and paid for school lunches and other incidentals like movies, penny candy, marbles, and my crystal radio set.

Some of my most vivid memories from this time are of my job at Safeway. The store opened at 7:00 a.m. and closed at 9:00 p.m., and on Saturdays, I worked the full day, fourteen hours. They paid me 25 cents an hour, and the $3.50 I earned was big money. Mother always worried about me being out so late; taking the streetcar, I would not get home until about 10:30. It didn't bother me; I enjoyed the night ride across the James River, through the darkened business district, and past the tobacco factories. The pungent smell of tobacco roasting was as familiar as the streetcars and the black A Model Ford cars.

One of my classmates, a red-haired boy named Fred, worked across the street in the A & P. We would meet at lunchtime and eat our peanut butter and jelly sandwiches. Then we walked down the street to a radio store and stood outside listening to songs like "The Music Goes Round and Round, Ho, Ho—Ho, Ho."

At the time, the Safeway store felt big to me, but actually, it was only about fifty feet wide and maybe one hundred feet deep. It had a fading Safeway sign over the entrance and display windows.

Upon my arrival, I hauled the fresh vegetables and fruits, delivered from nearby farms, off the sidewalk and arranged them in their display—red and green peppers, red and green apples stacked in neat rows; large, red summer radishes, lettuce, green onions, and a big stalk of not-quite-ripe, greenish bananas hanging by a cord from the ceiling. Upon completing the display, I walked out to the street in my long, white apron, and with fists resting on my hips, proudly eyeballed my handiwork and said "Good morning" to passersby. In the summer, sticky flypapers that were hung over the produce would be covered by dead flies by the end of the day.

I loved the smell of the Safeway—except for the occasional rotten potato hidden under a display table or the dead rat in the storage room. On the other hand, nothing could beat the aroma of fresh bread, fruits, and cheeses, mixed with the fragrance of gingerbread cookies. Even the brown paper bags had a clean, pleasant smell.

There were three ceiling fans with large blades rotating quietly. When the afternoon sun hit the front windows, we lowered a light green awning, which shaded and darkened the store. Customers coming in from the hot summer sidewalk experienced an abrupt coolness.

I learned a couple of tricks. It was common for a person to ask for ten pounds of potatoes. With experience, I could throw in the exact number of potatoes and see the black hand on the white scale move to the number ten. I could also hold a potato in my hand, palm up, flex my wrist just right, and pop the potato up to my biceps; this, in turn, would pop the potato into the air and right back into my hand. I could do the same thing with a can of corn or peas.

Another trick was to take the long-handled metal claws, grab an item from the top shelf up near the ceiling, drop the item straight down, and catch it in my hands. That was easy with toilet paper but more risky with a glass jar of blackberry preserves. If I broke anything, I had to pay for it—if the manager saw me do it, that is.

At the far end of the store was the meat department with ice chips spread over the meat and fish in the display case. There were no electric refrigerators, so we depended on daily deliveries of ice. The ice melted during the day, and it was my job to empty the drain bowl. If I forgot, the water ran out from under the display case and the butcher chewed me out.

The butcher had a way of cheating his customers. There was a ceiling fan exactly above the scale, and when a large piece of white paper was placed on the tray with the fan blowing down on it, the scale registered an eighth to a quarter pound. He was a master at putting the meat and the paper on at the same time so the customer didn't notice.

The checkout counter was another place where the store's profits were enhanced dishonestly. Many of our customers were poorly educated colored people (as we called them) who usually could not read or write, much less add up a long list of figures. The manager and clerks knew all these people, laughed and talked with them, but almost invariably cheated them. An old Remington adding machine printed the numbers on a roll of white paper. When the manager saw one of these customers come in, dirty and sweaty from working all day in the field or on the railroad, he would immediately hit the five and zero keys and register 50 cents in the machine. That would immediately be printed on the white receipt roll, but the manager tore the top of the receipt so the illicit 50 cents didn't show. Later, when the customer's actual purchases were added up, there was an extra 50 cents in the bottom line. The customer never questioned the tally. The manager defended this practice to the clerks by saying he would lose his job if he did not make a certain profit, and he couldn't make it without cheating.

If I was only a silent accomplice in this business of overcharging customers, there was another scam in which I participated more directly. Certain items didn't sell readily, and the inventory would pile up. For example, if we were stuck with a lot of canned peas, we would make a pyramid display of them at the end of the counter. When we bagged a customer's groceries, it was easy to slip in a can of peas, add the charge to the total, and at the end of the day, all the excess cans of peas were gone. I never saw anyone return a can of peas or ask for a refund. The manager said that if anyone did, we should apologize for the mistake and refund the money with a friendly smile. The regular customers who trusted the manager were the ones that usually got cheated.

◆   ◆   ◆

While I was still in high school, Mother acquired a new burden. Her mother and father, whom we called Hottie and Pop, moved in with us. I don't know where the name Hottie came from. My grandmother's real name was Sara, and my grandfather's name was Andrew. Pop was bald and a bit stooped-over. He was also eccentric and unhappy.

Hottie had fallen down the back steps while visiting us before my father died. She spent months in the hospital with a broken back, both arms broken, and a severe head injury. Mentally, she was never the same after that. Pop cleaned, dressed, and fed her, and took her for walks. He seemed devoted to her.

To accommodate them, Mother made our kitchen into a bedroom and developed a new, smaller kitchen out of a closet and a hallway. Except for their walks, Hottie and Pop stayed in their room. Pop sat most of the day chewing tobacco, spitting in an old tomato can, and reading the Bible. Hottie just sat. Outside their room, she seemed unaware of activities around her and stood in the way sometimes. One of our common household sayings was "Move, Hottie."

Previously, Hottie and Pop lived in Huntington, West Virginia, and Cynthiana, Kentucky. Pop managed a small hotel in Cynthiana, but it burned down. There was no Social Security or Medicare then, and he could not support himself and his wife. He must have been seething inside with frustration; he occasionally got angry with my mother, and once he chased her around the house, brandishing an umbrella. Although I didn't understand it then, the burden of rearing two children as well as caring for her parents must have exhausted Mother both physically and emotionally.

I never developed strong feelings about Hottie, and she took no particular notice of me. She and Pop became fixtures of our household and remained so until after I went off to college. Hottie died while I was a cadet at VMI, and it didn't even occur to me that I might return home for her funeral. Later, my sister told me Pop was so distraught that he had to be pulled away from her casket.

Sometime after Hottie's death, Mother acquired a small apartment for Pop across the street from our house. He lived there alone, sad and lonely. He had no friends, and he stopped attending church services, which had been such an important part of his life when he was younger. He was a teetotaler before, but now he began drinking heavily. I visited him when I came home on holidays from college, but neither of us had much to say.

After graduating from VMI, I came back to Richmond and lived at home again during my first year of medical school. From my study desk, I could see Pop as he headed for the liquor store. He wore his derby hat and carried an umbrella even when it was sunny. After a while, he returned with a bottle in a paper bag.

He developed a hernia that year and was fitted with a big leather truss because surgery was not the common treatment then. One day he asked me to take him to the doctor. We took the bus downtown to the doctor's office and got off opposite the medical building. We started across the street just as the traffic light turned red, and a car screeched to a stop. Pop banged his umbrella against the car's bumper and shouted, "Damn Yankee, damn Yankee!" Three-quarters of a century after the civil war, that was still a powerful curse to Pop—and to many other southerners.

Once mother asked me to go to his apartment and see if he was all right because he wasn't answering his phone. The door to his apartment had a window with a lace curtain, and through it, I could see him lying on the floor in the living room, an empty bottle close by. I ran home and got Mother, thinking he was dead. He wasn't dead, but dead drunk. Together, Mother and I hoisted him into bed. After that, Mother tried to get control of his little bit of money to keep him from buying whisky, but that didn't work.

When I think back now, I think how sad it was for all of them—Hottie, Pop, and Mother. As a younger man, Pop sang a beautiful bass in the Baptist choir. He wore his black suit to church and never played cards on Sunday. The last time I saw him, he lay in a nursing home, paralyzed by a stroke. He was ninety-five when he died. I was already practicing medicine in Seattle and did not go home for his funeral.

◆   ◆   ◆

Not long after my dad died, I heard Mother crying in the bathroom, "Oh God, Oh God, I want to die." I could picture her sitting on the toilet, her face in her hands, and I leaned against the outside of the bathroom door, sharing her misery.

She did not die then, of course; she lived another fifty years. Fifty years of widowhood, fifty years of loneliness and depression. All her expectations for happiness died along with my father. The life in her heart and soul stopped the morning he shot himself.

She tried to separate herself from the world emotionally. She all but cut off relations with her in-laws. I loved my paternal grandparents and missed them, for we hardly ever visited them. Many years later one of Dad's sisters told me how much she and her sisters had loved my father, what a loving brother he was and how they suffered from his loss.

Mother never played the piano at home after my dad's death, and once I asked her why. She dropped her head, her lips trembled, and she walked away. To my recollection, she never told me that she loved me.

She threw herself into her work and did what she had to do to support our little family. When Hottie and Pop moved in, she managed to support them, too. But her social life was limited, at least while I was growing up. If she had a soul friend with whom she could share her cares, I did not know about it.

She did eventually have a couple of suitors who wanted to marry her, but she turned them down. One courted her for several years and brought her expensive gifts. Another offered her $100,000 to marry him. This was after I had grown up, and when I asked Mother why she didn't accept his offer, she said, "He told me he wouldn't let me stay up after ten o'clock and watch TV." Somehow, it never struck me as a very good explanation.

Survivors of a suicide victim often ask, "What did I do? What could I have done to prevent it?" I never asked that question; it never occurred to me that I had anything to do with my dad's death. Who can say for sure why a person puts a gun in his mouth and pulls the trigger? How can anyone be so compulsive, have such a hatred of life? My father's death coincided with the collapse of the stock market and the crumbling of his business. These are facts, but not answers. Maybe he drank too much; I never saw him drunk, never smelled whisky on his breath, but many years later one of his sisters told me that he drank, especially during out-of-town business trips. Was he drunk when he pulled the trigger?

I have the feeling Mother existed from day to day with the thought that she may have been responsible for his actions. Certainly, she suffered through a lot of finger pointing by some of her in-laws, and I suppose that was why we avoided them. I never believed Mother had anything to do with Dad's death, but we never talked about it after that time when she told me he killed himself. There was never a moment when we sat together holding hands, touching, sharing the inner pain. Nor did my sister and I talk about it, either as children or as adults.

I wore a mask to hide the shame of my father's death. It was the mask of the honor student, the mask of the boy who dreamed he would one day be somebody, the boy who would be called Doctor and would drive a Pierce Arrow automobile. Keeping the mask on required me to follow certain rules of behavior: Don't talk about it. Act as if nothing ever happened. Hide the misery of being poor by walking down the alleyway rather than on the sidewalk. Earn more merit badges than any other Boy Scout. Hide in the linen closet and listen to the crystal radio set.

It was miserable behind the mask. When other boys' fathers picked me up to go camping on the weekend, I felt small and unloved. I felt ashamed and afraid someone would say something about my father. I was sure that when people looked at me, they knew I was no good, a boy whose father shot himself. I was the only boy in the whole world hiding behind a secret.

Decades later, it dawned on me that my mother and I had masks in common. When out of the house, she wore a mask like mine, to present herself to others as okay. She greeted people with a smile and a confident handshake. Steady and in control, she gave no hint of her inner guilt and insecurity. She had many admirers, and I doubt that any of them suspected what lay behind her mask

Late in life, Mother confessed to my sister that she felt she had failed with those she loved. Not only did her husband kill himself, but also both of her children left Richmond for distant places. We lived our adult lives and established our own families far away. We maintained contact with her, visited her occasionally and accepted her as a guest in our distant homes, but still she had reason to believe that when we left home, we left not just Richmond but *her* in particular. It embittered her that she could not hold onto her own family.

Mother's life epitomized courage, stamina, and a commitment to rear her children. There were some things she achieved that few women of her day could aspire to. She had a profession, did well at it, and became known among some of the most prominent citizens of Richmond. She prayed and worked and kept deep secrets of pain. She attended church regularly and was a popular lay leader, but it always seemed that grief covered her like a blanket.

4

Leaving Home

Leaving home means different things to different people. It can even mean different things to the same person.

I left home for Lexington, Virginia, and the Virginia Military Institute at the age of sixteen and a half. While a student there, I began to think that I never wanted to live at home again. Or, perhaps it would be more accurate to say that a part of me didn't want to live at home again.

My departure for VMI was not the first time I had gone away from home. The first was the summer I spent with Uncle Joe and Sister, just after my dad's death. That had been a wonderful summer, and I often wished it had not ended. Maybe that experience helped me understand that it was all right to leave home. For sure, my time with Uncle Joe taught me there were alternatives to living in the family house on Grace Street, which was saturated with my mother's misery.

In a true sense, however, the summer with Uncle Joe only *seemed* to take me away from home. I knew I would be returning, and no matter how much Uncle Joe and Sister loved me and cared for me, home was where Mother was. This remained true for me until well into adulthood.

It was because of Mother that I went to VMI. Mother's financial adviser was a trust officer at the First and Merchant's Bank in Richmond, and in those days, bankers had the reputation of taking care of widows. The man happened to be a member of VMI's Board of Visitors, the equivalent of a trustee or regent. He knew I was an honors student, and he knew about our family's tight financial situation. He managed to get me a full four-year scholarship to this prestigious military school. I knew nothing about VMI, but because it had a pre-med program, it sounded fine to me.

Military schools, of course, teach respect for authority because future officers must learn to follow orders even under the most threatening combat conditions. When I arrived at VMI, I soon found out exactly what that meant. First-year cadets were called rats, and upperclassmen treated me like every other rat—yelling in my face, poking me in the back, telling me I was a shit-ass. That was the way I felt, and I knew they could read me inside. They yelled at me if I was a second late falling into ranks, or there was a spot on my uniform, or I talked to one of my buddies in the rat line. This went on the first year.

The rat system was meant to teach the art of doing what you are told without questioning authority. Rats were described as the lowest form of humanity; the only humans we outranked were the "stoop niggers." Stoop niggers were blacks hired by the Institute to clean the toilets and sweep the stoops—the long concrete walkways, one on each floor of the barracks. (I hasten to add that this was still the segregationist South, where terms that would be unacceptable today, such as "nigger," were commonly used.)

I was assigned to what was called the "Squat Butt" company, officially C Company, because we were the short guys. A tall officer was not officially described as a superior specimen, but it was implied. This notion probably went back to the Civil War, when officers rode a horse behind the lines of the attacking foot soldiers. The height of an officer plus that of his horse enabled him to survey the enemy, and clearly, a tall officer had the advantage over a short one. As a child, I sometimes pictured myself as a general, like Robert E. Lee astride his horse Traveler, but I gave up that idea early on as a member of the "Squat Butt" company.

As a sixteen-year-old and the lowest form of humanity, I did not get it at first that the system was to be taken seriously. When I was a kid, I laughed often; sometimes other kids called me a "chesi cat." At VMI, I discovered that laughing at inappropriate times landed you in hot water.

Rats who didn't take the pathway of conformance were called gross. I quickly developed the reputation of being gross, beginning with the day that a certain upperclassman inspected the Squat Butt Company. The cadet stood very tall and had broad shoulders; it seemed he took up the space of two cadets my size. His uniform was crisply pressed, clean, and well fitting, and I couldn't help staring at the five gold stripes on each of his upper arms, signifying the rank of regimental commander. He was the height of power and the image of authority. In contrast, I weighed only 118 pounds. My uniform consisted of an ill-fitting gray shirt with a black tie, gray-blue pants, and black shoes with a bulge over the toe end. That was what the upperclassman saw when he scowled at me from under the visor of his cap. For a moment he did nothing but breathe down on me, as if uncertain what to say to such an unworthy creature.

Then he bellowed into my face, "Mister, you look like a bunch of shit."

I pressed my arms tight against my side, pulled my chin in, straightened my back, and said, "Yes, sir." I was sure he wondered how I was ever accepted as a cadet.

He barked, "What's on Stonewall Jackson's hat, Mister?"

A statue of the great general, a demigod who had taught at VMI, stood on a pedestal overlooking the parade ground. From the corner of my eye, I could see Stonewall's wide-brimmed cavalry hat.

"Sir, I don't know, sir."

I was straining to keep a straight face, but the giant standing before me with his nose descending toward mine saw my lips curl. Red-faced, he commanded me to report to his room that evening, where I had to stand in a half-knee bend with four rifles on my arms, and shout "Bird shit!" until my legs gave out and I fell over.

On another occasion, I got in trouble in the mess hall. Each table sat eight cadets, two or three of whom were rats. A rat was required to tell a joke while sitting up straight on the edge of his chair and looking down at the plate, with his arms hanging down at his sides. I never was much of a joke teller, but when my turn came, I told a story I had told back in high school when I was a candidate for vice-president of the student body. No one laughed except me. Again, I ended up in an upperclassmen's room that night, standing against a wall in a half-knee bend until my legs gave out.

It seemed I was getting in trouble all the time, mainly for minor infractions that I didn't entirely understand. Eventually, I learned to take military discipline seriously. And, in the meantime, despite being a rat, I applied myself intensely to my studies and became an honor student. That's how I survived that first, excruciating year. That and the fact that I couldn't see any alternative. I couldn't drop out and go home, or wouldn't allow myself to. I desperately needed to succeed, needed to get good grades so I would make it into medical school. I didn't want to pump gasoline for a living, or bag groceries. And for sure, I didn't want to live with Mother.

The worst was over after that first year and I became an upperclassman, no longer a rat. And by the time I graduated, I was extremely proud to be a VMI cadet. It helped being in the cavalry. The cavalry was a proud tradition in the South, and my self-image grew as I sat tall in the saddle. I learned to ride a horse as if I'd been born on one, and I loved wearing my snappy upperclassman's uniform with the gold stars of an honor student on my sleeves.

Despite graduating among the top ten students in my class, I was never promoted beyond the rank of private while at VMI. Years later, I found out that many of my classmates who had high military ranks envied me because of my scholastic standing, but at the time my lower rank made me feel as though I hadn't completely succeeded.

There were times when the secret I carried inside me hurt especially. Other cadets' dads would arrive on campus and take their sons off for the weekend, forcing me to remember that I didn't have a father. The pain weighed still more heavily at the end of the school year when dads picked up their sons to take them home for the summer. Not only did I have to ride the bus home, but also I had to confront Mother in her costume of misery.

However, being in the cavalry kept my spirits up. Now, I realize the cavalry was an anachronism by the 1930s, when across the Atlantic the Spanish Civil War was being fought with air power and many of the other twentieth-century technologies that would soon ravage all of Europe in the Second World War. VMI, however, was a grand Southern institution with a powerful connection to our region's history, and in my opinion, nothing represented the Southern military tradition better than the cavalry.

I became an expert at leading a machine-gun squad of eight men on horses into maneuvers, with a ninth horse carrying a water-cooled machine gun, its barrel strapped to one side of the horse and the tripod to the other. We would ride at a full gallop, stop and dismount, and hand over the eight horses to a horse holder who rounded them up in a circle. The horse holder stood in the center of the circle holding all of the reins, while the rest of us took only twenty seconds to remove the machine gun, set it up on the tripod, and start firing it at the enemy (an inanimate target).

In traditional warfare, the cavalry combined firepower with speed and flexibility, giving an army the ability to surprise the enemy. We were trained to charge at a gallop, firing 45-caliber pistols within 25 feet of the enemy. We could also dismount, remove our rifle from its scabbard on the near side of the horse, again turn the horses over to a horse holder, and attack the enemy on foot. It was the usual practice to dismount in the woods or behind an elevated area of earth, so the enemy couldn't see us coming.

At VMI, we didn't have spring vacation—we had spring maneuvers. We formed a regiment complete with cavalry, infantry, and field artillery. The field artillery was horse-drawn and had as its main weapon a 75-milli-meter cannon. One of my proudest memories is that day when I was a 19-year-old first-classman (senior), and the entire regiment formed for spring maneuvers in the Shenandoah Valley. The infantry marched out first with full equipment: rifles with leather straps and accoutrement belts of gray-green canvas, 45-caliber pistols with seven rounds in a clip, full backpacks, and bayonets. They wore canvas leggings and their field boots, as well as the brass on their leather rifle holds, were clean and shiny. The cavalry, the elite of the elite, brought up the rear. Our equipment was polished and our horses groomed. Each cadet sat erect like Stonewall Jackson, chin-strapped, with peaked, brimmed, felt hats. We were ready for whatever might come.

It was on a bright Sunday morning that the infantry, the artillery, and the cavalry advanced in military formation, accompanied by the post band. Our colors flew in the breeze, and deep down in our guts, we knew we were the best in the world. We passed a row of fraternity houses at Washington and Lee University, the school that shares the town of Lexington with VMI. We kept our faces pointed straight ahead, disdainful of the lowly, bathrobed civilians lounging on the porches and reading the funny papers. I didn't know what they thought of us, but we were ready to clean their butts if they made one remark. No question about it, we out-ranked and outshone those stupid asses. Not a word was uttered by any cadet. The silence was broken only by the rattles and squeaks of the artil-lery caissons, the clip-clop of the horses' feet, and the rhythmic slap of infantry boots against the street.

What a sense of power for a group of seventeen- to twenty-one-year-old boys, citizen soldiers, noble and strong, men dedicated to the defense of their country; men trained to meet any danger, any adversity, with cour-age; men who respected their officers and cared for each other.

There is a legend about the cavalry in Poland, another land that, like the American South, has a powerful tradition linking military valor and nobility. It is said that when the German army invaded Poland in Septem-ber 1939, the Polish cavalry rushed into battle against hundreds of tanks. No match for armored tanks, the cavalry fell into disarray and was quickly wiped out. Similarly, German tanks crushed French cavalry troops attempting to defend the Ardennes Forest in 1940. The day of the horse cavalry had passed.

Be that as it may, being in the cavalry or horse-drawn field artillery was excellent training for a soldier, and many of those who were so trained became excellent tank commanders, pilots, and even naval officers in World War II. VMI taught obedience, as well as how to be a leader with commitment, responsibility, and courage. With that kind of training fore-most, it was easy to hop off a horse and learn to fight in an armored tank. For sure, I'm glad I trained on a horse rather than in a tank.

◆   ◆   ◆

At VMI, I never lost sight of my boyhood dream to become a doctor, like Uncle Joe. My admission to the Medical College of Virginia took me back to Richmond. Mother pulled strings again and helped to get me an educational loan from the Masons; my dad had been a Mason, and that made me eligible. Without the loan, I might not have been able to afford medical school. Still, during the first year, I needed to live at home with my mother again to make ends meet, and so I returned to Grace Street and moved back in with Mother.

Although I did this with some misgivings, it worked out all right. One of my classmates, Bob Morrison, moved in with me. Mother set up one of the bedrooms for us, complete with bookshelves and two desks. Mother prepared at least one daily meal for us, usually dinner, and she always wore her public costume—a smart dress, her hairpiece, and so on. Bob and I rode the bus to classes, and we came and went pretty much as we pleased. I spent a lot of time in classes and laboratories, and after I was admitted to the medical fraternity Phi Chi, I hung out there quite often, too. Meanwhile, Mother was heavily involved with her work. When I think back about that period, I realize it was not at all unpleasant; an interlude, you might say, in my longer-term difficulties with my mother.

At the beginning of my third year, I moved away from home again and into the Sheltering Arms, a small charity hospital one block from the medical school. Along with three of my classmates, I became a student doctor. Each of us was given a hospital room that had been converted into staff quarters. We did what medical students do; we made patient rounds, did physical exams, kept the charts, and so on. Of course, we were always around nurses; we dated them and escorted them to Phi Chi parties on weekends.

I was still a student doctor working at the Sheltering Arms when the army took over the medical schools, paying our tuitions so that there would be a continuous flow of young doctors graduating and ready to be called later. We were enrolled as Privates First Class thus deleting my rank as a Second Lieutenant in the Reserve Corps acquired when I graduated from VMI in 1940. I attended classes, studied hard, and delivered babies at night. Despite the freedom I had by living in my own room at the hospital, I still hadn't left home—hadn't left Virginia.

This changed suddenly after I graduated from medical school in December 1943 and immediately took a train across country to the Virginia Mason Hospital in Seattle, Washington for further medical training as an intern. At the end of nine months, I received my orders from the army to report to Carlisle Barracks, Pennsylvania as a First Lieutenant in the Medical Corps. These were welcome changes, new adventures, but they certainly did not seem permanent. I was, after all, a Southern boy with a powerful sense of belonging to my hometown, to Virginia, and to the South. I developed a specific image of myself as an adult: I would return home to become a successful doctor. I would be a prominent citizen of Richmond, living in a beautiful mansion on a hill overlooking the James River. I would ride to hounds at the Hunt Club. I pictured myself on a crisp New Year's Day in a red jacket and black riding pants, with polished tan boots and small spurs. I would sit confidently astride a magnificent horse. Our party would stop at my house for refreshments, and Negro servants dressed in white jackets would bring us hot buttered rum. People would point me out and say to each other, "That's Doctor Barnes."

Certainly, this image would have thrilled my mother. She would have loved it if I had stayed in Richmond. I suppose this remained a possibility throughout the years I spent in the army and even for a while afterward.

Two incidents changed my fate. The first occurred while I was in the army, almost on the day that I was promoted from first lieutenant to captain in 1945. I was single and stationed at Tilden General Hospital in Fort Dix, New Jersey. I received a call from Mother, begging me in a wobbly voice to come home because she was sick. My request to spend a week with my sick mother was approved, and I arrived home proud to be in uniform and proud of my captain's bars.

Mother met me at the front door in her old costume of misery, a worn, pink bathrobe, and smelling of Pond's cold cream. She still had roomers upstairs, but she had turned the front parlor into a bedroom, and that's where I stayed. There was a small bathroom between my room and hers. Her bed was unmade, and the bathroom was home to cockroaches. Mother was only fifty-seven, but she seemed really old to me. Her illness was not physical; in retrospect, I realize that she was deeply depressed and lonely, with maybe some post-menopausal symptoms. Her life hadn't changed since the catastrophe of my father's death. I tried to cheer her up and encourage her, but all I could think of was how much happier I was in the army hospital where I enjoyed my life as a medical officer. Her misery was contagious, and I wanted out of there before it infected me.

The second incident took place in August of 1949. I had married June Yeakel the year before, and our first child, Julie, was about three months old. Never had I been at home with a wife and child before. I felt happy, proud and free. We were coming from Boston, where I completed my training in internal medicine, and Mother had visited us there the previous winter. She seemed to enjoy herself, and so I hoped that when we visited her back home in Richmond, Mother would not be wrapped in her costume of misery. She had moved to another house in the meantime, and I thought the new atmosphere might have changed her.

It was during this visit that I gave my last serious thought to setting up practice in Richmond. I went to see a physician whom I had worked with during my student days. He had stirred my interest in diabetes. Like me, he had been trained at the Joslin Clinic in Boston. He received me like an old friend. He had a solo practice not far from where my mother lived, and he felt I would fit into it very well. I thanked him and said I would consider it. Then I visited two well-known surgeons who worked in a clinic attached to the Johnston/Willis Hospital, named after them. They too, said they had a place for me. I was pleased at the reception they all gave me. It looked as if my old dream of being a prominent doctor in my hometown was within reach.

It wasn't to be. Back on the home front, our visit was a disaster. Mother's attitude toward June was cool. There were times when she spoke to June in clipped sentences and cut the conversation short. Behind June's back, she made critical remarks about the way June dressed. Once while June was taking a bath, Mother and I, in another room, heard her singing in the tub. I commented, "Doesn't she have a beautiful voice?"

Mother's reply was, "Hmmph."

June, of course, could not fail to pick up on Mother's attitude and quickly came to feel unwelcome, as I did. I didn't go back to the medical school, and I didn't follow up on the possibility at Johnston/Willis Hospital. I didn't even look up any old friends. June and I visited Mother's friends, people she felt were important for me to see. As the time wore on, it became increasingly clear that Mother just was not going to accept June. When I packed June and Julie into the car at the end of the stay, I knew I was leaving home for good.

What did I owe my mother? I never really asked myself this question. All I knew was that I could not live at home any more. I chose to make my own home in Seattle, 3000 miles from the one I grew up in. It was a moment both painful and liberating. I was leaving, moving on. I'm out of here.

The weight of my moving out of there was, if anything, even greater to my mother. Seattle was June's home, and Mother knew she was defeated. Once, out of earshot to me, she said to June, "You win, I lose."

Perhaps I needed an excuse to choose Seattle for another reason. I always pictured myself practicing medicine in my own hometown, but something disturbed that picture. I was known in Richmond; I would be seeing patients who, as Mother put it, were "my people." That meant they knew about my dad's suicide. Deep down inside, I knew that the family secret wasn't really a secret in Richmond. If I stayed there, I might have to face all sorts of people who knew, patients as well as people in church. But now there was a way out: I could live somewhere else, in a city far away, where nobody knew about me. My mask would be secure, and the pain I carried would go away. I would be accepted. The feeling that everyone who looked at me could read my inner thoughts would vanish. Even my wife would not be wise to my secret, and heaven knows, the last thing I wanted was for her to find out about my pain and humiliation.

Expecting my pain to fall away was an illusion, but a part of my dream came true immediately: I found acceptance in Seattle. My in-laws took me in, loved me, and introduced me to their friends. I bonded quickly with my father-in-law, Bill, and he became a surrogate father to me even before June and I married. Bill referred his business associates to me as patients. June and I had children, and I became established as a lay leader in St. Mark's Episcopal Cathedral, two blocks from our home. Lots of good things happened, and yet it didn't take long for doubts to set in. During the first years of my medical practice, if anything went wrong, I blamed it on Seattle. It occurred to me that if only I had stayed in Virginia, everything would be all right. I began to question my earlier feeling; Seattle could not relieve me of my burden. That could happen only in my own place, my home, among the people who knew me as a child.

With a family in Seattle, it began to feel as though I had one foot on one edge of the country and the other on the opposite edge. Many years later, I returned to Richmond to visit the cemetery where my father was buried and I still had this feeling. For the first time, I looked carefully at the Barnes family tombstones—about seventeen of them, going back to my great-great-grandfather. "This is where I belong," I thought to myself. Maybe when I die, I thought further, I can be cremated; half of my ashes can be put there and half in Seattle.

No doubt, the voice of my mother haunted me. I had been in practice in Seattle for fifteen years when she asked me, during a visit, "When are you coming home, Bobby?" She underscored it further by saying, "These are not your people."

That comment told me a lot. It told me about my mother's bitterness, and it said something about why she could never completely accept June. June was a stranger; she was not a Southern girl. She was not one of "us" and, as far as Mother was concerned, she never could be one of "us."

We are all products of our upbringing, and I am no exception. I was raised to be proud of my state's long history, and for a long time I really felt deep down that Virginians were in some way better than the people on the west coast. My state had produced seven presidents, plus the President of the Confederacy. Never mind that my wife, my in-laws, my patients, and all of my new friends were Seattleites; I was still a Virginian, and that made me different.

◆   ◆   ◆

Leaving home without closure leads to sadness and inner suffering.

I felt as if I had run away from something, and in a sense, I did. In another sense, though, I did not—because I could not. The mask covered my true self.

I had never mourned my dad. I didn't cry when I learned of his death. I didn't cry at his funeral, didn't cry at the sight of his waxy face, didn't cry as the strong men lowered him into the grave. I never looked at his picture or thought about good times together with him. The only thing I do remember from sometime after he died is looking at his shoes and his hat in the hall closet. The shoes were expensive soft leather oxfords, narrow and long, and they still had a shine. The hat was of felt, also expensive, in a light gray with a black band and a wide brim turned down in front. Inside, the manufacturer's logo was inscribed in gold on the leather band.

Physical objects—that's what I remember from that time after Dad's death. But not grief; at least, not conscious grief. I never said to my mother, "I miss Dad." I never put my head in her lap and cried. I never talked about it to my sister, my grandparents, or my dad's brother and sisters. The shame and pain, combined with my mother's warning never to discuss the subject, blocked me from talking to anyone. Just as I never mourned the loss of my dad, I never mourned leaving home. Leaving home, after all, has something in common with dying. You depart one life for another. The life you leave behind deserves mourning, or at least a coming to terms with its importance: closure, if you will. When I left home that final time, in 1949, I was too caught up in making a break with the past to think about closure. Good-by, Richmond; Hello, Seattle. I left behind even my connections to the medical school; I didn't attend reunions, didn't contact my classmates or professors, didn't even keep the school informed about my mailing address.

For me, leaving home and losing my father were deeply connected. Perhaps my failure to mourn my dad's death conditioned me to suppress grief and meant that I could not mourn the passing of my early life. This inability to grieve continued long into my adulthood. When our fourth child, Sarah, died three days post partum, I did not mourn. Even when my father-in-law died, the man who came to mean so much to me, I did not mourn.

If we do not know how to mourn or we deny our grief, we wear a mask. One of the requirements of growing up is taking off our masks and letting the tears fall where they may, like autumn leaves fluttering to the ground.

Whether we know it or not, we are deeply affected by our losses. We suffer with them forever unless we learn to mourn, to share our story, and even to reminisce with the dead.

It took me many years to confront the memories of my childhood and youth. June and the kids and I rarely visited my mother. It wasn't until after Mother's death that I was willing to return to my childhood haunts. I went back to Richmond several times then. I walked through the grade school and remembered that my dad sometimes drove me there if it was raining or snowing. I spent much time sitting on the steps across the street from the house on Grace Street where we lived. I always told June I wanted to be alone for a while. I took a picture of the windows on the second floor where his bed was. I peeked through the window into the living room where he lay in his casket. I walked around to the alley behind the house to see the window of the linen closet that had been my room. I went to the Second Presbyterian Church and sat down in the pew where our family sat. I sat there a long time.

Ironically, Mother's death freed me to return to my roots. Besides visiting my childhood haunts, I returned to VMI for the first time to attend my 50th class reunion, and what a thrill it was! My classmates told me how happy they were to see me, and tears came to my eyes. Most importantly, since my mother died I have confessed the secret about my father to several close friends. I was astonished by how understanding they were, and my heart was filled with warmth by their expressions of sadness for the loss I suffered as a child.

◆   ◆   ◆

How does one reconcile with the memory of a mother who worked so hard to raise her children but could not express her love to them? A mother who pinched pennies and pulled strings to put her kids through good schools but alienated them emotionally? A mother who silently wished to hold her family together and keep her children near her through their adult lives but rejected the spouses they chose and drove a wedge between herself and them? A widowed mother who bucked up and showed the world a mask of confidence but crumbled to dust within the walls of her own home?

In life, there are certain things that you simply have to do. For me, leaving home was one of them. Leaving home brought me a new life together with my Seattle family and my Seattle people. Yes, they became my people. I have learned that my people and my home can be wherever I am.

It is always tempting to ask, What if...? What if Mother had not been overtaken by depression? What if she had been able to say I love you? What if, instead of "These are not your people," she could have had the grace to say, "You have people in Seattle, but you also left people back home who love you"? But of course, we cannot change the past by saying What if...?

In my picture of leaving home, my mother stands at the curbside in front of her house on a scorching summer day. She has on a short-sleeved cotton dress. I am in the driver's seat of a two-door Ford coupe, and the motor is running. I am going away to live and practice medicine three thousand miles distant in Seattle, Washington. In the car with me are June, my wife of one year, and our three-month-old daughter Julie. Mother is waving good-by to us, and June waves the hand of our baby at her. I wave from behind the wheel, leaning forward to get a better look at Mother. Her lips are trembling. I press on the accelerator and shift gears. We slowly move forward, still waving. I turn the corner and Mother is gone.

PART II
The Clothing of the Physician

5

Putting on the White Coat

In the first year of medical school, you are hit by culture, language, and information shock. You are immersed in the world of chemistry, anatomy, pathology, and physiology. You deal with the living, the sick, and the dying, with new smells and new tactile experiences. To me, medical school was exhilarating and frightening.

Two things gave me anxiety: the possibility of flunking out and the nagging sense that I could never become a real doctor. I thought of Uncle Joe and all he did and knew. Me be a doctor? What a silly notion. To be responsible for life and death seemed a mystical notion, not a real possibility. We wore long, white coats for anatomy lab and carried notebooks, pens, and medical equipment in our pockets. We sat in amphitheaters, watched demonstrations and presentations of patients, and listened to lectures. We went to clinics and watched real doctors perform magic, make diagnoses and tell patients what to do to get well. It was amazing, beyond my imagination as a first-year student.

It all came together in the anatomy lab. The laboratory was a temple, a sacred place with the odor of formaldehyde and the sight of corpses on stretchers stacked in cubicles in a wall. Our first "patients" were dead persons to be dissected down to the smallest detail of nerves, muscles, heart, lungs, stomach, bowel, brain, bones, and more.

The lab was a large room surrounded by windows almost from floor to ceiling. There were metal-topped dissecting tables row on row, two stools on each side, four students to each body. On the walls of the lab were colored drawings of all the parts of the body: muscles red, bones yellowish-white, arteries red, veins blue, nerves whitish-blue—layer upon layer of drawings similar to architect's drawings, but of a human body rather than a building. The cadavers that we worked on had been soaked in formaldehyde so their tissue would not degenerate. They tended to be stiff, their skin leathery and dark. All body parts were preserved, although there was little fat. We eventually found out that cutting into a live person in surgery was very different, but we didn't learn that until our later years of schooling.

There is no experience like the anatomy lab. Even doing autopsies on the recently dead is an entirely different experience because the tissues are still soft, and facial features and skin look real. In contrast, our corpse in anatomy lab was more like a mummy preserved forever in formaldehyde.

The first day, the professor and his retinue of assistants faced us with the rules in the lab. There would be no funny business, no mockery of the dead, no jokes. There would be respect, and a sense that we were confronting the divine. We would each treat the body we worked with as a temple of the mystery of life. Horseplay would not be tolerated.

The professor was a small man with a gray goatee, pink cheeks, and light blue eyes. He spoke with a deep Germanic accent. He impressed me as a loving man, one who would listen to each student's problems with great intensity. He walked quietly among the lab tables, like an elderly father helping his children out of any distress as we delved into the intricacies of the human body. I respected him and always listened to what he said. When he watched me dissect an intricate nerve system, I did it gently with a sense of humility and an eagerness to learn. When he demonstrated to a group of students how to dissect an intricate part of the body, we watched in awe.

My student foursome began by going to the wall where the bodies were stacked. We pulled open a metal door and carefully pulled out a stretcher containing the body of a man, with whom we would live for months to come. The stretcher was made of a dull gray metal. There were dents in it and two metal handles on each end that we used to carry it to our dissecting table.

We had to be careful pulling the stretcher out of the wall. The body could slide forward if we lowered the head of the stretcher, or slide off if we tilted the side. I had a strange vision of myself awkwardly grabbing the cadaver and trying to keep it from falling to the floor—not an appetizing thought, as I still hadn't touched the body and felt somewhat repulsed by it. As I think back on it, never during our year in the anatomy lab did a student stumble or tilt a stretcher so that a body fell to the floor. Thanks in part to our professor, we were aware of the humanness of our cadavers, and we took care. As the days went by, we got more and more proficient at handling them.

As we laid the body out before us, I suddenly became aware that I was in a large room filled with corpses, one on every table. This was a visual experience new to all of us students. I don't know about the others, but I had every feeling in the book—squeamish, repulsed, awed. I hated the formaldehyde smell. I realized that as a medical student, I was different and separated from all other people in the world, who would never enter a room like this. At the same time, I was excited to get started. Deep inside, I remembered the time I was the little boy in a blue suit gazing at the waxy nose and forehead of my dad in his casket.

When it came time to start dissection, the professor demonstrated how to hold the scalpels and explained when to use other instruments such as scissors, tweezers, and retractors. We started on the thorax, or chest. By chance, I was picked to make the first incision. It was to be down the center of the chest over the sternum, a bone approximately two inches in diameter, to which the ribs are attached. I held the scalpel in my right hand and, with some trepidation, made the incision. The skin over the bone was dry and leathery, and I had to apply some pressure. Physically it was easy, but being aware that I was cutting the body of a human being created an emotional issue. I did it slowly and with care to keep the pressure appropriate. My cadaver was a black man, and the inside of the skin that opened along the incision line was a lighter tan than the skin on the surface of the chest. There was no bleeding; blood had been drained from all of the cadavers.

Several years later, I made my first incision in a live person and discovered that not nearly so much pressure is needed. A sharp scalpel goes through skin, fat, and muscle quickly, and doing it just right requires a touch gained by experience. Of course, in surgery, the blood vessels have to be cauterized or tied off to stop the bleeding.

In the anatomy lab, we sat on stools, leaning over closely to do the fine dissection. The nervous system is especially tedious. For example, exposing the complex nerves in the neck and following each one to its destination is an unbelievably difficult puzzle. The neck is a superhighway more crowded and snarled than an automobile freeway. All of the nerves, large and small, long and short, make their way between muscles, ligaments, and blood vessels to supply the facial muscles, tongue, and all things that move on command from headquarters, the brain.

Within a month or two of almost daily communion, we developed a strange kind of bonding with our cadavers. No two were exactly alike; mine was probably middle-aged, with a slim body and a head of short, kinky, black hair. Never before or since have I spent so much time sitting beside a body, living or dead, getting to know every detail of his anatomy. After months of observation, each body part was cemented in the visual storage section of my brain. Sixty years have passed and still, as I write these words, I can see that man's body as clearly as if I were sitting on the stool beside him. If I were to see my cadaver again, I would be awestruck and respectful. I am forever grateful for the gift that man gave me by making his body available for my education after his death.

A visitor peeking into the anatomy lab might be amazed at the sight: students sitting at the table with a cadaver, intact in places but split wide open in others. A student might nonchalantly eat a sandwich at lunchtime and wipe his hands on his white coat, now smudged and wrinkled. How could one sit by a cadaver and enjoy a peanut butter and jelly sandwich? If the visitor came back a few months later, the scene would have changed. A leg might be on the table, the rest of the cadaver gone.

At the end of the session, the visitor would see each student put a tag on the leg he has been working on, and take it to a large vat containing other parts. The student would lower the leg into the vat, wipe his hands on his coat, and go back to the lab table. He would wash the table off with soap and water. Finally, he would close his anatomy book, which had lain on the stool, and leave the lab through the swinging doors. The next morning, the student had to fish around in the vat to find his cadaver's leg, identified by his name on the red tag.

Sets of bones were loaned to each student and stored in a wooden box long enough to hold the leg bones, in particular the tibia and femur. During my first year, I often took the box home with me on the streetcar to study the bones. And one time the inevitable happened: While I was boarding a crowded streetcar on the way to school, the lid on my bone box popped up and some of the bones fell to the floor. I scrambled to get the bones back in the box while the people around me watched with a mixture of amusement and horror.

In those days, many people in the community looked upon medical students as morally questionable and not to be trusted dating a nice girl. After all, we studied subjects like sex. It was assumed that we had learned and inspected the female private parts in detail. With this knowledge, we should have been able to overwhelm any normal young lady. Such was the hidden fear of any respectable mother with a daughter who was brought up properly. Personally, I felt more comfortable dating nursing students, and they fitted right in with the raucous medical fraternity parties on the weekends. I must add, however, that working on cadavers, examining female patients, delivering babies, and doing circumcisions faded into the background and didn't enter into the same thought pattern as dating a beautiful girl.

◆   ◆   ◆

I was a second-year medical student when Japan attacked Pearl Harbor on December 7, 1941. Like many Americans, I had no idea where Pearl Harbor was. When President Roosevelt announced the attack and asked Congress for a declaration of war against Japan, I was in a physiology lab, operating on a big, black street dog. Along with three other classmates, I was trying to put a catheter into a blood vessel in the dog's neck. Of course, we were distracted by the news of the war; I don't remember what we did or failed to do, but our dog died, leaving me with a vivid personal memory of the war's outbreak. Having had four years of military training at VMI, I received a telegram the next day ordering me to report to the army for duty as a lieutenant. When I reported to army headquarters in Richmond and they learned I was a medical student, I was deferred from active duty and returned to medical school.

In 1943, the army took over the medical school. All of us in the army reserve were inducted into service at Camp Lee, Virginia. Our work at medical school was accelerated so we could graduate as soon as possible. We went to school in army uniform, taking no spring or summer breaks, and we graduated in a total of three and a half years. I was only twenty when I entered medical school, so I was not quite 24 when I received my medical degree.

By 1942, the war reached a fever pitch. Hitler's forces had subdued the European continent, but they were meeting Allied resistance in North Africa. Allied troops moved in quickly, staging tank attacks from El Alamein against the Germans, who were led by General Rommel. One of my VMI roommates, Dick Miller, was a tank commander in Africa.

Meanwhile, during that summer, I drove to Rochester, Minnesota, with three classmates whose fathers were doctors on the staff of the Mayo Clinic. It was a great trip from the start—lots of laughter, good camaraderie, and beer drinking. I was impressed by Rochester, a quiet and lovely small town filled with trees and flowers, and yet the home of the world's most famous medical clinic. The town's hotels were often filled with families of patients from around the world, or patients themselves if they did not need hospitalization.

The Mayo clinic and hospitals were the town's centerpiece. The clinic was a handsome red brick structure, fifteen stories tall, containing most of the doctors' offices, laboratories, and the clinic administration. There were several hospitals, each of which occupied an entire city block.

I remember watching my first surgery at St. Mary's Hospital. Over each surgical suite, there was a glass-enclosed balcony, located almost directly above the surgical table. Visiting doctors or students could observe as the great surgeons operated. In the neurosurgical suite, a famous brain surgeon was operating, along with a number of associates. A microphone hung over the table, connected to a speaker up on the balcony, so that the surgeon could explain what was happening every moment. Because the glass enclosing the balcony was slanted, there were times when I feared I might fall off my chair, crash through the glass, and land on the surgical table.

As I watched the operation, the head surgeon suddenly whacked his assistant's gloved hand with a steel retractor and told him to leave the surgery. The young doctor turned from the table and walked out. After the door to the surgery room closed, the surgeon spoke to the visitors. "This young man is an excellent surgeon," he said. "He has been with me for five years, but in spite of his experience, he did something that is inexcusable. He crossed his hand over mine, obstructing my view, and interrupted my focus. I scolded him in front of everyone so that he will always remember never to do that again"

I thought the doctor's behavior was arrogant, and it made me think that I never wanted to be a surgeon. It was not the last time I would witness such arrogance; as an assistant in surgery at a hospital in Seattle, for example, I saw the chief of surgery squirt a syringe full of saline in the face of a nurse who had made a mistake. I was watching surgery in a period when at least some excellent surgeons acted like bullies, with the idea that perfection can be taught through punishment.

On another day, I met some urological surgeons in their dressing room, gowning up to do a prostate surgery. Two of them were wagering on how much the tissue obtained from the prostate would weigh. As a neophyte just through his second year of medical school, I was both surprised and pleased by this relaxed jocularity. It made me realize that being a surgeon was not always a life-and-death situation. There was time for fun.

It was also a time that changed my life. While in Rochester, I asked to meet the staff physician who was in charge of selecting candidates for advanced medical training. I asked him how I might be considered for an appointment after I graduated from medical school. He recommended that I seek an internship at Johns Hopkins in Baltimore, or Virginia Mason in Seattle. This was how I happened to land eventually in Seattle. But that's getting ahead of the story.

Why had I decided to become a doctor? There may have been several reasons. Becoming a doctor would enable me to help people. It would make me *somebody*, a person others would love and respect. It would save me from my shame and the doctors white coat might elevate my self-image. Most of all, I believe it was my experience with Uncle Joe. He was my childhood role model. My memory of Uncle Joe making his rounds never faded. I knew from the time I spent that summer with him, when I was ten years old, that I wanted to be like Uncle Joe.

And what if Uncle Joe had been a carpenter, a journalist, or a grocer? It's quite possible that whatever he was I might have wanted to be. Certainly, it occurred to me while I worked at the Safeway that I could be a store manager. But no, Uncle Joe was a doctor. And that's what I became.

It wasn't that I was so intrigued by the science of the profession. My medical training was interesting, but that wasn't what drew me in. After all, no one ever said to me that to be like Uncle Joe I would have to go to medical school and operate on dogs. No one told me I would have to study a tubercle bacillus through a microscope. It was the *human* part of Uncle Joe's role model that captured my imagination. Uncle Joe may have been a simple country doctor, but to me, he was a hero. I had a sense that his patients thought so, too.

◆   ◆   ◆

At the beginning of my third year in medical school, I took off the long, white coat of the anatomy and physiology labs and put on the shorter white coat of a student doctor to join the house staff of a fifty-bed charity hospital. It was not the usual thing for medical students to work in a hospital, but the opportunity came up and I needed the modest salary offered for the position. Three other students took similar positions. Two of us were in our third year of medical school, and two were in their fourth. As living quarters, we each had a hospital room with a toilet. For the first time, I was called "Doctor," even though I hadn't received my degree. I was twenty-two years old, and being called Doctor made me both impressed with myself and a little intimidated.

Along with our status, our routine changed. We had been exposed to sick patients during our first two years, although we mostly interviewed them to write the medical history in the chart. We never participated in a case, not even to the point of diagnosing the disease or condition. When I arrived at the charity hospital on a sunny Sunday afternoon in September 1942, I had never delivered a baby, never been in surgery, never sewn up a wound or ordered a medicine. My experience in obstetrics included some lectures, book study, and demonstrations of a delivery using a doll and observing it passing through a plastic model of a female pelvis. I had never been in a nursery with newborns

The first thing that happened to me as a student doctor took place while I was on duty and the other three student doctors were off. I got a call that there was a woman in labor on the third-floor obstetrical wing; I was to go there immediately and examine her. I had never examined a pregnant woman in my life—nor any other woman, if we exclude my adolescent observations of our comely tenant through the keyhole.

Rather than take the rickety elevator with its heavy iron door, I ran up three flights of stairs. Breathlessly, I pushed open the fireproof metal door, stubbed my toe, and sprawled onto the hallway floor, my stethoscope sailing through the air. Standing there in the hallway were the husband, a grandmother, and two small children. As I jumped up and grabbed my stethoscope, the husband asked, "When is the doctor coming?"

I said, "I am the doctor," and pushed the door open into the delivery room, embarrassed.

My duty was to count the woman's contractions and do a rectal exam to determine the dilation of the cervix (the opening into the uterus). The wall between the rectum and vagina is thin, so you can easily feel the cervix—if you know what you're doing. After I examined the woman, I was to call her real doctor and report her condition to him.

Feeling and counting the contraction was easy enough. When it came to the rectum, however, not only had I never put my finger in a woman's rectum, but I had never seen one before. I dutifully put on a rubber glove the nurse handed me and held my index finger out for the lubricant. The nurse had already turned the patient onto her left side, with her right leg pulled up. By pushing her right buttock up, I exposed her rectum. I reassured the mother-to-be that I wouldn't hurt her. (It occurred to me at the moment that that was what a real doctor would do.) I inserted my finger into the woman's rectum as far as it would go and hoped to feel the opening of the cervix. I had no idea what I was feeling. I poked around in all directions and then, with an air of great authority, said I would call her doctor and give him the information. Hurriedly I pushed the door open, smiled at the waiting family in a manner as professional as I could muster, and headed down the hall to the phone booth. I told the real doctor that I thought the cervix was dilated about four fingers and that the lady would deliver soon, and I asked him to come immediately.

The doctor must have broken all speeding laws, because he was there in no time. He tore his coat and suit jacket off while running up the stairs, and burst into the delivery room. He immediately examined the patient, noting that all contraction had ceased. Upon examining her rectum, he stated that the cervix was barely dilated at all. The woman was having a few false contractions and didn't deliver for several days.

The doctor was kind to me. He told me I had been a help to him and got me to do another rectal exam. He instructed me what to feel for and explained where I would find the cervix. I have always been grateful to him, because before the year was over I considered myself pretty good at determining how far along a woman was in labor. I never forgot how wonderful it is when a neophyte is given a guiding hand by an experienced doctor. Fortunately, I didn't bump into the patient's family in the hall again.

◆   ◆   ◆

Another of our tasks as student doctors was performing circumcisions. I had never thought about it before, but—if you'll pardon the anatomically incorrect metaphor—circumcisions can be a pain in the neck. They are not difficult to do, but if a hospital is delivering a lot of babies, male babies can pile up in number.

The usual procedure in those days was to tie the baby down to what was irreverently called a "frog board." The board was curved like a baby's frame so that the baby's little legs could be secured to leg boards and his arms stretched out on arm boards. Babies showed their dislike for frog boards by howling as soon as they were fastened down, with their howls reaching a higher level during the actual circumcision. It was assumed that babies didn't suffer pain like adults—or at least the procedure didn't take long—so an anesthetic wasn't necessary. As a student, I didn't think too much about the pain, but I did get tired of the howling.

Sometimes there would be a run on male babies and, what with working hard at medical school, I would get behind and have to do five or ten circumcisions in an afternoon so the newborns could go home with their mothers. At that time, most mothers stayed in the hospital after delivery for as long as a week for rest and observation, and the circumcision had to be done sometime before they were released.

Because mothers stayed longer than they do today, the nursery was an active, noisy place. I performed circumcisions in a little room off to the side of the nursery. There were two ways to perform the operation. One way was to place a small metal cup made to fit the head of the baby's penis, pull the foreskin over the outside of the cup, and simply cut the foreskin off, guided by the edge of the cup. A few stitches were needed to hold the edges together and stop the bleeding. The other way was to use specially made scissors. This method involved slipping the blade beneath the foreskin, cutting in a straight line along the top of the penis, and then cutting in a lateral circle along the edge of the head. It is so simple that any housewife could learn the procedure.

Rabbis, of course, are experts. Most rabbis I have watched pull the foreskin forward over the top of the penis and then, using a knife, cut it off in one whack. Personally, I prefer the cup, finding it much neater.

If I had been paid by the piece, so to speak, I could have received a fairly decent income just by performing circumcisions. As a student doctor, however, I received a flat salary of 50 dollars per month plus room, board, and laundry service. Actually, I didn't mind because in 1942 fifty dollars was a lot of money for incidentals.

I got tired of doing circumcisions, though, and have never performed one since graduating from medical school. Today, circumcisions are controversial from a medical standpoint, but when they are performed, I'm glad to say that a local anesthetic is used to stop the pain. Remembering how those babies howled, I'm sure the procedure is painful. If I had continued to do circumcisions, I would eventually have had to wear ear plugs.

◆   ◆   ◆

It was unusual for a medical student to treat a white patient. This being the era of segregation in the South, the medical school had what was called a "colored" hospital as well as a large hospital and medical center for white people, which, interestingly enough, was not referred to as the "white" hospital. Segregation was a way of life. Today, the word "colored" is politically incorrect, and we are all aware that "nigger" is demeaning. I use these words only for the sake of capturing the vernacular of the time. In those days, we didn't often use the word "black," and when we did, it wasn't a positive term. I don't remember using "Afro-American." I hasten to add that, because I grew up as a white southerner in a segregationist culture I thought it was normal for colored people to sit in the back of a bus, to enter a "white" house through the back door, and to use a separate toilet and not eat in a white restaurant. As I worked with colored people in my days as a student doctor, I began to change.

I enjoyed working at the colored hospital. The patients were grateful, easy to work with, and very human. The hospital was not as clean or up to date as the white hospital, and the wards were larger; as many as twenty-five patients filling a large ward. Medical students, who were from the same segregationist culture, soon discovered that colored people's blood was just as red as that of the white folks—and on the inside, both look the same. It seems strange to say it now, but we learned that a wound or fracture hurt just as much to a colored person as to a white person.

The emergency room at St. Philip's on Saturday night was a madhouse. Patients came in with gunshot wounds to the head, blood pouring out of the hole, or long slash wounds to the abdomen, with their bowels hanging out. The floor became slippery with blood. I sometimes worked at one of the operating tables, helping to sew up people's bodies. I never asked questions about why coloreds knifed and shot each other. I didn't feel squeamish or shocked by what I saw, and learning how to sew up wounds and give shots for pain was very moving to me. Working in the emergency room is totally absorbing, and it gave me a sense of being special. To be sure, the sight and smell of blood and guts are, to say the least, unpleasant; however, I quickly got used to it and didn't let the unpleasantness keep me from doing what I had to do.

◆   ◆   ◆

In those days, many women had their babies at home, especially the poor and the colored. Medical students occasionally did home deliveries, but only for colored mothers, not white mothers—and only for women who had successfully delivered babies before; we never delivered a mother's first baby at home. A fourth-year and third-year student went together by streetcar, carrying an OB (obstetrics) box containing sterile sheets, towels, gloves, scissors to cut the umbilical cord, and a piece of sturdy line to tie the cord. We did not use forceps, because we performed only uncompli-cated deliveries at home. If there were complications, such as hemorrhag-ing or abnormal fetal position, we called the ambulance and sent the mother to the hospital.

I had assisted with several deliveries at the hospital, as well as one that took place in a taxi. Then the moment came late one night when one of my fellow student doctors and I got the call. We hurried out of the hospi-tal and boarded the streetcar, carrying our OB box. With our white medi-cal school coats on, we didn't have to pay the five cents fare. There were only a few people on the car, but everyone stared at us. I felt important to be delivering a baby. The streetcar took us deep into the colored section of town, a neighborhood of old, two-story, wooden row houses with sharply pitched roofs.

We found the address and walked up three steps onto a porch. To the right of the door was a window with lace curtains pulled close, but we could see through them into a room where a lighted floor lamp stood beside an empty chair. I knocked on the door, which had a long, elliptical window covered by another lace curtain. Inside, a beam of light suddenly struck the hallway floor as an interior door opened.

A woman opened the door and said, in her African-American vernacular, "We sure is glad to see you. I'm Rose. I lives next door and I'm here to help Isabella."

I introduced myself as Dr. Barnes, and my partner introduced himself. I didn't admit that this was my first home delivery, but I felt sure Rose could detect my ineptness just by looking at me. I suspected she could hear my heart beating.

The two of us picked up the OB box and followed her into the hall, which ran the length of the row house to the kitchen in the rear. We turned right into the first room, where our patient lay propped up on pillows under a sheet that outlined the curve of her enlarged abdomen. It startled us to see four small children asleep on the same bed with the mother, the oldest about six and the youngest a baby, perhaps one year old.

We set our box down and introduced ourselves to Isabella. She was a big woman with a round, heavy face and very dark skin, highlighting her beautiful, white teeth. Her hair was curly and short, and she had on gold earrings. I had the feeling she was a pro at this baby-delivering business. Her neighbor Rose wore her hair braided in pigtails and looked younger than Isabella. Isabella's husband had gone out to a tavern "with the boys" and would come home after the baby was delivered.

The room was small, and the bed pushed up against the wall both at the head and at one side. There was an old rocking chair with a worn-out brown pillow and a couple of straight-backed chairs, and throw rugs of a nondescript color and pattern. The only light came from a small bulb hanging by its cord from the ceiling.

I sat down by the bedside, took Isabella's blood pressure and pulse, listened to her heart and lungs, and recorded the data on a chart. She said the contractions were slow and not too strong yet. Her water had broken about an hour before we arrived. Rose cleaned everything up and changed the sheets. Isabella told us she'd had no serious problems with any of her previous pregnancies, although she bled a lot after the last one; the bleeding stopped after the doctor packed her vagina with gauze, stuck pillows under her buttocks to elevate her pelvis, and gave her a shot.

I examined her abdomen. She was at full term, and according to her menstrual history, she was due. My partner listened to the fetal heart tones, recorded the rates, and described the sounds as full and regular. We took turns counting the contractions and recording them on the chart. I put on a glove, did a rectal exam—correctly this time—and felt the cervix dilated about four fingers, which told me that the baby's head had descended into the pelvis. Isabella was coming along, but had a ways to go.

We opened the OB box and checked the equipment. Rose had newspaper nearby to put under Isabella at the time of delivery, and she was heating water in a bucket in the kitchen. Everything appeared to be in order. By palpating the abdomen, we confirmed my judgment based on the rectal exam that the baby was in a normal position. We were not absolutely sure of that, because there were certain things we were unable to see. For example, the head could come down with the face looking up at the ceiling; that can make for difficult delivery. Or the umbilical cord could be twisted around the baby's neck or body. But as far as we could tell at this point, all seemed well. There was no phone in the house, but Rose had one, so my partner went next door and reported the patient's status to the OB resident at the medical school.

We expected the contractions to increase in strength and number, but for some reason they quieted down for an hour. I dozed off while my partner counted contractions and talked to the mother. Finally, at about two a.m., the contractions got stronger and Isabella began to holler, "Jesus, Lord, have mercy!"

She raised her arms up and held onto the headboard. The baby's head was way down in the birth canal. We spread the newspapers under Isabella. She opened her legs wide, and before long we could see the black hair of the baby's head through the dilating vaginal opening. The contractions were building to a crescendo, Isabella shouting out for Jesus and occasionally throwing in a "shit" or two. Finally, the baby's head came out, face down and turned a little toward the left. Out came the shoulders, abdomen and legs, black like the mother, covered with blood and amniotic fluid. It was a healthy boy.

We laid the baby on the papers, which immediately became wet and bloody. We clamped off the umbilical cord and cut it. I tied the cord securely, and we wrapped the baby in a clean towel and laid him on his mother's belly. We used a small syringe to suck out the mucus from the baby's mouth. Then we took out a set of scales from the OB box, gently laid the baby on it, and recorded the weight as six pounds, fourteen ounces.

Rose brought warm towels and washed the baby. He let out a few loud howls and then was quiet. We listened to his heart and lungs, put drops in his eyes, checked his feet and hands. Everything appeared to be in working order. I was exuberant.

Before long, the placenta came out. There was minimal bleeding. My partner and I cleaned up while Rose wrapped the baby in warm towels and transferred him to a crib. She then washed Isabella's legs and abdomen, and helped her into a clean nightgown. Rose would stay the night, a wonderful friend to her next-door neighbor.

Three of Isabella's children had woken up and watched the whole process, wide-eyed and silent, but the smallest baby slept through it all. I never did see their dad.

We congratulated Isabella, thanked Rose for her help, and assured them the baby was healthy. We put our dirty equipment in the OB box and said goodbye. The streetcar was empty of passengers except for the two of us. When we got back to the medical school, we proudly reported in, completed the chart, and went to bed. We had performed our first delivery with success. I couldn't help remembering Uncle Joe, and I felt he would be proud of me.

6

The Psychiatrist's Ring: Caring for the Mentally Wounded

In September 1944, after completing an internship at The Virginia Mason Hospital in Seattle, Washington, I took off the white coat of the civilian doctor and put on the uniform of an army officer with silver first lieutenant's bars on the shoulders and the gold caduceus on each lapel. I felt even more excited wearing the dark green jacket, brown shirt, and black tie than I had putting on the white doctor's coat. I wore pants that were called "pinks" because they were beige with a slight pinkish tint. I had no decorations and wondered for a moment if I could wear the Mounted Sharpshooter medal I had won as a cavalry cadet at VMI, but my intuition told me no; why would a medical officer wear a cavalry medal?

I bought my uniform in a men's clothing store in downtown Seattle, and it didn't immediately hit me that in a few weeks I would be back on the east coast, caring for battle casualties from Europe. The Allied Forces had landed at Omaha Beach in France and were trying to break through the German army to liberate Paris. Reports reached us from Ernie Pyle, the famous Press Corps reporter beloved for his descriptions of GI Joe in the horrors of war. General George Patton, described as the toughest son-of-a-bitch in the Armed Forces, was commanding the troops in Europe. The war was raging, and there was a shortage of doctors available to care for the wounded.

My orders sent me to Carlisle Barracks, Pennsylvania, a military orientation camp for newly inducted medical officers. Young doctors were not thought of as competent field officers—and for good reason: medical schools didn't teach their graduates how to function as military officers. The great majority had no military training whatsoever; some wore their insignia upside-down, saluted awkwardly, and didn't know how to stand at attention properly. Later, when they reached the battlefield, they would get more respect; the presence of doctors and medical corpsmen behind the front lines gave the morale of the GIs a tremendous boost, and they were worshipped for their ability to stop pain and save lives. But for now, they had to be quickly converted into military officers, something that wasn't easy for many of them.

I got off the bus at Carlisle Barracks with all of my possessions in a duffel bag and gave the sentinel at the gate, an enlisted man, my snappiest VMI salute, determined to show him I wasn't one of those medical officers who didn't know their rear end from a hole in the wall. Once inside, I saw a long line of soldiers marching in a column of fours, all looking as if they'd been stamped with a cookie cutter—green, bucket combat helmets, first lieutenant's silver bar on each shoulder. My God, I thought, those are all doctors. There were a thousand of us, all civilian doctors about to be converted to medical officers.

Before dinner that evening, we lined up in three battalions, each with three companies. A colonel walked the lines, inspecting each officer. When he came to me, he stopped and looked me up and down. I stood straight, shoulders back, chin in, cap on straight, hands at my trouser seams.

He asked, "Where did you get your military training, Lieutenant?"

"At the Virginia Military Institute, sir."

He said, "I'm assigning you to be a battalion commander."

"Yes, sir," I said.

I broke ranks and marched out in front of the battalion. Later, along with the two other battalion commanders, I gave the orders as the flag was lowered at evening retreat. I was twenty-four years old, a temporary commander of a battalion made up of all doctors, and it was wartime. I felt proud that I could perform not only as a doctor, but also as an officer. In the army, no matter what your specialty, you are an officer first.

Basic training was tough, especially for the new medical officers who arrived with no military experience. One of the hardest experiences was drilling with gas masks. We had been told this would happen without warning. We were making our way up a hill, steep, when there was a loud explosion and dense smoke rolled towards us. An officer yelled, "Gas!" A thousand doctors stopped in their tracks and struggled to cover their faces with gas masks amid smoke that quickly became so thick it was hard to see. It was panic time getting those masks on. I put mine on too tight, and when I reached the top of the hill where the smoke was clearing, I was short of breath and my head was pounding. Fortunately, it went better the next time we did it.

We also had target drill with 45-calibre pistols. It might seem odd that doctors were taught to shoot, but in combat, doctors occasionally have to defend themselves. Moreover, there are times when a doctor has to take command of his combat unit. One example was on Guadalcanal, where a doctor assumed command of a company amid a fierce battle against the Japanese in which all other officers in the company were killed.

One morning at the Carlisle center, all one thousand of us marched into an auditorium to learn about how to locate, set up, and use a battalion aid station, or BAS. On the stage was a set representing the headquarters of a battalion. A colonel sat at a table along with his staff of majors, captains, and lieutenants. Behind them was a large, detailed map, which the colonel used to describe a hypothetical battle situation, with a U.S. Army division on the move against the Germans. The colonel called on the battalion medical officer to tell where he would locate the BAS. At the end of the table sat a young first lieutenant with Red Cross patches on his helmet, his arms, and even the seat of his pants. The medical insignia on his shirt collar was upside down. He gave the impression he didn't know forward from backward. He stood up awkwardly, and all of us in the audience laughed uproariously.

He walked toward the map, tried to locate the main line of departure and the main line of resistance, and then figure out where the BAS should be. He pointed with his finger at a place and said, "Right here."

The colonel jumped up and yelled, "My God, man, that's on top of a hill. You'll be wiped out in minutes, you and all your wounded!"

The lieutenant, seeming (or acting) shaken by the colonel's ire and the audience's laughter, made another wrong choice before hitting on the right spot: behind the hill, where the station would be protected from enemy fire and water was available from a nearby stream. The humorous skit taught us all something important about how to locate a battalion aid station—and the crucial need for a doctor to know how to read a map.

◆   ◆   ◆

I made a fateful decision one day while standing in formation among a group of about fifty medical officers. A staff officer, not a doctor, read off an announcement: Volunteers were sought for two special training programs. The first, a program for medical paratroopers, didn't sound appealing. I had visions of myself jumping out of the sky into the thick of battle, being shot at on the way down, getting caught in a tree, plucked out by the enemy, and hauled off to God knows what fate. It's not that I wished to avoid combat; in truth, I wanted to be sent to the front, felt that was my duty and my destiny as an officer. But I just didn't see myself jumping out of an airplane.

The second request was for training in military neuropsychiatry. The staff officer explained, a bit cryptically, what that meant: helping servicemen who develop mental and emotional conditions during the heat of battle. I remember precisely the officer's words at the end of his announcement: "Any officer who wishes to volunteer for training as a military neuropsychiatrist, step one pace forward."

I punched the lieutenant next to me and whispered, "Sounds better than being a medical paratrooper." I stepped forward, but he didn't.

Too late, I remembered the old army slogan, "Keep your bowels open, your mouth shut, and never volunteer for anything." I immediately wondered if I shouldn't have just let the dice fall where they might. I didn't have to volunteer for either of these programs.

Deep down, however, I felt drawn to the idea of being a military psychiatrist. In medical school, I had seen many patients with anxiety states—insomnia, fatigue, stomach gas, difficulty concentrating, and so on—when no physical diagnosis could be made. We used terms like psychosomatic, body-mind disorder, or psychoneurosis; or we simply wrote down something like "pain in the back, cause unknown." Such cases fascinated me, and I got along comfortably with the patients even if I wasn't able to cure them. The thought of caring for people in emotional distress hit me somewhere deep inside. Maybe the fact that I myself carried the weight of personal anxiety—the secret of my father's suicide—gave me a special feeling for others who had their own inner burdens. It was almost by instinct that I volunteered to become a military psychiatrist.

I didn't know exactly what I'd be doing, but I knew I'd soon find out. I reported for duty at Pilgrim General Hospital on Long Island, joining a class of approximately 100 doctors for a crash course in the care and treatment of neuropsychiatric casualties. The need was great, for the number of psychiatric casualties in World War II was very high. According to Dr. William C. Menninger, chief consultant in neuropsychiatry to the Surgeon General from 1943–1946, around one million American servicemen were hospitalized for psychiatric reasons. The peak occurred in April 1945, when the number of neuropsychiatric patients in army hospitals at one time reached nearly 50,000.

We were not well prepared for such numbers, despite the fact that the problem had been well documented after World War I, particularly by the British. In fact, the U.S. armed forces had no medical plan for psychiatric care until 1944. When I went on active duty in September of that year, there was a critical shortage of doctors knowledgeable about military psychiatry, and many of us had to be trained quickly.

Something else I didn't know at the time was that many "real" physicians looked down upon psychiatrists and thought they were a bit nutty. Some doctors seemed threatened by psychiatrists and tended to avoid them, as if they feared that the "shrinks" could read their minds or had the power to hypnotize them against their wishes.

Such attitudes, of course, were absurd. From the moment I began my training at Pilgrim General in October 1944, I was submerged in serious business. We had an outstanding faculty that included neurologists from Columbia University Medical School, psychiatrists from the famous Menninger Clinic in Topeka, Kansas, and other prominent specialists. The students, too, were of a high calibre. We were all MDs who had completed at least our internships, but none of us were specialists. Now we had three months to understand and become comfortable with a complicated medical specialty. We were ready, and the army's first-rate staff taught us well.

They taught us the logistics of evacuating patients from the front lines to a BAS. We learned that in some cases a short rest period, together with sedation and reassurance, were all that was needed to return a soldier to his unit. If a soldier had amnesia, wandered around aimlessly, or appeared psychotic and totally removed from reality, he would be transported further behind the lines to a regimental or division hospital. There the soldier would be treated for a short time. Those who required longer or more advanced treatment were shipped back to the United States. Generally, these were patients whose symptoms were so severe or so fixed that it might take months or more before they could be returned to duty or discharged from the service.

Of course, we learned about the various forms of treatments then practiced. Among other things, these included the standard medications, such as Phenobarbital and intravenous Pentothal, a sedative, mainly used for reducing anxiety and insomnia. In those days, we had no modern antidepressants like Prozac and Zoloft.

I was selected to study electroencephalography, something I had never heard of before. I learned how to use an electroencephalograph, or EEG, to measure electrical impulses from the brain—just as an electrocardiograph records heartbeats and indicates signs of damage to the heart. The army wanted to examine soldiers with head injuries to determine if they had brain damage that didn't appear on x-ray exams. The technique was so new that I became something of a pioneer in this field—and a charter member of the American Society of Electroencephalography.

Our instructors presented civilian cases for us to become more familiar with psychoses such as schizophrenia and manic depression. We learned about types of anxiety in which soldiers had dreams reliving combat every night and woke up hollering for help. Others had amnesia, a method their brain devised to block out the horrible sights and sounds they had experienced.

We were taught to show compassion for those with psychiatric problems. We learned how important it was to listen to their stories and use appropriate medications to help them rest and sleep. We were taught how to be a facilitator of group therapy sessions. We learned the importance of making sure that soldiers with psychiatric conditions were well fed and given daily, intensive physical exercise to keep their bodies in shape. Those who were physically sound were not allowed to stay in bed all day but were kept busy with therapies and recreational activities. On weekends, those who were well enough to go into town, or even go home, got passes.

◆　　　◆　　　◆

At last, it was time to use the skills I had learned, and I reported to Tilden General Hospital at Fort Dix, New Jersey, about an hour and a half south of New York City. The army had paid my tuition to stay in medical school at a time when most of my friends and VMI classmates were fighting and many, including a former roommate, were killed. At times, I felt guilty about still being in school. But finally I was headed for a large army hospital to do my part, and I was excited.

Fort Dix was a major army post, a training area for soldiers heading overseas and also a large detention camp for German prisoners of war. The commanding officer at the hospital, a full colonel and a fellow VMI graduate (class of 1929), welcomed me and, out of the blue, told me I would be promoted to captain within six months. Boy, did I feel well received! I thanked him, and he ordered a car to take me to the officer's quarters, where I met my new roommate, first lieutenant Ernie Cotlove, who worked closely with me in the 400-bed unit for the next two years.

I was assigned two patient wards, each containing twenty-five beds within a long, narrow wooden building. The rooms had ample window light but were otherwise plain—no pictures, no flowers, no bookshelves; just cots along each side, a few feet apart. My first glimpse of the ward took in the two rows of cots, covered with army-brown blankets and with a soldier's head resting on each pillow. Under the pillow was a round, four-inch speaker, connected to a central radio system so the patient could listen to music or the news. It didn't look like most military hospital wards; nobody wore a cast on his leg or a bandage on his head. At the far end of the ward was a small office where I could interview a patient in privacy and without interruption. The door was always shut when I listened to a soldier's story.

I made ward rounds each morning, escorted by a nurse and an orderly. The nurse, a major, outranked me; the orderly was a sergeant. The orderly commanded the patients to roll out of bed and stand at the ends of the cots. If a soldier stayed in his bed in spite of the order to stand, I sat at his bedside and listened to him tell me why he couldn't stand, and we made an appointment to talk in my private office during the day. After the morning rounds, my staff and I met and exchanged information about the patients.

The relationship between a medical officer and a soldier is different from that of a civilian doctor to a patient. The medical officer is first and foremost an officer, defined by his rank and uniform. It was my responsibility not just to rehabilitate my patients for their own sakes but, ideally, to return them to duty. Very few of these patients would ever return to combat, but they might be able to drive a truck, be a cook or carpenter, or serve in some other capacity that helped support those in the front lines.

An important part of my responsibility was to evaluate and document the severity of each patient's disability and his progress. I met weekly with the chief of the psychiatric unit and made recommendations about further treatment or medical discharge. Some of the soldiers were seriously ill with psychoses of one form or another and generally had to be transferred to an army specialty center equipped to give intensive care for a long period. I never saw a soldier faking a mental disorder to avoid return to duty.

One question I had to confront at the beginning was how I could treat combat casualty patients when I had never been in combat myself. Back in training, my classmates and I were advised to read the war reportage of Ernie Pyle. He was the epitome of the "soldier in the trenches" reporter, and reading his stuff gave you a pretty good feeling of what it was like to be in combat. Beyond that, our instructors taught us to tell it straight to individual soldiers or groups: "I have never been in combat, and when I see what can happen to soldiers, physically and mentally, I'm glad that, at least so far, I have not been shot at. However, I am committed to help you any way I can."

I found that, invariably, the response was, "That's okay, Doc. Hope you never have to go into combat!"

I listened to the soldiers' stories with deep concern, trying to understand and visualize the horrors they had been through. In group sessions, some shared their stories and wept. Others kept everything inside. As time went on, most opened up and talked about their experiences.

Emotional injuries show no physical wound. There are no bandages, no orthopedic casts on which friends can scrawl their names or draw a funny picture or scribble the message "Get well quick." Soldiers do not receive a Purple Heart for being wounded psychologically. Morale in the neuropsychiatric ward runs low, and many of my patients felt a severe guilt for falling apart mentally.

Imagine the situation: You have seen your buddy blown to bits, his blood turning a brown field red. A minute later, you see someone else's head lying on the ground separated from his body, the eyes staring into nowhere. The next day, a guy you didn't know too well saved your life and as you turned to thank him, his guts exploded out of his belly. Or maybe you were in a tank that got hit during an air attack. By some miracle, you crawled out through the turret and escaped, but then you heard the other members of your crew screaming as they burned to death inside the tank. You were found wandering through the rubble of a demolished farmhouse, unable to remember where you were or even who you were; the stretcher bearers had to tie you down, give you morphine, and haul you to the rear. Now you're separated from your outfit, you feel like you've gone crazy, nothing makes any sense.

Almost every soldier has his breaking point. Maybe you hit yours while marching through thick mud up to your thighs, fatigued beyond sensation. Maybe it came while you were crawling through snow in sub-zero weather with artillery shells landing nearby. Maybe it happened when you realized there is no limit to the cruelty in war, and all you can do is crap in your pants and try to keep moving forward through the smoke and the darkness and the stench.

During the time I worked at Fort Dix, ships were constantly landing in New York, loaded with patients who were then sent by train to the various hospitals and psychiatric units across the country, including ours. Sometimes we received new patients at night, and we immediately had to find beds for them. They were a sorry-looking lot as they staggered off the train. They had been traveling for a week or more. They were unshaven, and their uniforms were wrinkled. They were silent, anxious, and smelly.

Each patient had an emergency medical tag, or EMT, hanging on a string around his neck, indicating his general condition. They were crucial to our deciding where to send the patients. Those whose tags indicated they were suicidal or psychotic were immediately taken to locked wards for careful evaluation and protection. The large majority were labeled "Psychoneurosis" and went to open wards like mine. After a few months of meeting trainloads of patients, we became very efficient at sorting them out. We reassured them that we were their friends, there to help them, and that we were proud of them as American soldiers.

Some of our cases were truly bizarre. One day, a soldier arrived whom I couldn't help noticing. He was stooped over deeply, with his nose not far from the ground. As he walked, he pulled himself forward with his right leg, which was continuously bent, and dragged his left leg behind. I stopped him, and he peered up at me, his eyes wide with fear. His tag said "Possible schizophrenic." I had never seen such a peculiar gait. My first thought was to suspect a spinal injury, but there was no evidence of that in his record.

The soldier was assigned to my ward. Lying in bed, he seemed able to straighten out fairly well. The next day I asked him to get up and walk down the ward. Of course, all of the other patients were watching. He got into the same posture as before, looking crippled and pitiful.

He was perpetually confused and could give very little coherent information. I checked him out neurologically and found all reflexes normal, no loss of sensation, no paralysis. Subsequent x-rays of his back and legs showed normal bones. When I asked him what happened to him in combat, he couldn't remember. His military records told of his tank being blown up in the Battle of the Bulge, his buddy torn to bits and flung onto a barbed wire fence in several pieces.

At a staff meeting, we came to the conclusion that the patient's gait was a form of conversion hysteria, as it was called. Later, I learned there was a specific term for the soldier's illness: *camptocormia,* a rare psychogenic condition in which a person assumes a posture characterized by a forward-bent trunk. We decided to sedate him intravenously with sodium pentothal and observe him to see if he would stand and walk normally. While he was under Pentothal, we tried to get him to talk about his battle experiences. He did exactly that—to a degree we didn't expect. He yelled and screamed, and as he came out of the sedation, he took a wild poke at me. We had to restrain him.

I continued Pentothal therapy on the patient and spent some time carefully coaxing him to share his story, listening with care to what he was able to tell me. He improved a great deal, but ultimately we weren't able to handle him long enough for me to see him recover. He had a lot of anger and fear, and he constantly expressed them in ways that disturbed the other patients. Morale was a fragile thing on an open ward such as ours, so we couldn't keep him. He was transferred to a specialty psychiatric hospital where he could be isolated while undergoing further treatment. I have often wondered what happened to the poor fellow, whose condition so dramatically demonstrated how a person's body can respond in combat to the terrible fear of death.

◆   ◆   ◆

One patient on my ward had a severe and disabling tic. His neck muscles went into spasms, causing him to throw his head back and jerk it up and down. It was frightening to watch. It started in the Battle of the Bulge amid freezing weather and snowstorms, when the soldier was exposed to repeated artillery barrages and buzz bombs whistling overhead. His spasms got worse whenever I approached him, and sometimes he fell to the floor. It dawned on me that hypnosis might help him.

I had never hypnotized anyone before, but all of us who trained at Pilgrim General on Long Island learned that hypnosis can be useful for treating certain cases. One of our professors had given a convincing demonstration involving a young, German-born soldier who immigrated to the U.S. with his family before the war, was inducted into the U.S. Army, and had been evacuated from combat with severe hysteria, loss of memory, and other psychiatric symptoms. Under hypnosis, the young man started crying and described in detail how the majority of his unit were killed. The professor then took him back in time and got him to recall a happy incident when he was a little boy. To my amazement, the soldier brightened and even started speaking in German. Just before the professor brought him out of hypnosis, he asked the patient to smile. When he awoke, the soldier was at peace and smiled for the class.

It seemed worth a try. I asked my patient with the severe neck spasm to come into my office one night when the ward was quiet. The nurse and I gently explained what we planned to do and reassured him that he wouldn't be harmed. Going into my office at night accompanied by a nurse made him particularly anxious, however, and his spasms were at a high point when I started the procedure. I attached a string to my military ring with a ruby stone in it, and swung it back and forth in front of his face. In no time, he was hypnotized. I told him to raise his right arm, and he did. I told him to lower it, and he did. Speaking softly, I told him he was back at the front, he could see his buddies dying and hear them screaming. He began to cry, and his neck muscles twitched. He threw his head back and screamed. Calmly, I told him everything was going to be all right; he would be cared for, and his muscle twitches would go away. He gradually quieted down, and the muscle twitching stopped. Eventually I said it was time for him to wake up. I suggested that if I said "A-B-C" and snapped my fingers when he was asleep, he would wake up; if he were awake and I wanted him to go to sleep and have the muscles stop twitching, I would say the same thing. I also told him when he awoke he would feel refreshed, not frightened, and his muscles would be at ease.

He woke up feeling wonderful. There were no muscle spasms, and he thanked me for whatever it was I did to help him. He went back into the ward and told some of the other patients I had performed a miracle. The next morning, there was a lineup of patients asking for the treatment. Word got back to the commanding officer of the hospital, and I heard that he didn't want me to come into his office for fear that I might hypnotize him. Later, however, we had a good talk and he told me to keep up the good work.

When I made my rounds the next morning, my pride-and-joy hypnosis case was standing at the end of his bed, his neck muscles in severe spasms. The closer I got to him, the more nervous he became, and soon he crumpled to the floor. The nurse put a pillow under his head and I knelt down beside him. The ward became deathly quiet, and I felt everyone's eyes on me. I whispered to the soldier "A-B-C" and snapped my fingers. His entire body relaxed and the spasms stopped. Again, I reassured him, telling him that when he woke up his spasms would stop and he would feel better. Once more I whispered in his ear, "A-B-C," and snapped my fingers. He opened his eyes, glanced around at everyone staring at him, and stood up at the end of the bed, appearing quite normal.

The rest of the room remained silent. No one cheered, no one said a thing. To tell the truth, I myself was just as surprised and moved as they were.

That morning at the group meeting, I explained a few things about hypnosis. I told the patients it was not for everyone and, like medications, it was not a cure. Their fellow patient, the soldier with the neck spasms, would need a lot more care, like everyone else.

For about two months, I continued to hypnotize the patient in the privacy of my office. With the support of the staff and his buddies, plus sleep medication, good food, and exercise, the spasms finally stopped and he went home to Philadelphia on furlough. On the day he left to go home, he was happy—but anxious about how he would get along. I gave him my phone number. The night he got home, mild spasms came back and he called me, afraid they would get as bad as in the beginning. I reassured him, said "A-B-C" and snapped my fingers into the phone, and told him his muscles would relax and that he would be all right. When I brought him out of his telephone hypnosis, he felt much better. He returned from furlough and continued to do well on the ward. In time, he received a medical discharge from the army.

I continued to study hypnosis and had good results with patients who had amnesia and hysteria, particularly some with hysterical paralysis—soldiers who believed they had a severe arm or leg wound, for example, when in fact there was no physical injury. Occasionally I treated patients referred from an orthopedic ward because the doctor suspected they were malingering. A typical case was a soldier who couldn't raise his right arm up over his head. Under hypnosis, with strong suggestions that his arm was not injured, the patient still could not raise it. My report to the orthopedic service was that the soldier was not faking it—there was something physically wrong with the arm.

◆   ◆   ◆

In psychiatric medicine, as in so many other areas, the armed forces excelled at training fast and effectively in the midst of war. Military doctors have far more training than any other specialty in the armed forces—more, even, than bomber pilots or bridge engineers, and in some cases more than a two-star general. The main weakness of medical officers, at least when first called to duty, is that they don't understand much about how the armed services work, but most military doctors adjust well enough to the culture of the armed forces. All understand the vital role they play, especially in wartime.

For our work during the war, the hospital staff at Fort Dix received an American Theater victory award, as well as the Presidential unit citation award. The latter, a cloth patch with a gold wreath displayed on the left sleeve above the wrist, was sometimes jokingly likened to a toilet seat cover; all jokes aside, though, we were proud to wear it.

I thoroughly enjoyed my experience in the army. I felt competent and appreciated; I learned a lot that was helpful later in private practice. I enjoyed the comradeship in the officers' quarters and at the officers' club. In the officers' mess, where we were served by German prisoners of war, there was no shortage of good steaks, and we could order whatever we wanted for breakfast.

Perhaps this sounds like an easy life, especially compared with conditions on the front lines. A 5,000-bed hospital was not like a battalion aid station, a few yards behind enemy fire. I could just as easily have found myself overseas, and in fact, those of us who had not yet been in combat were in reserve for a possible invasion of Japan, where by some estimates there would be a million Allied casualties. I was mentally prepared for Japan when on August 6, 1945, President Harry Truman ordered the dropping of the atomic bomb on Hiroshima. As dreadful as that bomb was, those of us in line to go to Japan leapt with joy when, following a second A-bomb, the Japanese surrendered.

There were still thousands of casualties in hospitals across the country. I stayed at Fort Dix for some months longer and was offered a promotion to major if I stayed in still longer. I thought about it seriously. Being a medical officer was great experience in both the professional and personal sense, and the army would have paid for more medical training. However, I had an equally attractive opportunity awaiting me at the Virginia Mason Hospital in Seattle. I had always seen myself in private practice. With some mixed feelings, I left the army.

7

I Thee Wed

To every thing there is a season,
and a time to every purpose under the heaven…

—Ecclesiastes 3:1 (KJV)

There is a time and place for everything: a time to be born, a time to die, and—most exciting—a time to fall in love and marry. This happened to me when I was twenty-eight years old. World War II was over, and I had returned to Seattle to complete my specialized training in internal medicine. There I met June, my true love. It hit me like a brick. We met in March, became engaged one month later, and got married on August 18, all in the year 1948.

People have often asked me how I got from Virginia to the state of Washington, about as far away as I could go back then, and still be in the USA. Neither Hawaii nor Alaska was a state yet. I did not mention my mother or my secret. One answer I liked to give is that God sent me there so I could meet my future wife.

The story, however, is a bit more complicated. Recalling the advice I received in 1942 from the physician who selected advanced trainees for the Mayo Clinic, I applied during my final year of medical school to both Johns Hopkins and Virginia Mason for an internship in internal medicine. To my surprise, both accepted me. I weighed the options and chose Virginia Mason. I am not sure exactly why. Johns Hopkins, of course, was very prestigious, and Baltimore was known territory two and a half hours north of Richmond. Virginia Mason, on the other hand, was across the continent in the Pacific Northwest: Indian Territory, as far as I knew. It was a hard decision; Seattle's exotic lure was strong, but at the same time, it seemed almost inconceivable that a person born and reared in Virginia would go so far away. At least, that's how my mother saw the question. I flipped a coin and got what I was really wishing for.

I completed my internship at Virginia Mason in 1944. That was when my military duties took me to Pennsylvania, Long Island, and finally Fort Dix. Upon leaving the army, I had a chance to return to Virginia Mason for a residency. It was an attractive opportunity because I had enjoyed my internship very much and thought it would be a great place to continue my training. Now, however, I faced another difficult decision, for I was also offered the chance that I had hoped for back in 1942: I was accepted as a fellow at the Mayo Clinic. After some correspondence with the Mayo administration, however, I got the impression that there was a flood of young doctors returning there from the war. I decided for Seattle, knowing that I would receive good training there. This decision disappointed my mother, who would have loved to tell her friends her son was being trained at the world-famous Mayo Clinic.

In the second year of my residency, an intern set me up with a 20-year-old drama student at the University of Washington named June Yeakel. June was a friend of the intern's girl, who was staying at June's house while their parents vacationed together. The four of us planned to go skiing. It sounded fine to me; never mind that it was my first ski outing and they might as well have asked me to walk on water as to manipulate those boards down a hill. I took the rope tow up the children's slope while the rest of our party, having climbing skins on their skis, climbed to the top of the ski area and swooshed past me on their way down.

June had spent her first two college years at Middlebury in Vermont, where she was on the ski patrol. It didn't matter; she forgave me my ineptitude on the skis, and boy, was I turned on by her—blue-gray eyes in an honest face, English rose skin with no freckles or lines, shoulder-length brown hair pulled back off her face and forehead. She had no need for putting on, and she looked great in ski pants and sweater. She must have been attracted to me, too, because we hugged and kissed each other in the back seat all the way home.

Thus began a companionship that has continued to grow in love and respect over more than fifty years. I still remember many details about how she appeared to me in those first days. Her oval face and blue eyes framed by wavy hair caught my attention. I remember also noticing her feet, which were small with a high arch, and a dress that made her look particularly enchanting: fitted bodice, small cap sleeves, low rounded neck with a drawstring, and a full skirt in three tiers. The dress was navy blue with a print of small teardrop figures, each teardrop outlined by a series of little pears, and tiny white petaled flowers under the teardrops.

June is seven years younger than I and at the time we fell in love I had some concern that people would accuse me of robbing the cradle. However, we were perfectly suited to each other, I the talker, she the listener. June was a self-possessed, mature young woman who, when we met, was stage manager for a student production of the play *Daniel Boone*. There was calmness about her, and I soon learned that her musical talents equaled her theatrical skills. She played piano and violin as a child, and her violin teacher urged her parents to continue her training. She loved to sing. She has always had an excellent ear for tone and timing. After we were married, she sang for many years in the Seattle Symphony Chorale and the Cathedral choir at St. Mark's.

We had a short, happy courtship—short because I was scheduled to finish my training soon at the Joslin Diabetes clinic in Boston. Originally I was to report in June of 1948, but I arranged to postpone my start date until September so June and I could get married in Seattle that August.

June's parents welcomed me like a son in their home of white washed brick with its immaculate garden. June's mother had striking, prematurely silver hair and always dressed well. She seemed perpetually joyful, the opposite of my mother. She made it clear that she loved me and would do anything to help June and me be happy.

June's dad and I were comfortable immediately, and we had no difficulty bonding. Bill started a business in the 1920s, the Northwest Bolt and Nut Company, and he took me on a tour of the factory, where I was fascinated by the noise and activity: machines spitting out bolts and nuts of all sizes, and other machines with hot fires that bent rods for reinforcing concrete. My future father-in-law introduced me to the workers on the shop floor, all of whom called him "Bill," and I felt proud to walk with him amid blast furnaces blowing orange flames, the clanking of machinery, and the acrid smell of steel. Bill told me about the construction of Grand Coulee Dam, for which his company supplied thousands of steel rebars, used for reinforcing the concrete. Bill was a real American success story. He grew up in Chicago, where his father was a physician; that helped us connect with each other. Later, he helped me get my private practice in internal medicine established by referring his friends to me. In short, Bill became not just my father-in-law but a good friend and supporter, a true surrogate for the father I lost as a child.

That helped me overcome the only uncertainty I had about marrying June. As the date of our wedding approached, my old fear began to gnaw away at me from the inside. I had not told June that my dad committed suicide. I could not bear to. Something within me told me that to tell June my secret would make her stop loving me. I wondered whether I could keep the truth from her forever and even thought about wiggling out of the marriage to prevent being exposed. I am eternally grateful that I overcame this fear and went ahead with what my heart really wanted to do—but I continued to keep my secret.

◆   ◆   ◆

June and I were married on August 18, 1948 at an Episcopal church in Seattle. Mother came out for the wedding by train. It was her first trip to the Northwest, and she said she enjoyed the long, cross-country ride. Upon arrival, one of her first questions to June was whether she considered herself a Yankee or a Westerner, and she was relieved that June called herself a Westerner. From there, however, it was downhill for Mother.

Mother and I slept in hotel rooms the night before the wedding. The ceremony would take place the next evening, and I followed the tradition of not seeing the bride on the big day. That morning, I took my mother sightseeing around the Seattle area. I was edgy and uncomfortable, remembering all the unhappy experiences in the past. She was dressed well, but I couldn't help picturing her in her costume of misery, her face covered with cold cream. I could tell she was jealous of my bride, and perhaps I didn't help that by bragging about June, proclaiming my love for her, and expressing how lucky I felt.

Mother said, "It's not you who is lucky. It's her."

I ignored this caustic remark and drove on. Some minutes later, we crossed Lake Washington on the Mercer Island Bridge, whitecaps smashing against it. To the south, the snow-capped vision of Mt. Rainier floated 14,000 feet into the sky.

Paying no attention to the breathtaking scenery Mother said, "I've been thinking about committing suicide."

Her words hit me like the striking of a cathedral bell at one o'clock in the morning. I could not look or speak to her. Once past the shock, my insides churned with anger that she could say these things on my wedding day.

Somehow or another I put all that aside, and at 8:00 that evening, in white tie and tails, I watched with pride, love, and anticipation as the lovely figure of my bride in her flowing satin dress glided down the aisle toward me, on the arm of her dad. I could hear an occasional growl in my stomach, and I nervously folded and unfolded my hands behind my back. June's gown of off-white satin fitted tightly around her waist, cascaded to the floor, and trailed regally behind her. She wore a pearl pendant, and lace streamed from her headpiece down below her waist in the back. Her face was radiant as her eyes met mine. I was marrying the most beautiful girl in the world.

◆   ◆   ◆

The next day we packed my two-door Ford sedan and headed across the country for Boston. This trip was our honeymoon, and I have wonderful memories of it. I had to pinch myself to believe that this beautiful young lady seated beside me was my wife. I couldn't keep my hands off her or stop looking at her.

A lot happened that first year in Boston—renting an apartment, finishing my medical training, and most of all, having our firstborn child, Julie. It was a good year, even though our total assets upon our arrival consisted mainly of my trusty car. We lived on the top floor of a five-story brick building on Boylston Avenue, just across the alley from Fenway Park, where the Boston Red Sox played. From one spot on our rooftop, we could easily see home plate and the batter; by moving to the far side of the roof, we could see the pitcher—but not the batter and the pitcher simultaneously. Across the street from our building was a large park where June took walks while she was pregnant.

Our apartment had one bedroom, a living room that measured about ten by twelve feet, and a small kitchen with a window. The bathroom was off a hallway that led from the kitchen to the entrance door. Our "dining room" was a tabletop in the hallway that dropped down from a hook on the wall. Lifting it back up again after eating became a routine, because otherwise, it blocked the hallway to the door. In the living room were a sofa and chair with pinkish-red coverings from Sears, Roebuck. After Julie was born, we learned not to change her diapers on the sofa because if they were wet, they would turn pink. We also learned not to put her crib under the window in the hallway and leave her there for the night, because black soot blew in and completely changed her appearance.

Julie was born on May 20, 1949 at the Boston Lying In Hospital. Approximately eight months earlier, June had told me while lying beside me in bed with a slight smile that she was pregnant. She caught me completely by surprise. In those days people didn't *plan* to have a baby—they just had one. We were both excited, and June said she was proud to be pregnant.

June gave birth to our first child without complications. I first saw Julie through a window in the nursery. After a long look at her pink face and curly, black hair, I rushed down the hall and called Mother in Richmond. She sounded pleased at the news and congratulated me enthusiastically. June's mother arrived from Seattle and immediately set to work doing the laundry, changing diapers, cooking meals, and holding and walking the baby. She was a great help and wonderful company for June while I continued to put in my time every day at the hospital and clinic.

I wish I could have spent more time sharing the joy of our new baby with June. At the hospital, my colleagues gave me cigars and slapped my back, and I was given the day off. It felt great to be a father and my little family made me happy.

Recommendations from Virginia Mason had helped me to receive an appointment at the Joslin Clinic in Boston. My entire year there focused on the treatment of diabetes, in which I had become interested as a medical student. Dr. Joslin was a formidable mentor. He was an eighty-year-old New Englander who always wore a black suit with a vest, pocket watch, and gold chain. His slight, somewhat stooped body belied the man's energy and commitment to his work. His age didn't stop him from getting up early and working a full day, and he was constantly making clinical observations to add to the ninth edition of his authoritative textbook on diabetes, which was used at every medical school in the country.

Dr Joslin didn't smoke, chew, or drink. This made him a bit unusual. Back then, the medical profession was largely unaware of the connection between smoking and lung cancer. Smoking was common, especially among young military veterans like me, and some doctors would even offer a cigarette to a patient in their office to help relax him. Not, however, at the Joslin Clinic. No one smoked within sight of Dr.Joslin.

To have a smoke, my fellow trainees and I would take the rickety, two- to three-passenger elevator to the top floor of the clinic and climb the steps from there to the roof. One time I had a cigarette in my mouth while leaving the clinic and was just about to light it when I caught sight of Dr. Joslin coming in. I hid the cigarette behind my back and smiled innocently at the great white father.

Dr. Joslin was the kind of man who would stop his teaching rounds if he saw a spot on the hospital floor. He immediately would call a nurse and order her to clean it up. When we came back after rounds, he would notice whether the spot was gone. If not, he pulled a mop from a closet and cleaned it up himself.

We could not help admiring him, and we always told stories about him for the amusement and amazement of our wives and each other. At times, however, his fussiness could be aggravating. He would meet us in the hospital lobby at 7:30 on Sunday morning for ward rounds. We formed a circle, ready to listen to some pearls of wisdom from him. One Sunday he asked, in his wavery, high voice, "Have any of you read the article published this week in the *Berlin Journal of Medicine* about diabetes and retinal complications?" Of course, no one had; the article had just been published and was written in German. He proceeded to read the article to us, translating it. His act of one-upmanship annoyed all of us. Nevertheless, we respected his discipline and determination at the age of eighty to keep up with medical information from around the world. We knew he was also studying French at this time, in preparation for giving a talk in Paris.

When my year of training ended, Dr.Joslin offered me a junior position in the clinic at three hundred dollars per month. This was quite an honor and a temptation, but two factors weighed against my accepting the job. Being a doctor at the Joslin Clinic was demanding, indeed totally absorbing. It involved not only seeing patients, but teaching students at one of the medical schools and writing medical papers. Such an intense lifestyle didn't appeal to me. In addition, I could see that it was impossible in Boston for a family of three to live comfortably on three hundred dollars a month. We could have made it before Julie came along, because June worked as receptionist at the clinic, but in those days, mothers generally didn't work outside the home. It would have been hard, and probably costly, to find good care for our infant daughter, and in any case, June wanted to be a "real mother" to Julie. So, with some regret, I turned down the offer.

This was when June and I decided to go to Richmond, where my mother awaited the return of her son. I swept aside the stinging and pathetic comments she had made on my wedding day and focused on the pleasant time June and I spent with her when she visited us some months later in Boston. Our journey to Richmond now was to be my homecoming, the moment when I found my place in familiar surroundings, among my own people, and settled down for life as a respected doctor and a southern gentleman. As we have seen, however, it turned out to be a shattering visit during which I learned that Mother was not ready to accept June and I had to make a bitter choice. Without a moment's hesitation, I chose June and left Mother.

◆   ◆   ◆

Years later on the wedding day of our daughter Julie, I remembered the words my mother spoke to me on the day of my own wedding. No matter how depressed or lonely I might be, I could never say such things to any of my children. With years of hindsight, I could realize that my mother loved me, but her mask of misery hid her love. It was her mask that said those hurtful words, and it was her mask that kept her from saying anything positive about June.

An ironic and telling incident occurred toward the end of Mother's life. She was 97 years old and living in a nursing home in Richmond when I paid her my last visit. She was gaunt and almost bald. Her mind was a bit confused, but she had enough strength and lucidity to demand that I get her out of that place, buy her an airplane ticket, and take her to Seattle with me. I told her it was impossible. She made a fist, took a swing at me, and said, "June will look after me." This was the closest she ever came to expressing trust, respect, or love for June.

A few years after Mother's death, something occurred to me. While meditating one morning sometime before my eightieth birthday, I had a vision of my mother and me in the car on my wedding day. I asked her why she said she wanted to kill herself. She lowered her head and said, "Because I love you so much."

I have thought a lot about this. Mother had lost my dad through suicide, my sister had moved away, and I was choosing as my life partner someone from the most distant corner of the country. Already she sensed that her dream about my future—that I would wed a Virginia girl and practice medicine in my hometown, Mother's town, where she had already picked out an office for me—was fading. She did not kill herself. It wasn't she who expressed that doleful wish; it was her mask, or rather, it was the dark forces inside her that compelled her to wear her costume of misery, and that caused her to say things she didn't mean, blocked her from being able to tell me she loved me and wish me happiness. Once she said, with trembling lips, "Everyone whom I love has left me."

And I realize now that the words Mother spoke to me then, as well as many other words spoken and unspoken, were a cry for help. I didn't understand. I didn't listen. I didn't know how to help her.

We have all failed in similar ways. Our instincts, or our fears, tell us to ignore a cry for help. We don't want to confront misery. We have our own lives to live. And we might feel as though we don't know how to lift another person out of the depths. But if we open ourselves and become more aware of the human bonds we share with others, we might just find a way. We might learn that the opportunity to help someone who suffers is also an opportunity to move ourselves to a higher level of joy and sanctuary. With my mother, I missed just such an opportunity. I didn't know.

◆   ◆   ◆

My wife is a happy woman, and that is a blessing. We have been married now more than half a century, and I still love watching her. I see her ironing clothes in front of the television while Fred Astaire in a 1945 movie does a waltz; his legs dance as gracefully as June's hands move across the ironing board.

I loved watching her through an upstairs window of our former house as she worked in the garden, a Dutch matron in her wooden shoes and floppy-brimmed straw hat. I can close my eyes now and still see her. She stoops from the waist without bending her knees and plants a bulb in fresh dirt, packs fertilizer around it, does the same with another bulb. Later, she waters them all. She stands and arches her body backward to relieve the discomfort. She cannot pass by the garden without pulling a weed. She is beautiful in her seventies.

Skilled at arranging cut flowers for the house, she fills vases with multiple colors, branches with leaves of light green in the spring, red and golden leaves in the fall, bouquets destined for the table in the front hallway and the mantel over the living-room fireplace.

On Mondays, she meets with her book club. They take turns reading aloud, and June is a favorite; her accent, as well as the rhythm and feeling in her voice, is pleasing. On Wednesdays, she tapes for the blind, reading in a small room with modern recording equipment. On Fridays, she often hikes with a friend, choosing a trail in the foothills or a pathway in town.

Given my choices as I saw them in 1948, I made the right one. June and I have celebrated more than fifty wedding anniversaries. We have four grown grandchildren, three granddaughters, and one grandson. My life has gone through twists and turns, the joy of professional success, the loss of our fourth child, the virus of depression, the exhilaration of a new career, and the transformation of my consciousness. Through it all, the steady one has been June.

PART III
The Clothing of the Healer

8

The Doctor's Mask

At the end of my first week in private practice, I ushered a middle-aged woman into my consulting room. She was blond, overweight, breathing heavily, and a bit ill at ease. She had on a smart wool suit and a hat with a half-veil that extended down to the end of her nose.

She told me her name and said, "I'm pleased to find you. Someone told me you just started your practice. I remember you when you were a resident at Virginia Mason. You were so kind to me when I was sick."

For the life of me, I could not remember her and was thankful she said her name. She was my first patient in private practice, and my heart was probably beating faster than hers. Nevertheless, I put on my best professional smile and asked, "What brings you to see a doctor?"

I saw two patients the first month. I had no receptionist. A bell rang whenever the door to the reception room opened. I popped up from my chair in the consulting room and peered into the lobby to see who was there. Usually it was either the mail carrier, someone looking for a different doctor, or a pharmaceutical representative hoping to tell me about his company's latest "sure to cure" pill. When my new patient came in that first Friday, I said to her, "I'm pleased to see you"—and I really meant it.

To myself I said, "Finally, I am in practice." It had been nineteen years since my summer with Uncle Joe, and I thought he would be proud of me. I closed my eyes and tried to picture myself beside him. Of course, I was an urban doctor and he was a country doctor, but somehow the image seemed to fit. The only thing missing was that I did not smell like Uncle Joe. I carried a black bag when I made home calls, but I had no doctor's aroma, no whiff of antiseptic and ether, as my calling card.

June, Julie, and I had arrived in Seattle in the summer of 1949. We stayed in the home of June's family for a few weeks until we figured out where we would live and how I would start my practice. The family welcomed us with good food, a lovely room for June and me with our own bathroom, and a nursery for Julie. Edith, June's mother, had grown attached to Julie by being with her in Boston during the first few weeks of her life, and she was happy to baby-sit any time. On Sundays, she served the famous Yeakel dinner in the dining room on English bone china: leg of lamb, peas, and mashed potatoes with vanilla, strawberry, or chocolate ice cream for dessert.

June and I were busy, happy, and excited. We started looking for our own place to live, and before long, we rented a two-bedroom apartment overlooking Lake Union for one hundred and twenty-five dollars a month. It seemed like a lot of money, but we were confident my medical practice would succeed.

Starting a solo practice was the usual thing for doctors then, but it was not such an easy thing in a strange city. I knew practically no one in Seattle except for the doctors I had trained with at the hospital. One of them gave me a boost by welcoming me back to town and throwing a party at his home in my honor. Several dozen doctors and their wives were invited to the party, and I had an opportunity to begin the essential networking that is crucial to every new doctor.

Of course, I had to find an office. Office space was at a premium because many doctors had returned from the Second World War to either start or return to their practice. A lot of them clustered in the hospitals and clinics on Seattle's First Hill, known as "Pill Hill." Bill, my father-in-law, wisely advised me to avoid Pill Hill and instead take an office downtown where there was a lot of pedestrian traffic. The Medical-Dental Building, on Olive Way in the heart of the retail area, seemed like a good location. The manager of the Pharmacy on the street level of the building referred me to a surgeon on the ninth floor, who was looking for someone to share his office.

He was a gray-haired, middle-aged man who wasted no time in small talk. His reception room was small and windowless; it contained two straight-backed chairs, a small sofa, and a table holding a stack of magazines, old and wrinkled from use. There was an area where a receptionist would ordinarily sit, but since the doctor spent much of his time in surgery, he had neither a secretary nor a nurse.

The consulting room had a window looking at a concrete wall across an empty shaft. The examining room contained an old table with a black leather mattress and a hydraulic support operated by a foot pedal. There was dust under the table and a worn-out trash basket under the sink. I could have the office every morning until 12:30 p.m., as that was when the doctor performed surgery in the hospital. My share of the rent would be $100.00 per month. I was responsible for laundry charges, towels, and patient gowns; if I required a nurse or a secretary, I would have to hire my own.

Despite the unattractiveness of the place, I took it. I had no money or patients, and my new office mate did not offer to refer any to me. My thought was to take the space on a monthly basis and keep an eye open for something better. The building management gave the office a good cleaning, hung my MD diploma on the wall in the consultation room, and placed my license to practice in the examining room. I brought a small radio into the office, and that turned out to be a lifesaver as I waited for patients to find me.

I bought a five-cent notebook and penciled in four columns. The first column was for the date, the second for the patient's name, the third for service rendered, and the fourth for the charge. I checked around with other doctors and found the average charge for an office call was five dollars, and a complete checkup, twenty or twenty-five dollars. Obviously, the two patients I saw during my first month did not pay for my rent and laundry expenses.

I felt awkward, examining my first patient with no nurse present, but I left the door open a crack, and she did not require a pelvic exam. Later, I checked with the doctor next door, an orthopedist, and he said his nurse could run over for a moment or so if I got in a pinch.

June and I celebrated the startup of my practice over dinner at our home with June's family. Bill told his friends I was the best doctor in town. I picked up a fair number of patients through his referrals, and I always felt a great responsibility to give them the best of care.

Meantime, I still had a lot of self-marketing to do if I was going to pay my expenses and earn a living for my family. I made it a habit to eat lunch in the restaurant in the building, where I soon got to know other doctors. There were more than a hundred doctors in the Medical-Dental Building, and within a few months, many of them were referring patients to me for specialized care in internal medicine and diabetes. One doctor tipped me off about insurance companies that contracted with young doctors to examine applicants for life insurance. I followed up on their referrals and soon represented four insurance companies, doing home calls for their applicants in the evenings. I found I could do four or five calls per night at five dollars each. June, who knew Seattle well, made the appointments and drew maps for me so I would not get lost. These evening calls paid for my basic office expenses, as well as the rent for our apartment and my car expenses. In addition, my "night job" increased my patient load as a number of people whom I met on the insurance calls were looking for a doctor.

Bill's suggestion to locate downtown turned out to be good advice. The Medical-Dental Building was adjacent to Frederick and Nelson's, a department store with about four thousand employees. I introduced myself to the nurse in the store clinic, who saw employees daily about their colds, flu, and other minor complaints, and frequently referred patients to a doctor. She already had a doctor on whom she depended, but six months later he retired and she called me. In time, more than three hundred Frederick and Nelson's employees came to call me their doctor. When I walked through the store, it was like Old Home week because of all the staff people who knew me.

I moved out of the surgeon's office in a few months, sharing another doctor's office, which was staffed with a wonderful nurse and receptionist. Within two years, my practice having grown, I rented my first private office with reception area, secretary's desk, two examining rooms, and space for an x-ray machine and a small laboratory. My first employee was a young woman fresh out of high school, smart, friendly, and soon loved by patients. She played many roles, keeping medical records, developing x-rays, and doing lab work. She worked hard and took night classes to increase her skills. For many years, she ran the office.

At this time, the University of Washington was developing its new School of Medicine. Dr.Joslin in Boston had written a letter of introduction for me to the new head of the Department of Medicine, and I quickly got an appointment as Instructor of Medicine. I taught physical diagnosis to second-year students one morning a week at a teaching hospital as well as in nursing homes. I enjoyed teaching and felt close to my students, who were not a whole lot younger than I. The work was pro bono, but it included a number of "benefits." As a faculty member, I received half-price tickets to all University of Washington athletic events and ate in the faculty dining room. The school's leadership recognized that private practitioners could teach medical students from the basis of their practical, human experiences in the community and thereby form a bridge between the academic program and "real life." The school is now one of the top-rated medical schools in the country, and my affiliation helped me keep up to date with advances in medical science. Many of the faculty became friends

My work with diabetic patients expanded into the treatment of obesity, a common problem associated with adult-onset diabetes. Soon I got a grant from a pharmaceutical company to test an anti-appetite medication. As the program grew, I came to dedicate Wednesdays in my office to treating patients who were struggling with obesity. The word got around that I was becoming an expert, and other doctors referred patients to me for treatment of obesity. I wrote articles on obesity for medical journals, gave a series of presentations to colleagues and others, and in 1959 I was featured in a local television program.

I did not particularly relish this renown, and when publishers started urging me to write books on the subject, I decided enough was enough. I did not want to be a specialist on obesity. Obesity was and is a legitimate medical issue, relating to high blood pressure, heart disease, and other illnesses, but there were so many other medical problems, more serious ones, crying out for attention—diabetes, pneumonia, cancer, liver disease. Besides, it seemed to me that the practitioners who were getting rich on their weight-reduction programs, fad diets, and "fat clinics" were not completely honest about what they could deliver. My own experience was discouraging; among obese patients with whom I worked for a year, my cure rate was less than one percent. I could see that the fashionable and lucrative business of treating obesity was holding out false hopes for millions of people, and I wanted out of it. I drew a line: I was happy to treat patients who had diabetes, high blood pressure, and other obesity-related illnesses, and I would do my best to help them manage their weight, but I stopped treating obesity per se. I did not become a "fat doctor."

To this day, I still do not regret that decision. The various medications that have been tested and marketed have not solved the problem of obesity, which has in fact increased over the four and one-half decades since. The only thing we know for sure today is that no simple approach works; diet, exercise, and sometimes genetic factors are all important. There is no easy cure yet, but there is hope.

◆   ◆   ◆

The success of my medical practice had a positive effect on my family's lifestyle. After just one year in the apartment, we bought a three-bedroom, split-level house in the Magnolia neighborhood of Seattle. We added a second car for June—a used Buick for which we paid six hundred dollars—and a second daughter when Debbie was born in 1951. My income was still modest, but in contrast to my childhood during the Depression, I felt wealthy and more confident about the future than ever.

Our house was a short stroll from a bluff overlooking Puget Sound, where June and I liked to walk Julie and push Debbie in a carriage. Gazing westward, we took in the view of the distant Olympic Mountains. We counted the sailboats on the sound and watched tugboats pulling barges destined for Alaska. Sometimes we caught a rare glimpse of migrating whales.

I was the only doctor on the block, and some of our neighbors became not only friends but patients as well. June was happy, and I was proud of her. I loved to glance out from our living room on a summer day and see

June working in the garden or playing with Julie and Debbie. June was a wonderful companion and an excellent housekeeper. She was dedicated to looking after me and raising the children.

We started attending an Episcopal church in our Magnolia neighborhood. I was not sure I wanted to be an Episcopalian, because my mother had always taught me to be proud of the fact that I was born a Presbyterian. There were three underpinnings of my identity, as Mother seemed to see it: I was a Southerner, a Presbyterian, and a Democrat. Now I had left the South, so one of those underpinnings had already been compromised. June was an Episcopalian, and by attending services with her, I came to appreciate the beauty and dignity of the Anglican forms of worship. I loved standing beside June in church just listening to her sing the hymns.

We lived in that first house only a year and one-half. June was pregnant again when we bought a larger house on East Blaine Street. It was a beautiful house located on Seattle's Capitol Hill near St. Mark's Episcopal Cathedral. We felt we needed the additional space because our family would soon grow by one more child—and now we could buy the kind of place we could see ourselves living in for the long term. It was a stretch, though; we had to take out two mortgages, and we worried about being able to afford the payments if, for some reason, my patient load dropped off. As it happened, we stayed in that beautiful house for forty-nine years. All of our children grew up in it and, in time, brought their own children to visit us for holidays and other family get-togethers.

At the same time that we moved into our new home, we found our new church. St. Mark's was a short walk away, and we loved going there to hear the choir and the organ. The Dean of St. Mark's, The Very Reverend John Leffler, became my patient and friend as well as my priest, and I like to think it was because of him that I officially became an Episcopalian. The power of John Leffler's personality and the clarity of his teaching won me over.

Our third daughter, Tucker, was born in February 1953. She became our first movie star, for I bought a movie camera in time to film her coming home from the hospital with June. The film captured June, in a blue coat, carrying Tucker in a baby basket from the car to our front door. I also remember Tucker during a family vacation on Maui six years later, how she sat on the beach and let the waves wash her out a short distance into the sea; I rushed out to pull her back in and, far from being frightened, she was ready to do it again and again.

As much as I loved my family, I also enjoyed getting out with the boys and playing tennis. We joined a Tennis Club, where I met other men who became my regular tennis partners. As I read my own words now about this period in my life, I suddenly have a vision of a Norman Rockwell painting. There I was with my lovely wife, three beautiful daughters, and a home with all the comforts. I was established in the profession I had dreamed of as a little boy.

What could possibly go wrong with this picture?

◆　　　◆　　　◆

As my career advanced, I took on more responsibilities and gained more prestige in my profession. In the late 1950s, I gained a partner, a pulmonary specialist. It was wonderful because we were now able to take every other weekend off. After a few years, I became director of the weekly staff educational conference, at which we discussed medical cases and often listened to visiting speakers. In 1963, I was chosen Teacher of the Year at Doctors. These activities, together with my University of Washington affiliation, set up my next major career move. In the late sixties, the board of trustees at Doctors appointed me Director of Medical Education, a voluntary job.

The various pieces of my career added up to more than full-time. Now I was still maintaining my private practice, directing the medical education program at Doctors, and pursuing research. Eventually, I became Chairman of the Board of Trustees at Doctors. In addition, I began to develop a new professional interest, quality of care evaluation, which would later evolve into a full-time career. But that's getting ahead of the story.

9

Kairos

A rusty, dilapidated truck lumbered along the dirt road on the outskirts of Algiers. Two young Arabs sat in the back of it, their legs hanging over the tailgate. They took turns shouting to the passersby through a cardboard bullhorn, crying out in their guttural, throat-clearing language, "If you have red eyeballs, come get free medicine."

It was 1963, and blindness was rampant in Algeria, as in many other countries of the Third World. Much of the blindness was unnecessary, for its main causes—infection (most commonly trachoma), cataracts, and trauma (injuries)—were conditions about which something could be done. Injuries could be decreased through education, infection could be treated, and cataracts removed.

The young Arabs in the truck were working with volunteers from the World Health Organization (WHO), an agency of the United Nations. WHO was leading a campaign against unnecessary blindness. There were notices on telephone poles and the sides of buildings: People should not neglect red eyes; if they are untreated, the result could be blindness. As the truck made its rounds, stopping every so often, men and women clustered around it to get a tube of an antibiotic eye ointment. Sometimes, if supplies were available, they also received a supply of multi-vitamins and a bar of soap; skin infections of all kinds were common, and cleanliness could prevent some of them.

I spent a month in Algeria heading a team of five Seattle doctors sponsored by Care-Medico and the State Department. In 1962, the French had pulled out of Algeria following nearly eight years of bloody war, and Algeria was independent after 132 years of French rule. When the French left, so did most of the doctors, nurses, and technicians, the vast majority of whom were French. Fourteen million people were abandoned without adequate medical care. In the face of this emergency, countries around the world, including the United States, called on volunteer health care professionals to help. Our church treated us as missionaries to a developing country—which of course, we were not. We were dined and recognized before we departed. June shared my excitement and looked forward to the adventure. We arranged for a grandmotherly neighbor who had baby-sat for us many times to move into our house and take care of Tucker, Debbie, and Julie, then ten, twelve, and fourteen years old. June committed herself to learning French and for six months prior to the trip, she received tutoring from a young Algerian woman, who had an uncle in Algiers. June learned French well, and once we got to Algiers her ability to understand it over the phone proved invaluable. She also played an important role in the outpatient clinic where I worked, interviewing patients and recording their names, ages, and medical complaints.

Other teams of doctors from around the world had volunteered their services in Algeria before us. They had not taken their wives with them thinking it was too dangerous because Algeria was at war with its neighbor, Morocco, over the ownership of oil fields in the Sahara Desert. We were reassured by Care Medico. It turned out that we were never in danger, and June and I agreed that our Algerian adventure proved to be one of the highlights of our life.

Our team included an orthopedic surgeon, an ophthalmologist, an anesthesiologist and a general surgeon. Although I was a specialist in Seattle, I filled the need for a general practitioner on the team. We held numerous planning sessions together and grew to know and respect each other by the time we met up for our month in Algiers. Our ages ranged from early forties to mid fifties, and we were full of energy and excited about the adventure to North Africa.

For me, Algeria proved to be the first of several experiences during the 1960s that changed my consciousness. For one thing, Algeria brought home to me the fact that a great part of the world's population lives in conditions most Americans would find shocking. Third world doctoring is radically different from the way we practice medicine in our own country.

In Algeria I learned first-hand about the importance of public health issues, something I have been interested in ever since.

Every First-world physician who volunteers in a developing country knows that he or she can treat many diseases and reduce some of the widespread pain and suffering; yet, despite their skills, there's a limit to what even the best doctors can do because of underlying health standards, poor sanitation, and lack of health education. The key to improving world health standards lies in the area of public health—in the prevention of diseases—not in the hopeless race to keep up with illnesses that could have been prevented. In Algeria, for example, we saw young children with home-made crutches dragging their paralyzed feet and legs through the dirt—evidence of polio, a disease that had been eradicated in the Western world ten years earlier. We saw a great many people afflicted with other diseases, infections, and congenital defects that would have been prevented or treated routinely in our home countries.

The hospital where we worked was a modern, 1200-bed facility built by the French. In leaving it behind, the French had taken the medical supplies and destroyed much of the equipment. They tore out the telephones and cut the lines. They rendered the elevators inoperable, so the hospital staff had to climb lots of steps, especially awkward with an emergency. An appeal by me to the U.S. Ambassador got us some military field telephones, and a few of us on the staff used them to stay in touch with each other, but for most people the only means of communicating from one room to another in that very large building complex was to go in person or send a messenger.

Sanitary conditions in the hospital were poor. Patients lay on beds that were not clean, under sheets that were not changed regularly and often gray from dirt. In some wards, men urinated out the windows because the toilets sometimes didn't function and even when they did, there weren't enough of them. Patients threw banana peels, apple cores, and other food waste out the windows, and as a result, there was a persistent stench along the base of the building's exterior walls. Because the windows had no screens, there were flies everywhere.

One sunny afternoon, as I was making ward rounds with the surgeon, we came to the bed of a teen-age girl who had had abdominal surgery a day or two before. The Algerian nurse accompanying us pulled the girl's well-worn sheet down for us to examine her abdomen, and a mouse scurried out from under the sheet at the foot of the bed. The girl shrieked.

Our everyday business in the hospital and its adjacent clinic included cases of malnutrition, gastrointestinal parasites, seriously infected wounds and burns, and tuberculosis—enough cases of tuberculosis to keep a separate, 600-bed hospital filled most of the time. We treated soldiers wounded in the Moroccan war and toddlers with esophageal burns from inadvertently drinking a caustic cleaning solution.

On another day, I made my way through a corridor packed with about twenty people who were crying aloud and praying. They were the relatives of a six-year-old boy who was hit by a car and underwent emergency surgery. We could not save him because we didn't have enough blood.

In fact, we rarely had adequate blood supplies because there were no blood centers. Sometimes we were able to beg for a supply from a Russian-run hospital across town, but we frequently ended up throwing away much of what the Russians gave us, either because the blood came from a donor who was anemic or because it was contaminated with malaria or some other infectious disease. As a result, numerous emergency patients died from injuries that should not have been fatal.

A typical day for me began in the early morning when our American team gathered outside the hotel where we were staying and drove to our medical complex in a van painted with the Care-Medico logo. I would arrive at the hospital wearing my white coat and walk up a dirt pathway lined on both sides by a double queue of squatting patients waiting to be admitted to the outpatient clinic. Inside, I sat on a stool in the middle of a large room flanked by two interpreters—no desk, no charts. There were three examining tables in the corners, each closed off by a hospital curtain. June sat in a small reception area at the entrance to the room, taking notes on each patient's symptoms. When it was time for me to see the next patient, one of the interpreters called out to him or her, and the patient crossed the floor to take a chair facing me.

None of the patients spoke English, and so each one told his or her story to one of my interpreters, who in turn filled me in on the patient's symptoms. I listened to each story and made a quick judgment. Some I directed to one of the curtained areas and asked them to wait a few minutes for me to come and examine them. In the case of women, for whom physical examination by a man was a culturally sensitive issue, a female Algerian nurse always assisted me. Some I sent to the lab for tests. For some I just prescribed a medication or multi-vitamins, oftentimes as guess. The attending nurse then went to the hospital pharmacy and returned with the medicine for the patient. I was hardly a miracle worker, but I was uplifted and proud to be a doctor in such a needy place.

There were times when our task seemed to brush up against the miraculous. One day, for example, an Arab with a gray beard shuffled into the clinic, holding the hand of his ten-year-old granddaughter. Over a million Algerian fathers had been killed during the war of liberation, so grandparents and grandchildren were dependent on each other. An Arab grandfather can be an impressive person, and this one was. He was tall and handsome in his long robe flowing to his sandals, his turban wrapped around his head. He had been blind for years but heard through the grapevine that the American doctors might be able to help.

The ophthalmologist examined him, although he almost didn't have to because the whiteness of the old man's pupils visibly reflected the opaque lenses of his eyes. When surgery was done a week later, I watched as the eye doctor's wife, a volunteer like June, helped grandfather onto the operating table, still wearing his turban and robe, and she clipped his eyelashes. He had a lovely, peaceful face and it was clear that he was excited about the possibility of regaining his vision. The doctor focused the bright surgical light on one eye, and a local anesthetic was applied. Then the doctor used an instrument to retract the upper and lower lids, carefully cut a moon-shaped incision over the upper part of the pupil, inserted a pair of tweezers down into the eye behind the pupil, pinched the opaque lens, and pulled it up and out of the eye. He took a small, curved needle with fine thread and sewed the incision together. The doctor laid a bandage over the eye and taped it in place. Grandpa stayed on the gurney as sandbags were placed on each side of his head. An interpreter told him he would have to lie still for several days in the hospital and could return after a week to be fitted with glasses. He returned to the clinic with his grandchild, the bandage still covering his eye. His doctor took the bandage off, cleaned the skin around the eye, checked the incision, and peered through the pupil to the retina. All seemed well.

The crucial moment arrived. The doctor fitted a pair of eyeglasses with thick lenses held by a silver wire frame. There was a moment of silence as the old man looked around at the ceiling, at me, and the doctor. He saw his granddaughter for the first time in her ten years. He threw his arms up in the air and shouted, *"Allahu akbar! Allahu akbar!"*—God is great—and then he covered his face with his hands and fell to his knees in prayer.

My other consciousness-raising experiences during the 1960s took place back home in Seattle. One of them began when I got the news that Father John Leffler, the Dean of St. Mark's Cathedral, was being rushed to the emergency room after being hit by a car. The news shook me; John was a patient of mine, but he was much more. He was our priest, neighbor, and close friend—almost a member of the family—and I tasted the anxiety and dread that one feels when a loved one's life is threatened.

John's injuries were serious, but not fatal. His thigh was shattered, and his left shoulder fractured. He required orthopedic surgery, and it would take him months to recuperate. During the painful days in the hospital, he insisted that he owed his recovery to the many friends who consoled him. He always kept a bottle of gin in the bedside table and shared it with those who visited at cocktail hour. Never mind that he was bedridden with his left arm wrapped and his leg in traction; he enjoyed good fellowship—and a good, stiff drink.

It was during his hospital stay that John opened my eyes to something unexpected. One day we were having a conversation in his room when he asked, "Bob, do you know Mrs.Bodwin?"

I didn't know whom he was talking about.

"She's the woman who cleans my room," John said. "She's been working here for over fifteen years. She knows you, but she says you never speak to her."

"I'm sure I would recognize her if I saw her," I said, sheepishly.

"You should get to know her. She is one of the most important people in this hospital for me. If I'm feeling down, she always gives me a pick-up. She comes in, cleans the sink, changes the soap, and tells me I am looking better. She says she has seen many patients like me get back to a normal life. When she cleans the bedside table, she sometimes stops and holds my hand for a moment."

John insisted that I meet Mrs. Bodwin. He picked up his telephone, dialed the nurses' station, and asked that she be sent in. A few minutes later, a middle-aged, heavy-set woman in a hospital blue uniform knocked lightly at the door and stepped in with a quizzical expression on her face. I had seen her around the hospital, but I had never given a thought to her. Now I saw that she had a kind face with graying black hair.

John said, "Mrs. Bodwin, I want Dr. Barnes to meet you because he said he has never been properly introduced to you, and yet you already know him."

I shook her hand and immediately saw why she might bolster the spirits of a patient. She had a toothy, unassuming smile, and she radiated a caring and sensitive personality.

"John has told me such good things about you," I said, adding that I would like to get to know her better. She beamed. When we finished our little conversation and she turned to leave the room, she thanked John for inviting her in and introducing me.

After her departure John said, "You doctors are all alike. You are elitists. You only talk to each other and never notice these other hospital employees. They're important, too, you know, and patients are aware of what they do. Why aren't you?"

Somewhat defensively, I argued that I had a lot on my mind—I kept my mind focused on patient problems, checked the progress notes, studied lab reports, conferred with the nurse in charge. John told me I needed to know the other people who in their own way were true healers, people who were compassionate and took time to speak to patients. I realized he was right. A light came on. As a leader in the hospital, I had failed to appreciate these people. It simply hadn't occurred to me how important they were to good patient care. In the months that followed, I initiated a program to include all hospital personnel in the continuing medical education program. I drew up guidelines for new employees about patient relationships and their role with doctors, nurses, and all hospital personnel. The relationship has changed but not enough yet to elevate all personnel above second class. I am forever grateful to John for the insight he gave me. Prior to meeting Mrs. Bodwin, my picture of what a hospital is was incomplete: a hospital as a building full of medical equipment and staffed by doctors, nurses, lab technicians, and other health professionals. Now I knew that a hospital was also the custodial personnel, the food services employees, the grounds-keepers. It was people like Mrs. Bodwin, the hard-working housekeeper, who come into contact with patients every day. I realized how egotistic I could be. John Leffler opened my eyes

◆   ◆   ◆

Another clergyman who changed me was Bill Lewis, who came to Seattle from Nevada as the fourth Bishop of Olympia, the Episcopal diocese of western Washington State. I treated Bill for mild diabetes, which he successfully controlled with a daily tablet, exercise, and a simple diet. His illness certainly didn't diminish his energy to do God's work. On Sundays, he arose at 5 a.m. to visit as many as three churches and missions, where he baptized, confirmed, and preached.

Bill was a strapping man in his early sixties, about six feet tall with thinning hair. He always showed the faint notion of a smile, making those around him immediately comfortable. He was a great outdoorsman who loved to fish and take long hikes, and he was the kind of guy who would muddy his shoes to help you change a flat tire. He scoffed at pomp and seemed unmotivated by personal ambition. He was steeped in Christian principles, and he made many of Christ's teachings unfold before my eyes. He became a father figure to me, and I came to realize that a doctor needs a priest, just as the priest may need a doctor.

Shortly after Bill arrived in Seattle, a routine medical examination revealed the early stages of chronic lymphocytic leukemia. I often visited him at home, only a few blocks from mine, not necessarily to talk about diabetes or leukemia, but to exchange stories.

Bill always said, "Bob, there are many things more important than being concerned about my body. God's work in this diocese is the thing that counts."

For three years, his wife and the two of us kept his leukemia a secret. Not even his secretary knew about it. In the hospital laboratory, he watched the automatic counter click off his white blood count, and together, we checked its rise or fall on a graph sheet. Bill's charm and good cheer captivated the technicians, and they always looked forward to his monthly visit. Sometimes a doctor or nurse would stop me in the hallway and say, "Gee, you're lucky to have a patient like that. It must make you feel good to take care of him." It did.

Things went along smoothly until one day the automatic counter began clicking off the white cells at a much greater clip. Instead of the normal count of about 5,000, Bill's rose to 20,000, to 40,000, to 50,000, and finally almost to 100,000. The leukemia specialist and I decided to start aggressive medication, and with real excitement, we watched Bill's white count drop over a period of some weeks. Bill felt strong. He made light of his illness and continued working full-time.

I sat with Bill and his wife in their living room one evening to discuss his future. Even though his blood count was responding to treatment, we all understood that his time on earth was running out. We talked about whether he would go suddenly or slowly, whether he would have his mental faculties to the end, and how much warning he might have before he died. He wanted to carry on his work as long as possible, and he didn't want to release the news about his condition until necessary; he could picture his parishioners helping him on with his coat or showing sympathy in small ways, which he wanted to avoid. At the same time, he wanted the diocese to have enough time to choose his successor.

That night we philosophized about death. Bill felt he had prepared throughout his entire life to meet his Lord. No true Christian should have fear when his time drew near, and Bill was ready. His face shone, and it occurred to me that I was in the presence of a saint, a Gibraltar of inner strength. At one moment I could almost hear Christ say, "Let not your heart be troubled: ye believe in God, believe also in me."

Bill's illness could no longer be kept secret when, in November 1963, he injured his right shoulder while lifting his dog. An x-ray of the bone showed destruction by leukemia infiltration. By this time, x-rays showed that the disease had also spread to his thighs—an unusual and grave sign. It was clear that Bill probably had no more than six months to live. Bill informed the diocese, and soon I found myself with tears in my eyes explaining the Bishop's condition to a special meeting of the diocese's Standing Committee. Within two months, a new bishop from California was elected to succeed Bill.

This transition took a few months; in the meantime Bill Lewis's red blood count was plummeting, and bone lesions were spreading in spite of radiation therapy and transfusions. Bill was growing weak and short of breath, but he refused to let his condition keep him down. He tended to his pastoral work, continued to confirm members, and held a retreat for the clergy. Bishop Curtis arrived in June, and the transition began, with Bishop Curtis filling in whenever Bill's condition didn't permit him to fulfill his duties. We instituted heroic treatment with massive doses of cortisone, but this aggravated his diabetes and he began to take large injections of insulin three or four times a day. His leukemia lessened, but his legs became so swollen he could hardly get his shoes on. His body chemistry became so abnormal that it was a constant fight to maintain balance. His thirst was unquenchable, and he drank large amounts of water. It seemed he was taking medications by the handful. Nutrition became difficult, because he was not allowed any salt or sugar and he had to eat according to a precise schedule.

Bill hated all this attention to his body and insisted on making his rounds to parishes. In time, however, his legs became so weak he could barely shuffle, and it was heart wrenching to watch him pull himself up at the altar. Two weeks before he died, he went to Portland alone by train and conducted a three-day retreat. He was determined that as long as he could possibly function, he would keep going.

Finally, the body would not do what the spirit wished. Bill entered the hospital and fell into a semi-coma within 48 hours. He lay on his deathbed with nurses tending to him around the clock. His eyes were closed, but he had a constant smile on his face. He received communion daily and did not appear to suffer, in spite of the fact that his bones were crumbling. He recognized his family and most of the priests who came to pray for him. He died quietly as the nurse turned him to sponge his back. As I held his still-warm hand and a priest said a prayer, all I could think was, "Dear Bishop, thanks for the privilege of being your doctor."

I meant this in more ways than one. In truth, doctors generally find it inspiring or gratifying to treat patients who are powerful or famous. The doctors in Dallas who tended to President John F. Kennedy after he was gunned down told afterwards how moved they were; the same is true of those in Washington who treated President Ronald Reagan after he was wounded by a would-be assassin. I have been proud to treat such people as the renowned conductor Sir Thomas Beecham, the CEO of the Boeing Company, and of course Bishop Lewis. Treating notable people made me feel important. Bill Lewis, however, was special not only because he was a bishop, but also because of his courage and his unyielding devotion to God.

I treated Bishop Lewis's bodily ills for four years and finally stood in awe beside his deathbed. Never had I seen a man so willing to face death on its own terms, so much at peace with his mortality. I was filled with wonder about the meaning of his life and death. In a way, I was his student as much as his doctor. I wasn't a very good student, though. He gave me a book about dying, and I am ashamed to say that I didn't read the book until years later; I wasn't ready yet for the lesson Bill Lewis tried to teach me.

◆   ◆   ◆

The time of which I am writing was one of turbulence within me, but not yet one of growth and transformation. Whatever it was that I learned from my experience in Algeria, my lesson from John Leffler, and my closeness to Bishop Lewis, it did not make me whole. It did not save me from the weight of the stone I still carried within me.

Three years after Bishop Lewis died, I sat in another hospital room with my father-in-law, Bill. Perched atop Seattle's First Hill, Swedish Hospital looked toward the downtown business district, and Bill watched as construction proceeded on the Seattle First National Bank tower, on its way to becoming the tallest building in the Pacific Northwest. Every week it reached new heights.

Bill said, "I don't think I'll see it completed."

He was right. Bill, the father-in-law who had become my close friend, the man who accepted me wholeheartedly into his family, helped me establish my medical practice, bragging about me to his friends, died before the new tower was finished.

In the funeral parlor, I stood beside the casket in which Bill lay and I thought what a gift it was to die honorably, unlike my own father. I wished I could have told him this, but in fact, I had never allowed myself to talk to Bill about my father. As far as I knew, Bill didn't know how my dad died.

Bill was 67 years of age—not very old—and yet his death didn't affect me deeply; at least it didn't seem so at the time. I didn't cry when he died, and I didn't cry at his funeral. I loved him and missed him after he was gone, and yet to this day I have the feeling that I never mourned him properly, just as I never mourned my dad properly. The fact that I did not grieve for my father-in-law, just like my failure to grieve for my baby daughter Sara, was an indication of something not quite right within me: an unwillingness to let myself *feel,* an inability to grapple with the loss of a dear one, and at the bottom, a profound denial of death. From my vantage point today, it seems almost unbelievable that I could go through the deaths of my dad, my daughter, Bishop Bill Lewis and my father-in-law, and still be in denial of death, but that is how it was. Death happened to them; it did not happen to me, and therefore it didn't have much to do with me.

Something was bothering me. The same issues that gnawed at me before continued to frustrate me. My medical practice was a success by any standard measure, and yet it failed to satisfy me. The driving ambition I had since childhood, the nagging feeling that I wasn't living up to my mother's expectations, or my own: These demons ate away at my soul. My everyday life was filled with patients who began to look alike to me, suffering from diabetes, obesity, or some other ailment. My work seemed routine, predictable, and without meaning. I reached the point at which I felt I could not stand to see another overweight diabetic. And yet, I had to. My caseload was unrelenting. My workday was an endless parade of patients, an endless series of medical charts, an endless book of prescription forms, an endless lecture on dieting and insulin, endless hospital staff meetings. I felt overwhelmed by the pressure to keep up with the latest information in medical journals, which bored me as much as my patients did. And despite being recognized as a good doctor and teacher, I felt incompetent.

In 1969, June talked me into getting away from it all. Still acting like the typical survivor of the Great Depression, I felt we could not afford the trip. We took the three girls, who were now 20, 18, and 16, and set out on a trip around the world. I didn't really want to go; there was too much to do, too many patients, so much in my routine that I was afraid to leave. I had never taken a sabbatical in my life. We flew from Seattle to Hawaii, and from there to Hong Kong, Malaysia, Singapore, and India. We spent three weeks in East Africa, flying around in a small plane with our own pilot. We took dancing lessons on the Greek island of Spetse and visited the world-famous organ builder D.A. Flentrop in The Netherlands, whom we had met when he built the grand organ at St. Mark's in Seattle. It was the trip of a lifetime for all of us, and although I enjoyed it, I fretted about the money we were spending. We traveled for almost three months, the longest time I had ever been away from work; I worried that my patients wouldn't be there when I returned and that we would then find ourselves penniless. My patients didn't desert me, and soon after our return, I found myself back in the routine, overworked, and frustrated by the feeling that I was going nowhere.

Part of my problem was my specialty, internal medicine, which deals mostly with chronic conditions that do not require surgery. The internist is a thinker, a scientist, who takes in information and makes a diagnosis, who knows how to take cultures and read slides, knows how to keep body chemistry in balance—cholesterol, serum ammonia, blood urea nitrogen, glucose, and a hundred other factors. Internal medicine is about reading chest x-rays and electrocardiograms; it's not about implanting an artificial hip socket or putting a stent into a failed artery of the heart. It tends to be a *maintenance* practice, not a *fixing* practice.

Perhaps I chose wrongly when I decided on my specialization. Perhaps my temperament wasn't really suited to internal medicine. For me, it did not offer the satisfaction of curing an illness or delivering a baby. Indeed, I came to envy doctors who could restore the use of an injured hand or remove a tumor and cure the patient. Of course, I had a flashback to Uncle Joe, who received so much recognition, and personal satisfaction, out of making people better.

I cannot blame my malaise entirely on my choice of specialty. Some of the frustration about not being able to fix my patients was present when I watched Bishop Lewis die. I didn't want him to die but was helpless to stop his demise. I didn't get it. In my frustration over his inevitable death, I closed my mind to the lesson he wanted to teach me about dying.

In November of 1965, the Episcopal Diocese of Olympia awarded me a Bishop's Cross because of my care for both Bishop Lewis and Dean John Leffler. I accepted the award with great pride. Perversely, however, the medal became another piece of my masquerade, another Boy Scout merit badge, symbolic of my eagerness to be recognized for my deeds while those inner insecurities still burned at my soul.

Midway through this stage of my life, a nurse named Bobbie, who was a member of my church, asked me to participate in a panel discussing the care of the terminally ill and the grieving process. I had in fact done a lot of research on this and given lectures for programs training hospital chaplains. We held a planning session for the panel, and I brought along a briefcase full of books, lecture notes, and articles. I felt proud of my experiences and studies, and assumed I would be "the resource" for the group. I placed my references in front of me on the table, around which sat the other participants: Bobbie, acting as chairperson, plus a recently widowed woman, a psychologist, and a college student whose mother had died. No one else brought any books or papers, and my stack of materials stood out on the otherwise empty table.

Bobbie said, "What's all that stuff, Bob?"

"These are references I've collected for my lectures about grieving and care of the dying to chaplains, doctors, and medical students," I answered.

"Would you mind putting them on the floor, please? I thought we might start the meeting by having you tell us your thoughts about your own death."

I was stunned and speechless. I put all of my references on the floor and stared at the group. To my surprise, tears started rolling down my cheeks.

I felt naked. No one had ever asked me that before; not in medical school, not during my lectures, not anywhere.

Bobbie's face softened, and she said, quietly, "It's okay. We'll come back to it later." She turned to the woman on her right.

We never did come back to it. I don't know if she simply forgot about it in the ensuing discussion, or if she felt she had pushed me too far. For sure, it must have seemed strange to her, as a nurse, that she could have such power over a doctor, and perhaps her professional instincts told her she had overstepped a boundary.

As I think back on that incident, I have to admit that Bobbie's request was a wise and reasonable one. Death, hope, and resurrection are key issues in human life and in most religions. It makes perfect sense to start a discussion about grieving by talking about one's own mortality. And yet, the moment in which I faced that small group of people with Bobbie's challenge ringing in my head was the first time I ever consciously faced the question of my own death. I was a captive of the unspoken myth in the medical profession: Doctors don't die; patients die.

I escaped having to grapple with the question for the time being. I swept it under the rug. I didn't tell anybody about it, and the incident passed from my immediate consciousness. Certainly, I didn't change my behavior or my approach to patients and colleagues. Under the surface, however, the issue affected me. The question of my own death began to pop back into my mind at unpredictable times. Eventually I would have to confront it head-on.

◆   ◆   ◆

Kairos is a Greek word used in the New Testament to mean a time of decision or moment of truth. *Kairos* carries the connotation of a miraculous experience so powerful and life changing that it is remembered forever. When Saul of Tarsus was thrown from his horse on the road to Damascus and blinded, he experienced a revelation from God that changed his beliefs, and his life, forever.

When the Algerian grandfather regained his eyesight, he experienced a *kairos,* although he probably did not know the Greek word. I shall certainly never forget the moment. Far from home, I felt the presence of a mystery and shared the joy of a man with a deep faith. Did I experience a *kairos* then? Did I experience one when John Leffler healed *my* blindness to the everyday people around me? When Bishop Lewis died? Or when nurse Bobbie flattened me with her question about my death?

The events I have related in this chapter present moments when something essential occurred in my life. It is hard to say that any one of them represented a *kairos,* and yet by the end of the period I'm describing, I had stared into the face of a great truth and reached a moment of decision. My *kairos,* the moment of truth that changed my life came in 1971 when a patient, who happened to be a career counselor, said to me, "If you're not happy with what you're doing, you don't have to keep doing it."

At first I thought he was crazy; once a doctor, always a doctor. But eventually I saw his point, and his comment prompted me to make a big change the following year. I was already Director of the continuing medical education program at my hospital. They offered me the opportunity to expand that role to a paid, half time position. I took it and gave up my private practice. In 1974, I took a further step, setting up a consulting business in quality health care. I continued my education work at the hospital, but my larger effort soon centered in a non-medical office in another part of town. In time, my new career took me around the state of Washington and indeed into the national health care arena. I had taken off my white coat and put on my business suit.

10

From Private Practice to Medical Administrator—And Beyond

On a day in 1972, I sat at my desk listening to a woman telling me how she had not yet recovered from the death of her husband a few months before. She was about sixty years old, white, a bit overweight, wearing a gown tied together in the back, and I had just finished examining her. She had been my patient for a long time and I felt attached to her. I would be seeing her no more, for this was my last day in private practice. I was about to take my new position at the hospital.

"I'm sorry to see you go," my patient said.

I left the room so she could get dressed in private. As she left the office, I gave her a hug and told her good-bye. Really, though, my mind was on the fact that there was no one in the reception room waiting to see me and there would be no one the next morning. I felt as though I, too, was dealing with a death.

Truth be told, I had become miserable practicing medicine. I cared for my patients, but even so, they became tiresome to me. There were so many who had multiple symptoms and disorders—diabetes, arthritis, lack of energy, menopause. I could not fix them; I could only help them live with their illnesses. My frustration with my specialty grew intense, and I felt that I could not stand dealing with chronic illnesses any longer. Wouldn't it be great, I thought, to deliver a healthy baby and hand it to the proud mother, as I had done in medical school? Here you are, Mrs. Jones. Congratulations.

While still in private practice, I co-authored an article, published in *Northwest Medicine,* about what it is to be a good doctor. I desperately wanted to be a good doctor and like many doctors, I wondered if I was.

As director of continuing medical education at the hospital, I threw myself into the emerging field of quality of care. My new work coincided with a growing interest in the quality of patient care, monitored by both state and national organizations. Doctors was a 150-bed hospital, small as modern hospitals go. Our program quickly became a model. My job grew supported by grants locally and nationally. It was the beginning of an exciting new journey, which I embarked upon for both good reasons and others not so good. On the one hand, I saw a need in the health care community for serious work in improving the quality of patient care; I could make a difference in my new line of work. That was a positive objective. On the other hand, I left private practice because the work did not fulfill me. Even the honors I achieved at Doctors Hospital failed to satisfy me. It seemed that the more I achieved, the more my work served to isolate me from myself and others.

By 1974, my quality-of-care programs were flourishing. Demand for my experience grew quickly, making it clear that I needed more office space, my own staff, and complete independence. I moved out of Doctors Hospital and expanded into a wider consulting enterprise. I teamed up with an educator from the medical school at the University of Washington and together we founded the Health Care Review Center dedicated to advising hospitals and other medical organizations on how to improve the quality of patient care.

HCRC proposed a practical approach to monitoring and evaluating the quality of care a hospital gives its patients. We encouraged hospital staffs to organize themselves in a way that made collecting data on patient care a part of their routine. Our working assumption was simple. Every member of the medical profession wished to give patients the best care possible. We believed we knew how to help them. We proposed to take medical education to a higher level within each institution we worked with so that staff members would be continuously involved in assessing their patient-care procedures and finding ways to address any shortcomings.

Soon into our work, we became aware of a growing national concern about the rising costs of health care. We saw a connection between the quality and cost of care, and it wasn't necessarily a direct correlation; that is, in health care, you don't always get what you pay for. Higher costs may mean treatments and procedures that are unjustified, such as inappropriate use of antibiotics, excessive laboratory studies, and unneeded blood transfusions. Unnecessary procedures frequently mean increased risks of infection and other complications. Thus, by paying attention to cost control, the quality of care can actually be improved.

My background in medicine proved crucial to our success. I could talk to doctors in their own language, and they usually understood that I was not a health care bureaucrat with little knowledge of medical practice. Because of our pioneering work, we became known throughout the Northwest, spreading our services into Alaska, Idaho, and Montana. In time, we visited over half of the more than one hundred hospitals in Washington State and obtained enough contracts to keep busy.

Our program was a success, and for a while, my responsibilities and professional standing helped quiet my inner demons. I was involved in pioneering work, something to be proud of. Yet, my achievements and reputation ultimately failed to satisfy me. Whatever I achieved, it always felt insufficient. I did not enjoy life. But even as I craved more, deep inside I feared the next step, whatever it might be. I was not sure I would be up to par, might not know what I was doing. My mask would be torn from my face, and everyone would realize I was not what I appeared to be.

Unknown to me, a low-level depression had taken hold of me. With so much to do in my evolving professional life, however, it was easy to ignore the signs. One day I would no longer be able to ignore them, and by the time I reached the peak of my influence on the national scene, I would suffer a serious mental crisis.

◆　　◆　　◆

My work became that of an administrator, a job description that I never found acceptable. I was a doctor, not an administrator. I avoided the implications of that unacceptable label by thinking of myself as a medical educator, but that, too, left me feeling unfulfilled. I lived in a painful ambivalence, conscious that I was a doctor and yet not a doctor. If a friend or relative asked me why I quit my practice, I always had an answer, but it never sounded quite right to me. The day I left the hospital in 1974, the staff gave me a stethoscope with a gold-plated chest piece, and when the Chief of Staff made the presentation, a wise guy in the back of the room, a doctor, piped up, "What's he going to need that for?" It was a joke, of course, but I took it as a put-down.

Once I attended the monthly dinner meeting of a hospital Board of Trustees, where I spoke about collecting data on cost controls and quality of care. While speaking, I noticed that many of the doctors in the audience were staring down at their empty plates. I called this the "nose in the plate" syndrome. There were no nods of agreement, no smiles at my attempts to be witty. In short, my audience was uncomfortable with what I had to say. Collecting data meant monitoring doctors on the job, looking over their shoulders, figuratively speaking, questioning their ability to do their work properly. Their unspoken question was, "Who gives you the right?"

I became aware some doctors considered me a threat, as if I were a government inspector who was out to catch them for making a mistake in patient care. This rejection stung me. I wanted to say, "But I'm one of you. Trust me." Instead, I swallowed hard and went on with my work. It comforted me to have the endorsements of major medical societies, and it pleased me that my strong medical background made it easy for hospital administrators to accept me as an authority, but it pained me that my fellow doctors often did not. Like them, I was untrained in dealing with rejection, but unlike them, I was not practicing medicine.

During Jimmy Carter's presidency, Congress passed a law mandating the establishment of quality of care programs for all hospitals. Connections were made with state medical societies and organizations like mine, the aim being to establish federal agencies known as Professional Service Review Organizations (PSRO). In line with this initiative, the government offered to adopt my Health Care Review Center and turn it into a PSRO in the State of Washington. I would keep my staff, but instead of developing our own guidelines and protocols, we would be federal employees. I did not wish to be in such a position. On the positive side, the arrangement would have meant financial security for my organization, as we would have been included in the federal budget. In other words, we would become a branch of the large public network being developed to administer the new federal quality-of-care and cost-control program.

The prospect of becoming a government employee appealed to me even less than the thought of calling myself an administrator. I was dedicated to private medicine and local control. I was concerned that the government's approach would cause doctors and hospital staffs to lose control of their quality of care at the local level. The image of the government inserting itself between the doctor and the patient troubled me, for it seemed to involve serious questions of patient privacy and make doctors accountable to an outside party wielding a powerful degree of financial control.

The tide was turning against my position, but I decided to reject the government's offer for HCRC to become a PSRO. We would maintain our independence and, based on the reputation we had already established, we would find our own niche in the quality-of-care enterprise. There were areas the federal government was not entering, at least for the time being. We saw opportunities to offer our services in areas such as outpatient care, hospice care, and corporations that provided health care to employees. We would fill these gaps.

It did not work. We downsized HCRC and put together a new program. With the federal government moving in, however, it was hard to find new clients. Our funding dried up. With no more operating funds, we closed up.

The organization I had created within a pioneering field of public health, the organization that had given me a sense of accomplishment and a national reputation was gone. And even though HCRC hadn't made me whole, its death was like the death of a loved one. When I locked up the door of our offices, it felt as though I was throwing the last shovelful of soil onto a grave.

Now I was unemployed. I was headed for a condition of the mind, body, and soul that would test my survival.

11

Who Looks After the Doctor?

In the early evening of a day in January 1983, I sat in the living room of our second home in Sun Valley, Idaho, in front of a wood fire that crackled and hissed while June prepared dinner. She could look across the counter into the opening between the kitchen and the dining area and see me leaning forward in the armchair, holding my head in my hands. Slowly I got up and wandered over to the window, where I watched large snowflakes float downward and saw the lights of a car passing along the road at the bottom of the hill, far below. I felt as if I were in a tomb.

In bed that night, I twisted and turned. My breathing became rapid and a kind of fear gripped me, an indefinable fear that had no form and seemed more frightening because it was something I could not fathom. I got out of bed and walked slowly into the living room. It was still snowing outside and cold inside; the fire had gone out long before. I returned to the bedroom. June was awake and frightened. She spoke a few words of comfort and asked if there was something she could do. I don't remember my answer, but I climbed back into bed and she rubbed my back tenderly. I must have drifted off eventually, for I recall waking up in the light of the morning and feeling exhausted.

June had dearly wanted the house as a place for us to live six months of the year. The girls were grown up and I was no longer working, and after a lengthy time of stewing about it, procrastinating, planning, and negotiating with the architect, it had been built. First, we had bought the land, one acre with a spectacular view across the valley to high mountains, very near some of the best skiing in the world. I hesitated even then, thoroughly ambivalent about the property and the plans for building a getaway. Once we bought the land, I wavered again for about a year. We had friends in

Sun Valley who encouraged us. The location was beautiful, and architect's drawings promised a lovely home. I had no enthusiasm for it, however, and although we were able to afford the house, I worried about spending the money. June pleaded her case and couldn't get a yes or a no out of me. Finally she said, "I'm going to do it and we will both love it."

I didn't look forward to the day in the dead of winter when we headed east to move into our new house. I rode in a rented truck, together with my son-in-law Bob Morrison; June and Julie followed in our car. It was more than a day's drive from Seattle, and as we pulled into Sun Valley, we caught our first glimpse of the newly completed house from the road below. Bob cheered. I cheered, too, following his lead, but in fact, I felt it was the bleakest place I'd ever seen, sitting atop that treeless hill with the snow flurries blowing hard through the frigid air.

That is when I began to sink into a melancholy such as I never before experienced. This was different from the low-level depression I had had off and on for so many years. This was serious, clinical depression.

The best way I can describe how I felt is in visual terms. Years afterward, I created a poster illustrating what happens to people when they confront themselves without their protective masks. From a magazine, I cut out a cartoon that showed a man sitting at the bottom of a deep pit with his legs crossed and his shoulders hunched. There are dark bags around his eyes, and his mouth is drawn tightly shut. Above him, flowers grow in the soil outside the pit, but the man is unaware of them; he stares straight ahead toward the side of the pit. He can't see the flowers, and perhaps he wouldn't see them even if he were looking right at them. He believes the pit is his grave, and he cannot climb out. He is alone, miserable, and without hope. That cartoon man was I.

Even though I felt miserable, something kept me going to fulfill my limited professional duties. I served on the National Committee on Vital and Health Statistics, and continued to attend meetings in Washington, D.C. and elsewhere. As far as I know, none of my colleagues suspected anything was wrong with me, and I tried to deny it. Depression, like death, was not something that happened to *me*. I had another secret to hide.

One day while I was in Washington, something came over me as I walked into a Metro station and rode the escalator down, down, down. Although I had been in that station many times, it now felt as if I was plunging into the unknown. My body was heavy, and I could feel my heart pounding. At the bottom, I trudged uncertainly to the vending machine where by force of habit I slid a dollar into the slot, punched a button, and pulled out my ticket. I passed through the turnstile and approached the track, feeling suddenly alone and isolated; there were other people around me, but I knew none of them cared about me in the slightest. I became acutely aware of the train as it approached with a rushing, clickety-clack clangor, its headlights penetrating the darkness in the tunnel off to the side. And then, all of a sudden, I felt an urge to leap in front of the train, and an image of the impact flashed across my mind, my body flung around in pieces, blood squirting over the rails. The demons within me told me it wouldn't hurt, and it would relieve what I felt in the dark place of my soul.

But I didn't jump. A flash of reason penetrated my mind, telling me I didn't want to do what my father did, I couldn't cause my family such suffering. I shrank back and grabbed a support pole, hugging it for dear life, while dozens of other passengers stepped forward to board, totally oblivious of me. The doors slid open, and I gathered all my strength. I dashed across the platform and just made it into a car before the doors clattered shut. The train moved, and I sat down trembling. For a moment, I still didn't know what happened, but some higher force had kept me from self-destruction.

◆　　◆　　◆

June knew a little about depression but, like any spouse, had a hard time understanding what was going on with me. She thought if I would exercise, read a good book, mix with friends and so on, I would be all right. Back in Sun Valley, I tried to keep busy. I played tennis on an indoor court, visited the library, went to parties. I even went skiing on the children's slope. I succeeding in putting on a front for other people, but when June and I were alone in the house on top of the hill, I wanted to retreat to my armchair in front of the fireplace. No matter how many activities I imposed on myself, I still felt alone in the world.

Unable to deny my problem any longer, I decided to get help. I was eager to do it. I made an appointment with a psychologist who was listed in the Sun Valley yellow pages. A couple days later, I walked into his office, a simple suite in a separate wing of his home. I sat in a comfortable, leather-upholstered chair. There were potted plants in the room and a calming view out his window to the snow-covered mountains.

"What brings you here?" he asked quietly.

I told him my story, struggling through thoughts that were hard to articulate and dredging up facts about myself that were painful to confront. He listened carefully, interrupting me occasionally with questions and comments. He integrated some Buddhist principles into his approach. He taught me, among other things, that success and happiness come not from conquering the world but from knowing yourself and bringing harmony between your inner and outer self. He recommended books to read, and we discussed the stages leading to that state of internal harmony known to Buddhists as nirvana.

We talked about the human ego as a great deceiver. I became aware that the desire to have wealth and power, to accumulate material possessions, and to be "Somebody" (with a capital S) are not about who we *are;* they are about appearance and image, about who we *appear to be.* The desire for approval and renown are externally driven. What humans desire is not what makes them whole; all too frequently, externally driven desires turn out to be false ideals, and if we do achieve them they do not satisfy us but only lead us to desire ever more.

It dawned on me what he wanted me to do when he drew a picture of a man trying to climb a mountain with a sign on the top:

YOU CAN'T CLIMB TO THE TOP OF THIS MOUNTAIN

He told me a story. The man sees the sign but scoffs. "Who says so?" And he continues to climb. There are boulders in his way, and rivulets of muddy water. The grade becomes steeper the more he climbs; a wind kicks up, and the air gets colder and colder. He returns down the mountain to get a down-filled jacket, a warm cap, and gloves. As he starts up on his second try, he sees an elderly man with a gray beard sitting at ease behind a small table holding a pitcher of lemonade. The old man lifts a glass to salute the climber, takes a drink, and smiles contentedly. The climber laughs at him and sets off for the top. This time he gets some distance farther and runs into a wall of sheer rock. He realizes he can't make it up without better equipment, and so he returns to the base for rock shoes, ropes, carabineers, pitons: the whole outfit. The old man smiles at him and sips his lemonade; the climber laughs.

This cycle repeats itself several times, with the climber always reaching an obstacle he cannot get beyond. Finally, he is worn out and frustrated to the point of madness. Back at the bottom again, he approaches the old man, who continues to smile and sip lemonade. "Why don't you sit quietly and have a drink?" the old man says.

The climber sits, takes a glass, and drinks. He looks around himself and sees that he is in a lush, green valley. It is quiet except for the babble of a brook and the sound of birdsong from a nearby tree. The old man says, "Getting to the top will not quench your soul's thirst." The climber knows the old man is right.

Whatever it is we desire, if the force driving us toward it is something other than the will to realize our true inner selves, we won't achieve it. There are warning signs that tell us this, but it's easy to ignore them. As human beings, we want what we want, and we prefer not to be told that what we want is meaningless. The psychologist taught me that we need to pay attention to the warning signs, for the man struggling to climb his mountain ignores them at his peril.

When I think about it now, I can identify in specific terms what some of the warning signs were for me as I tried to climb my mountain. Some of them came in simple forms, for example when June's Aunt Helen, whom I loved deeply, contentiously asked me, "Bob, why do you have to think you're always right?"—a question that I wrote off as coming from an old lady who didn't have a clue.

Some of the warning signs were more complex. I recall a time at Doctors Hospital, for example, when I stopped the chief surgeon in the corridor and began to discuss with him my ideas about quality of care. I was so wrapped up in my world, so obsessed by my program, that it didn't occur to me he might be too busy to stand there and listen to my lengthy monologue. He was too polite to pull away from me, but later the hospital administrator called me into his office to tell me the surgeon had complained about my interrupting him and talking too much. There was my flirtation with a high government position. I was endorsed by the State Medical Society and my two Senators to be a candidate to become the Assistant Secretary of Health in Washington, D.C. The desire to achieve this office became my ultimate mountain. It was a position of great prestige and perquisites, with an impressive office in our nation's capital, and a big, black car with a driver at my beck and call. In fact, the job didn't really suit my personality or my skills. June, in her wisdom, feared I was on the wrong track. In the end, I wasn't offered the position—and in retrospect, that was a good thing. Although I had had relevant experience in medicine and quality of care, I was not at all prepared for the political aspects of the job and I doubt that I could have fit into the Washington power scene.

There were other signposts along my way up the mountain, and I had consistently ignored them all. It is not that I ignored them intentionally; I didn't recognize them, or my sense of who I was and what I should be caused me to deny them. It was only through therapy that they became clear to me.

One of the most important things I learned in therapy is that I wasn't alone, wasn't unique. Everyone is susceptible to desires that represent external, false ideals. A great many people, if not all of us, are at one time or another driven by illusory goals and counterfeit self-images; some of us spend our entire lives pursuing them and never feel content. Doctors are by no means immune to these viruses of the spirit.

This is not to say that it's wrong to strive for a high purpose, or that the desire to achieve is necessarily an illusion. Wanting to be a good doctor is certainly not a false ideal. Doctors who are motivated by the desire to heal are on the right track. However, if a doctor seeks mainly to be recognized, if his or her goal is to become rich and famous, or to be named Doctor of the Year, or if he elevates himself in his own mind to a position of infallibility—then that doctor is on the wrong track.

For me, it was an epiphany to learn that others are struggling, that they, too, are trying to get up that mountain and can't make it. To learn that I wasn't alone was a liberating experience. One of the people who was in the same boat with me was my daughter. Tucker, having suffered bipolar disease for years, knew all too well what it was like to be in the pit. Bless her, that lovely person helped me greatly during my struggle. I called her, often at night from my bedside phone, and she listened as I poured out my feelings. She asked what I was learning from therapy and offered practical advice.

"Dad," she said one time, "when you're in the pit, get up and wash windows. You'll be surprised how much that helps."

She was right. It wasn't my custom to wash windows, but I did. And it helped. I knew I could count on Tucker, who could read me clearly even when I was unable to articulate my feelings. She'd been there herself, and she always knew what to say. I am forever grateful to her.

By the time my therapist helped me to grasp the concept of the mountain, I began to understand what it was that was trapping me. I began to believe there really were flowers blooming, and I wanted to climb out of my hole and see them. I had gotten only partway through the stages of my own inner development, however. There was still a considerable distance to go.

In 1987, June and I sold the house in Sun Valley. For me, this was a necessary step toward healing. My need to abandon Sun Valley may seem odd or superficial. You might ask, wasn't my problem deeper, more personal; wasn't it really a problem within myself and not a matter of my environment? For me, however, being in Sun Valley was being removed from everything that gave my life purpose. My committee and commission work took me away from Sun Valley to Seattle, Olympia, or Washington, D.C. My primary social contacts were in Seattle, as well as St. Mark's Cathedral, my children and grandchildren, and most of our friends. Other crucial elements in my personal support system were in Seattle, including our lovely home in Seattle's Capitol Hill neighborhood, where I always felt comfortable. It was important for me to feel immediately connected to this support system, and not to be in a place where I felt isolated and cut off. On the day in 1987 that we moved the last of our belongings out and left Sun Valley for good, I felt elated.

Leaving Sun Valley meant leaving my therapist, who seemed to have figured me out. Surprisingly, this was not so hard for me. He had helped me over the first excruciating hurdles in my path to healing, and I am forever grateful for his wisdom and sensitivity. But it was time to move on. There would be a new therapist in Seattle, and another one after that. In all, I was in therapy for six years. There were times when my healing process advanced and times when it seemed stuck on a plateau, but on the whole I was moving forward.

In those days, I did not think in terms of *transformation*. I thought in terms of making it through the day, struggling to find my purpose, and learning about my true, inner self. When I looked in the mirror, I saw a self-centered person who had spent most of his life seeking success in terms of external markers: I'd always been concerned with proving myself to others, and I hadn't paid enough attention to just *being me.* And yet, when I reflected on my career in medicine, I liked the image of myself as a doctor. I was an excellent caregiver; as a physician, I was genuinely concerned about my patients. I believe I was a good doctor. But I didn't give myself enough credit for that, because just being a good doctor didn't bring me peace.

I was learning to let it go, learning that I was all right, that I could be content with doing the things I myself wanted to do.

Transformation can take a long time. I wasn't there yet. One important step remained. That step would take me into the territory of my own inner self that so many of us dread the most, the contemplation of our own death, the letting go of ego, the development of a quiet mind. It would help me grapple with the deep-lying, heavy stone I carried within me, the stone representing my father's suicide. That last crucial step would come as I made yet another change of vocation.

◆　　◆　　◆

"Who is looking after the Doctor?" a priest once asked me. He stopped me after I had just completed a report at a church meeting on the health of the Dean. It was 1967, the day after the Dean, John Leffler, nearly died. I was dog-tired after spending most of the past twenty-four hours caring for him, and the emotional strain was catching up with me. My voice faltered as I related how John narrowly escaped death from shock and blood loss. I described his shattered leg and shoulder and the surgery he underwent. My audience was amused when I told them the Dean raised his head off the gurney and said to me, "Bob, you look green. Don't worry—I'm not going to die."

The canon pastor, an assistant to the Dean, was a tall man who liked to wear a cowboy hat. He gave the impression of not quite being "with it," and many of us considered him a poor preacher whose rambling sermons left the congregation wondering what the point was. Many questioned why he was a staff member. I didn't know him well and usually tried to avoid him.

His question now stopped me dead in my tracks. Tears welled in my eyes as I gazed into his. He had seen that I was fatigued. He took my hand caringly, lovingly, and spoke in a quiet, calming voice, "God is with you. Any time you need help, don't hesitate to call me. Take care of yourself". He hugged me, and left. At times, the healer needs to be healed. It was a great awakening for me.

The experience flashed back to me many years later after I had pulled through depression and learned more about myself. I've come to realize there's a type of burnout that results not just from spending long hours on the job, but from feeling indispensable, trying to be perfect, or trying to please everyone. Burnout can result from playing God. Doctors, not only me, but many doctors, are vulnerable to this. We expect too much of ourselves, and we let others expect too much of us. We ignore our vulnerability and crash headlong into the reality of what we can and cannot accomplish.

Not only that. We get wrapped up in the task of treating patients scientifically to the point where we sometimes neglect treating them *humanly*. On the bureaucratic forms we fill out for reimbursement, there is no code number for listening to patients, touching them, or calming their fears. What's the diagnosis, what's the treatment, what's the prescription, what's the cure?—these questions all too frequently lead us away from the most important question of all: Who is the patient, and how can I truly care for him or her?

And who am I? What is it that makes a good doctor a good doctor? It's not only an up-to-date knowledge of medical science, familiarity with the latest drugs, a skilled hand with the surgical tools. It is all of these things *plus* compassion, responsibility, and trust that make a good doctor. It is being available when needed, and sensitive to the needs of others. I know many doctors like this and others who are not.

These human qualities, ultimately, are unattainable without a sense of personal wholeness. Doctors don't find it easy to consider their inner selves, and it's very hard for them to admit they need help, whether it be therapy or just love and understanding. True compassion and responsibility for others are intimately tied up with a sense of peace within oneself. The doctor who reaches the pinnacle of his or her success is one who knows not only how to care for others but also how to care for himself or herself.

12

How to Rid Yourself of Prejudice

June and I were in Philadelphia for a medical convention when a doctor friend of mine invited us to a private party in Camden, New Jersey, just across the Delaware River. We joined Al and his wife Faye, an Afro-American couple we knew from Seattle, for the cab ride to a lovely brick home occupying almost half a city block, with a manicured lawn and expensive cars parked in front. We were met at the door by a handsome woman in a sequin-covered formal dress. She graciously ushered us into a large room, where a crowd of people dressed to the nines milled around tables beautifully laid out with food. I glanced around and realized June and I were the only white people there—except for the waiters. I whispered into Al's ear, "Why didn't you tell me it was an all-black party?"

My friend smiled and said, "Because I was afraid you wouldn't come."

I whispered again, "Who do they think we are?"

"Friends of mine. They think you're black, too." Looking at June's blue eyes, he added, "A lot of black people have white blood in them, you know."

I was sure he was pulling my leg and everybody knew we were not black. It didn't matter at all. We met doctors, one an army General, lawyers, teachers, and politicians. This was in the 1970s, long before America knew Colin Powell, and it struck me that despite my military experience, I had never met a black general before. I didn't even know there was such a person. I wasn't sure what to talk about with him, but soon we were exchanging stories about our grandchildren and becoming friends. It was a wonderful party, and by the end of the evening, I had lost all my discomfort about the possibility that June and I might be considered black or that everyone there was black. As June and I returned to our hotel in Philadelphia, I felt very distant from the boy who grew up a half-century before in segregated Richmond, Virginia.

How I became aware of my many prejudices, and subsequently opened my heart and friendship to people different from me, and became an advocate for inclusion of all people, is an important part of my story. My struggle to become a whole, integrated human being could not have succeeded without overcoming some of the attitudes I grew up with, attitudes that limited my ability to love and relate to humanity, attitudes that represented yet another mask concealing my inner self and another stone weighing upon my soul.

I was born a white, Protestant, middle-class Southerner, with all of the white, Protestant, middle-class, Southern prejudices prevalent during the first part of the twentieth century. My community kept an unwritten list of people we treated as second-class citizens. This list began, of course, with colored people, as we called Afro-Americans. We considered colored people inferior to ourselves, and we also took it as a given that Jews, Catholics, Yankees, Native Americans, and foreigners were second class citizens Additional categories of lesser people included poor white trash, chronic drunkards, the mentally ill, and (ironically enough, given my own family's secret) families in which there had been a suicide. We also looked down upon people who were not well educated or spoke poor English, as well as those who lacked Southern manners; if a person did not know which spoon to use for the soup or where the butter knife was, that person deserved our scorn. Garbage collectors, junk dealers, the ice man, the milkman, anyone associated with labor unions, and indeed manual laborers in general—all of these, and their families, were beneath us. At the bottom of our scale were convicts and "ex-cons," especially those who were black and had been on a chain gang.

While I carried these prejudices, I meant no harm by them; they were a part of my culture, and I inherited them by dint of birthplace and the social standing of my family. The lines were drawn most sharply in terms of race. No colored person ever ate with us while I was growing up. It would have been shocking for a colored person to come to our front door; we had a back door for them. We attended an all-white church, and the schools I attended were all white. Whites and coloreds did not use the same public rest rooms. In high school, I heard that black boys had large penises and craved blond girls. In fact, a lot of white prejudices toward African-Americans centered around an obsession with the notion that white girls might fall prey to the ravenous sexual appetites of black males. White parents were horrified at the thought; colored people were not quite human, they were dirty and they would contaminate white girls by spreading venereal disease and destroying their moral purity. Our attitudes toward Afro-Americans were conditioned by these and other myths. No one that I knew questioned our assumptions about race and social standing.

I cannot help commenting, in retrospect, that white people too easily forgot how many slave owners had considered it their right to take sexual advantage of attractive, young slave women. Today we know that Thomas Jefferson, the man many consider the greatest Virginian of all, appears to have fathered several black children, but during my childhood it would have been blasphemy to suggest such a thing.

From my childhood, I remember Josh, the "colored" man who served as verger at the Second Presbyterian Church. Josh cleaned the church, kept the kitchen in order, tended the furnace, and handled other custodial tasks. He lived in a small apartment within the church building, and on Sundays, he put on his suit and tie and posted himself outside the front door to greet worshipers as we arrived. He always bent down to greet me with a handshake and a question about how I was, and I liked him because he made me feel special. He did not worship with us. I am sure the parishioners would have been shocked if Josh had come into the sanctuary while we were gathered there.

Another memory takes me back to the summer I spent in North Carolina with Uncle Joe and Sister. One day Sister got wind of a chain gang that was working on a nearby road, and she took me along as she drove out to see them. She went out of curiosity, but when she saw the "colored" men bound together by heavy chains attached to iron ankle rings, working with picks and shovels to prepare the roadbed and dripping with sweat under the hot Carolina sun, she cried. How quiet they were, I recall. They were not singing spirituals, nor did they smile. A burly white prison guard with a gun kept a wary eye on them. Parked nearby was the van that carried them between the prison and their workplace—a grim jail-on-wheels with no windows, only two-inch square perforations checkered along the sides of the compartment in which the men rode. I, too, felt deeply sad to see these men suffering.

At home in Richmond, we had an Afro-American maid named Mary, a stocky, very dark-skinned woman. Mary did not say much, and when she laughed, she put her hand over her mouth, where most of her front teeth were missing. She was a hard worker who had toiled in a tobacco factory—one of the lowliest jobs within our social order—before coming to us. Mother paid her three dollars per week, plus a streetcar pass to get her home in the evening. Mary also had toting privileges, which meant she was allowed to take home leftovers. Not every housemaid had toting privileges, and Mary was always grateful for the food she could take to her family. I never knew how many kids she had, or who else lived in her household. The subject never came up.

One day Mother and I were in the kitchen with Mary when two colored men came to the back door. They had on black suits, and their faces were somber. They spoke only a few words, quietly informing Mary that her husband had died. For a long moment, Mary stood stock-still and didn't say a thing. Then she said, "Well, ain't that something."

My mother said, "Mary, I'm so sorry. You go home and take care of things. We'll get along without you for a few days."

Mary followed the men out through the back gate and out the alley. She returned to work several days later, and I never heard another word about this incident.

It impressed me to see those colored men all dressed up and with such a serious demeanor. I knew something was wrong before they said a word. But their exchange with Mary was the closest I ever got to knowing anything about her personal life. We liked both Josh and Mary, and we appreciated what they did for us. In turn, we did for them what we believed was appropriate—but no more. As I think back, it is clear that we had no understanding of their lives apart from how they interacted with us. Our relationships were clearly defined by roles, and our social masks were essential to those roles. Whites wore a mask of privilege and authority. Blacks were there to serve our needs. We white people played out our roles toward blacks as they were written for us: not without kindness and even a degree of affection, but with a definite sense of who we were and what our respective places were in our community. I have no idea how much Mary or Josh saw of us beneath the surface of our masks, but we saw almost nothing of them beneath theirs. Their masks expressed the fact they, too, knew their place in our world; they did what we expected of them and behaved as we expected them to. But they showed us nothing of their personal selves, their passions, their real feelings about themselves or about us. I still marvel at how Mary kept her composure in front of us when she learned of her husband's death. I knew even then, as I do now, that among themselves, black people mourned their loved ones with an expressiveness that exceeds some white people's.

Mary came to work for us after my dad died. Thinking back before that, I don't have any memory of Dad talking about race relations and I don't recall any incident involving him and black people, positively or negatively. I am sure, though, that he accepted segregation as natural and proper.

On the other hand, I knew my mother's attitude very well. She took it for granted that colored people needed to keep their place, but she also believed they had rights. She even campaigned once for an unsuccessful white mayoral candidate who favored desegregation. As a principle, Mother opposed segregation in the buses and streetcars long before the civil rights movement, but she was not comfortable to sit by an Afro-American. In other words, her attitude toward race was benign and even caring, but she stopped short of considering black people her equals. Cultural habits were hard to break.

Mother spent her last years living in Stratford, a high-quality nursing facility named after the home of Robert E. Lee, the great Confederate general. The Stratford nursing home fit Mother's social self-image. It was the place to be for white people in Richmond. The Stratford remained segregated throughout my mother's life. The staff was Afro-American. Mother appreciated it when they waited on her, brought her food, and helped her get from the bed into a wheelchair, but she would never have shared a room with a black person. She was, after all, the daughter of white Southern parents who had lived during the Civil War, and were a product of their time.

I cannot deny that my mother's attitude influenced mine throughout my youth. I never had an Afro-American friend during my childhood, nor in college, medical school, or the army. It never occurred to me that segregation was wrong. While at VMI, I never wondered why the only African-Americans around us were the so-called stoop niggers, men who cleaned the lavatories and the "stoop," the porch-like platform that wrapped around each of the four floors of the barracks. It never occurred to me then that there was anything wrong with the name "*stoop nigger*".

Although there were no Afro-American students in the medical school, it was while I was a medical student that I woke up about colored people. My experiences in the emergency room showed me things that my childhood experience with Mary did not. I recall a weekend night when a young boy was brought in after a street fight. He had been sliced open with a straight edge razor and lay on a gurney barely conscious, with his guts hanging out. There were half a dozen other patients on gurneys, and the room was a frenzy of activity. I quickly clamped off a severed artery in an attempt to stop the boy's bleeding and checked to see if his bowel, kidneys, and other internal organs were cut. It would be up to the doctor in charge to make the decision about whether or not to send the boy into surgery. Meanwhile, his mother stuck her head in through the open door of the emergency room and shouted at us, pleaded with us to save her boy. A nurse patiently but firmly escorted her back to the waiting area, along with other family members, and gave her a sedative. Through the open door, we could hear the boy's loved ones crying and praying. If there was any doubt in my mind before, it was gone now—I knew that black people bleed red blood, they hurt when they are wounded, and they feel pain and agony when a loved one suffers. Just like white people.

Whether the victim of a street fight or the mother of a new baby, I found my black patients warm and human. Still, my world remained segregated until I went to Seattle and stepped, for the first time, into a medical facility that served members of all races. Early during my internship at Virginia Mason Hospital, I assisted in the delivery of a black baby. All went well, and afterward the delivery room was cleaned up and readied for the next patient. When I saw that the next patient was a white woman, I was astonished. It didn't seem right—didn't they have separate rooms for black and white deliveries? It was also disconcerting to see black and white babies together in the nursery.

It was not long before my fellow interns let me know they thought my reaction was strange. Integrated medical facilities became a natural part of my life. By the time I finished my internship, neither Seattle nor the integrated hospital was foreign to me.

Seattle in the 1940s was not free of racial prejudice and stereotyping. Most residential neighborhoods were segregated, and social divisions tended to keep people apart, not only black from white but also whites from Asian Americans, of whom Seattle had many. In this light, it should be remembered that Seattle's Japanese population, even though American citizens, spent the war years in the infamous internment camps.

◆   ◆   ◆

There was no one moment when I saw the light about racial prejudice. My attitude evolved over time. I had a few black patients in my private practice, and the church June and I joined, St. Mark's Cathedral, had some black members. I paid attention to the beginnings of the civil rights movement back in the South, and on that fateful day when Rosa Parks courageously sat down in a Birmingham bus and refused to give up her seat to a white man, I said "Good for her." I admired Martin Luther King, thought George Wallace was a fool, and had nothing but disgust for those ignorant local sheriffs and Ku Klux Klansmen who used intimidation and violence against the civil rights workers. I disdained the rednecks in Mississippi and Alabama whose hate-filled faces and ugly words assaulted us through the news media; they were not the Southern gentlemen I once aspired to be. At the same time, I recognized myself as a Southerner, too, with a trace of Virginia in my speech and manners, and there were times when I felt embarrassed for the way black people were being treated in my home region.

While on vacation in Jamaica with June in 1977, I met a man who helped give my racial attitude one last, crucial boost forward. I happened by chance to get into a conversation in the bar of our hotel with an Afro-American, a tall and dynamic attorney from Chicago. Bob and his wife Shirley joined June and me for dinner, and the four of us hit it off from the beginning. We spent a lot of time together during our week in Jamaica, and when we parted, I knew I had found a friend for life.

Sometime later, I hesitated when June suggested that we invite Bob and Shirley along to Maui, where we planned a group vacation with some wealthy and influential Seattle friends. I worried that my black friends from Chicago wouldn't be accepted into that company. It was my old Southern prejudice speaking, however, and June was right: Bob and Shirley blended in with our other friends beautifully, and we had a wonderful time.

I have learned much about African-Americans and their struggles by knowing my new friend and listening to his story. He grew up in the company town of Alcoa, Tennessee, where his father was a laborer in the aluminum smelting plant. Bob pulled himself up by the bootstraps. He worked his way through college in his home state and went on to earn a law degree at Northwestern University. As a young attorney in the Chicago area he discovered how hard it was for a black man to succeed in white society. Nevertheless, he joined the law faculty at Northwestern, and for a number of years he served as an attorney for Jesse Jackson's PUSH coalition. He became very close to Chicago's former mayor Harold Washington.

June and I have always been proud to know them and over the years we have traded visits in Chicago and Seattle. Bob's family has always made me feel welcome, and I know they feel perfectly comfortable with us in our home. After many talks over a cocktail, he has me figured out, as only a deeply loved friend can do.

◆   ◆   ◆

A very important opportunity to confront my prejudices came in 1977, when the Bishop of the Episcopal Diocese of Olympia asked me to chair a new commission on the study of human sexuality. The committee's brief was wide-ranging, but the key question was whether homosexuals should be ordained as priests. I accepted the appointment and considered it an honor. The Bishop probably thought I knew all there was to know about sex since I was a doctor. I had treated syphilis and gonorrhea, and in the army, I gave lectures on prevention of venereal diseases, but I was by no means an expert on the subject. At the outset of the commission's work, I was leaning against the ordination of gay people.

A number of other denominations throughout the United States were appointing committees to discuss the same issue. In the more conservative Protestant churches, of course, clergy were blasting out from their pulpits against what they considered the abomination of homosexuality. The Roman Catholic Church also stood firm on its position that homosexuality was a sin, and gay people could not be admitted to the priesthood. I had been in the medical profession for more than thirty years and had never before given these questions much thought. I don't remember the subject of homosexuality ever coming up in my education, either at VMI or in medical school, and not even during my service in military neuropsychiatry. I am sure there must have been what we now call closet gays in the military services during World War II, and that they did their part in winning the war.

Physicians reflect the culture from which they come, and up until the 1970s, homosexuality was a taboo in our culture. Most of us in mainstream America knew little about it, and tended to see homosexuals as abnormal, deviant, or at the minimum different. In fact, the subject was so far off-limits that it didn't come up in polite conversation. The term *sexual orientation* didn't exist, as far as I knew, and even the word *gay* still meant *merry* and was used most often to describe a happy or gala event. Throughout most of the twentieth century, a good many doctors were naïve not only about homosexuality, but also about heterosexuality.

I was not totally in the dark. While in private practice, I noticed the occasional male patient who seemed effeminate, and one man even knitted me a pair of socks. Even if I had my suspicions, I would never have brought the subject up with a patient or anyone else. From today's perspective, it seems almost unbelievable that all of our controversies about gays lay submerged for so long. You might think that doctors should have known something about them and their particular medical concerns. Only since the onset of AIDS have all of us changed.

Personally, the only experience I ever had with a homosexual before my work on the Bishop's commission was an unpleasant one. While visiting the Mayo Clinic during my summer break from medical school in 1942, I met the Clinic's chief of research in high-altitude flight, which Mayo researchers were studying to determine the medical effects on military pilots. The research chief—let's call him Steve—showed up one day at the tavern where students gathered to drink beer in the late afternoon. I was very much interested in medical flight research, and to my delight, Steve took an interest in me and answered all of my questions. He invited me to spend the evening at his home, where we could continue our conversation. I was thrilled that this important man found me worthy of his attention and assumed it was because he thought I was bright and full of professional promise. His place was small but comfortable, with floor-to-ceiling bookshelves and original artwork. We talked late into the evening, and he invited me to spend the night. His bedroom was furnished with twin beds, each fitted with only a white sheet and pillow because the weather was hot and there was no air conditioning.

Steve was an attractive man, lean and suntanned with an easy smile and a full head of light-brown hair. It surprised me that he was not married, and I reflected (not without some envy) that he must have had it easy with the hospital nurses. We both undressed down to a tee shirt and boxer shorts, washed up in the adjoining bathroom, and made a little small talk as we turned in. Then he suddenly started talking about the disadvantages of being a research physician. For one thing, he said, he didn't examine patients and sometimes wondered if he was losing his skills as a practicing physician. He then asked if I would mind letting him do a physical exam on me. He said he hadn't checked a male for a hernia in a long time. With that, he moved over to the edge of my bed and laid his hand on my thigh.

I may have been naïve, but I realized this was not an appropriate request from a doctor. When he moved his hand up close to my groin, I jumped up and said, "Hey, quit that!"

He pulled his hand away, dropped his chin, and began to cry. He apologized and confessed that he was a homosexual. He was afraid he would be caught and lose his position at the Mayo Clinic. His mother and father didn't know, and he was sure that his father, in particular, would be devastated if he found out. He told me he had first recognized his attraction to males when he was about sixteen or seventeen and that he had no choice about his attraction to other men. He assured me he would not make any further attempts at intimate relations with me.

I have never forgotten that physician, who was highly respected in his work. Indeed, Steve popped into my mind when I once again met people like him while on the Diocesan commission. Our group included two Episcopal priests, a psychiatrist, two housewives, a university professor, and a psychologist. We met approximately every two weeks before the fireplace in the living room of my house. June was a member of the group and, like me, learned a great deal. She and I had never before discussed such a taboo topic.

We began by studying the Bible, under the leadership of John Leffler, the Dean Emeritus of St. Mark's Cathedral. We called him the "Great Bald Ego." He was a knowledgeable scholar of the Bible, and he knew how to combine his long experience with a keen sense of humor to make Bible study fascinating.

Many people believe the Bible condemns homosexuality in as many as eleven or more passages. Dean Leffler pointed out, however, that opinions vary widely about what the texts mean. Jesus is silent on the subject. The passages that are perhaps the most explicit are several precepts in the Jewish Holiness Code, for example Leviticus 18:22, which reads, "You shall not lie with a male as one lies with a woman; it is an abomination," and the teaching of St. Paul in 1 Corinthians 6:9–10, that "neither the immoral, nor idolaters, nor adulterers, nor sexual perverts, nor thieves, nor the greedy, nor drunkards, nor revilers, nor robbers will inherit the kingdom of God." (Both translations are from the *Revised Standard Version.*) Dean Leffler, however, helped us understand that even these passages, which appear to be straightforward, are open to differing interpretations. In the case of St. Paul's letter, written in Greek, the explicitness of the passage rests on the translation of a two-word phrase, *malakoi arsenokoitai,* translated in the *Revised Standard Version* of the Bible as one term, "sexual perverts." Some modern translators chose to translate these two words into "effeminate" and "homosexuals" (as in the *New American Standard Bible*), but the King James Version rendered them into the phrase "abusers of themselves with mankind." These translations are highly controversial. The first word, *malakoi,* was used commonly in St. Paul's time to mean "soft," and the meaning of the second word, *arsenokoitai,* seems to have gotten lost over the years. Translators have had to guess at what the second word meant, which explains the difference between the King James Version and more modern translations. St. Paul's meaning is not at all clear. One reasonable interpretation is "persons of soft morals," which is hardly the same as homosexuals.

The passage from Leviticus, among others in the Old Testament, is a bit more complicated. The Jewish Holiness Code was written when male homosexual sex was associated with idolatry, and the rule in question, like numerous other precepts in the Code, may have been aimed at combating the practice of idolatry. In addition, a good many of the associated rules forbade such things as eating rare meat, wearing clothes made from a blend of fabrics, cross-breeding animals, and sowing mixed seeds in a field—rules that Christians do not consider valid today. Other rules in Leviticus about not wasting one's seed had much to do with the need of the Israelites to increase their population to better protect themselves from their enemies.

The bottom line in our commission's opinion was that the Bible does not condemn homosexuality, and those in the church who do so rely on faulty interpretations of the language or context in the Biblical passages.

Over the course of two and one-half years' discussions, we had the opportunity to listen to many gay people tell their stories. For me, this was a remarkable experience. The people we met told the same story, over and over: As teenagers, or perhaps sometime later, they made the frightening discovery that they were different from others. They told about their fear of being discovered by their parents or friends, a fear so devastating that depression and thoughts of suicide were common. For some, the desire to be like others was so overpowering that they saw psychologists or psychiatrists in the hope of being cured, that is, converted to heterosexuality. Some psychologists claimed they could perform such a cure, but of course, they could not. We heard devastating stories of people who tried to change their sexual orientations but could not. We met couples, man and wife, who had married out of a desire to be culturally accepted, only to end up in heart-wrenching divorces. We heard stories, in other words, of people desperately trying to be something they were not, because society demanded it of them. Failing in the attempt, they suffered from colossal feelings of guilt and self-hatred.

I recall one couple that met with us, Anthony and Marilyn (not their real names). We gathered, as always, before my fireplace, some on chairs and others relaxing on the floor. Anthony and Marilyn sat next to each other on the sofa and, after I welcomed them and introduced them to the group, they told their story. They were both Episcopalians in their thirties, both attractive, college-educated, and well-spoken. Anthony was gay, but he loved Marilyn dearly and she loved him. For years, Anthony denied his homosexuality, and when he could not deny it any longer, he began seeing a psychiatrist; he wanted to be changed, wanted to be like other men. When he found that he could not change, he became deeply depressed and thought very often about suicide. Marilyn confirmed his story, confirmed her love for him, and expressed similar feelings of misery, sexual frustration, and a sense of being separated from society. Both worked hard to conceal their problem, fearful of being stigmatized. They were considering a separation.

None of us on the commission heard from them after that evening, but we all sympathized with this unfortunate couple and wished we could do something to help them. They cried as they told their story, and some of us cried, too. I felt both sorrow and anger—sorrow for the pain Anthony and Marilyn were undergoing, anger at the way society and the church looked upon people like them. All of us on the commission deeply regretted that the church in which we believed could not give them comfort.

Today, one often hears the argument that homosexuality is not a natural condition but a lifestyle choice. My experience on the Bishop's commission convinced me beyond any doubt that sexual orientation is not a matter of choice. Why should a person choose to subject himself or herself to the kind of hatred, ridicule, discrimination, harassment, and even violence that we know gays and lesbians often suffer? Why should they choose to be so different from the social norm that their difference makes them miserable?

Today we know that homosexuals are sometimes the targets of violence perpetrated by heterosexual men, but this came as a shock to us back in the 1970s. We learned that a significant cause of suicide among teenagers is the discovery by a kid that he or she is homosexual. We also learned a few things about our own homophobia and the cultural rules it produces; for example, that in many countries it is considered acceptable and normal for two men to hold hands, embrace, or kiss publicly, or for two women to link arms as they walk down the street—behavior that "straight" Americans feel uncomfortable with.

We discussed some of the negative myths about homosexuals: that gays are sex addicts; that they are kleptomaniacs; that they commonly molest children, or would if they could; that they sexually harass each other and try to proselytize or recruit converts among heterosexuals. Certainly, some gay people are guilty of these behaviors. But, as we know all too well, sex addiction, theft, child molestation, and sexual harassment are behaviors widely found among straight people, too. In fact, the overwhelming proportion of child molesters are heterosexual men who abuse girls; only about six percent of child molestation cases involve men abusing boys. All such behaviors are wrong no matter who practices them, and gays who behave offensively are no more wicked than straight people.

From our Bible studies, we learned one thing for sure: The Bible contains prophecies and revelations, great stories and deep wisdom, but it is a lousy reference book on sex. The authors knew nothing about sperm and egg cells, testosterone and estrogen, or how to prevent sexually transmitted diseases. The Bible has little, if anything, to say about the joy in sex, the pleasure of it, the naturalness of it. In biblical times, no one had much understanding of the psychological dimensions of sexuality and love. The lifestyles of the tribes in the Old Testament were primitive compared with the complex cultures of the twenty-first century, and science was at a very low level.

As for our modern civilizations, it became crystal-clear to me how our church, which at its best is a place of love and a house that reveals the presence of God, can also be a place of the devil, where people become separated from each other. The church can even become a partner with other organizations in precipitating hatred and violence. The people who make up the church, after all, are imperfect. In the process of searching for a meaning to life, these imperfect beings sometimes imagine they know all the right answers and are prone to condemning those who do not conform to their narrow conceptions of right and wrong.

There is such irony in the behavior of the church. On the one hand, it stands steadfast on the teachings of Christ. "Love your neighbor" is a bedrock Christian principle, taught by Jesus and preached from every pulpit of every denomination, along with the more demanding commandment, "Love your enemy." And yet, many in the church have acted as though there are exceptions to these rules. From the Crusades through the great European wars of religion to today's crusade against homosexuals, church authorities have led their followers away from Jesus' central teachings. The church creates a climate for prejudice whenever its spokesmen interpret the Bible in a way that encourages us to set culture against culture, religion against religion, and race against race.

So, too, with people of differing sexual orientations. The essential ingredient of any complex community is learning to trust, love, and bond with those who are different from ourselves. It is the devil's work to twist the meaning of the Bible and condemn gays. If God is love, as the Bible says, then aiming a prejudicial hatred toward any person or group is the work of the devil.

In *The Good Book: Reading the Bible with Mind and Heart,* Peter J. Gomes argues the importance of awakening Christians to a view of their faith that values charity and humility over mean-spiritedness and arrogance. To put this into practice, we in the church need to commit ourselves to love and put aside our tendency to judge others. God asks us to love all of our fellow humans, including those who are different from us. It is our duty to accept them into our midst, get to know them, and avoid the temptation to assume we are right and they are wrong. When we truly accept these precepts and follow them faithfully, we will realize that it is a burden to hate, but it is uplifting to extend our hand in peace and love.

At the end of our deliberations, we wrote two resolutions. The first recommended that the diocese develop a program of sex education for its parishes. The second asserted that sexual orientation should be neither a qualification nor a disqualification for candidacy to Holy Orders. We figured the first resolution would be relatively uncontroversial, and we worded the second resolution as carefully as we could.

I was a bit nervous when I delivered our final report to several hundred people at the western Washington Episcopal convention in September 1979. This is a group composed of clergy and elected laypersons from all parishes in the diocese who meet annually to discuss diocesan business and make policy recommendations. I said as clearly as I could that sexual orientation need not be a barrier to priesthood, nor did the church need to write new canons (Church laws) to deal with the issue. After I finished, several people stood and praised the report, and there was a motion that it be accepted. But that was not to be. The discussion was heated. The first resolution passed, but the second was voted down.

We on the commission were not surprised by this outcome. We felt we had done our work thoroughly, but we were ahead of our time. Personally, I was delighted by what we all learned and proud of the stand we took. We opened the door within the Episcopal Church to a long discussion of homosexuality. This question continues to generate much heat today, but the momentum within the Church has shifted. In 1996, a national

Church court exonerated a retired bishop who was charged with violating canon law when he ordained a practicing gay man as a deacon. Since then, the Church's official position is that there is no canon law that applies to the ordination of gays, and sexual orientation should not be an issue in considering candidates for Holy Orders. If the question happens to arise, it is essentially left to the discretion of each parish and the Bishop of the diocese.

In 1997, the Diocese of Olympia Convention passed a resolution asserting that homosexuality is "morally neutral." Two years later, St. Mark's, the cathedral of the Diocese of Olympia, chose as its Dean the Very Reverend Robert Vincent Taylor, a white South African whom we hired because he is an outstanding priest—and who just happens to be openly gay. Thus, twenty years after my report to the Diocesan Convention, I rejoiced to see the commission's work brought to fruition in my own parish.

There are still many denominations that do not accept the moral neutrality of homosexuality. I believe the momentum will continue, though. It is well known that there are openly gay students in many seminaries, and in time I believe more and more parishes will be willing to accept them as priests and ministers. Cultural change takes time; people learn only gradually to release their doubts and anxieties about those who are different from them. But we do learn—through openness, prayer, and understanding. Justice for all, both in churches and throughout the world, cannot be argued. It was little more than a generation ago that women were admitted to the priesthood, and now we are seeing their numbers increase.

Such changes are evolutionary. People overcome prejudice by getting to know others not as gays, blacks, and so on, but as friends, equal but different. The process grows through a kind of ripple effect. Once we get over one prejudice, the next one is less difficult; and so on, until eventually we accept the beautiful diversity of our world without thinking twice.

Serving on the Bishop's commission was a significant milestone in my personal development. It was a time of learning, growing, and becoming more sensitive to others. The experience helped me rid myself of one more bias. Meeting with gays gave me a more sensitive vision of all people, including myself. I learned that if a person lives with and gets to know individual members of a minority group, the chances are he will become an advocate of the group in due time.

At the end of the commission's work, I felt that I had come out of a closet. I tore off my mask of prejudice and discarded the notion that gay people were sinners because they were gay. I stopped worrying about what they _do_ in their private lives and accepted them for what they _are_—fellow humans who deserve my love, understanding, and support. Gay people are God's children. It is our sacred calling to care for them, support them, and defend them as citizens and human beings. If we do these things we become one, each at peace with the other.

Sometime around the beginning of the commission's work, I bought my first book about homosexuality. I walked into a bookstore and found the section on sex. Glancing from side to side to make sure no one I knew was watching me, I picked out *The Church and the Homosexual,* by a Jesuit priest, John J. McNeill (1976). I carried it so the title could not be seen, and on my way to the cashier, I hastily picked up a book on how to draw. While standing in line, I spotted a doctor friend who, to my great anxiety, approached me. I stuck the McNeill book in my jacket and grew more and more anxious as our conversation went on and I got closer to the front of the cashier line. I began to fear I would be stopped, searched, and arrested for trying to steal the book. Finally, my friend said good-by and I was able to pull the book out of my jacket in time to pay for it at the counter. A year or so later, I bought ten copies of *The Homosexual Matrix* by C.A. Tripp (1975). Not only did I feel no discomfort about buying the book, but I talked about it with a stranger standing behind me in the cashier line. Later, it struck me how far I had come.

Today, June and I enjoy friendships with numerous gay persons, both in church and socially. These friendships have enriched our lives, and we feel in our souls that we have become more complete and more human by overcoming our prejudices.

I have been asked how I, a Southerner, was able to discard so many of the cultural biases I grew up with. Part of the answer is that I simply allowed myself to be open to the different kinds of people who came into my life. At the same time, I believe something deep within me has helped me empathize with people who have felt the pain of rejection. I have felt the threat of rejection because of my dad's suicide. That terrible family secret made me self-conscious and afraid of discovery.

In an earlier time, we heard the term "passing" to refer to light-skinned people with African blood who were able to disguise their ethnic identity in order to fit in with white society. Reba Lee's book *I Passed for White* (1955), which was made into a movie (1960), told the story of a young woman who concealed her true racial identity, married a white man, and suffered from her secret. I think of this story, and then I think of all the gays and lesbians who tried so hard to pass for "straight." I think of myself, living with a deep, dark secret in order to pass for "normal" and be accepted by others. My secret was not the same as the stigma experienced by racial and sexual minorities, but we do have the commonality of hiding in the closet and wearing a mask to cover our pain.

The scourge of prejudice is at the root of many of the contemporary world's most urgent problems. In the twenty-first century, human survival may very well depend on learning to love all people, being comfortable with them, seeking them out as friends and learning about them. Human beings are more alike than different. Christians, Jews, Muslims, Hindus, Buddhists, Zoroastrians, all must seek common ground. White, black, yellow, and brown; Israeli and Palestinian, Russian and Chechen, Serb and Kosovar, Hutu and Tutsi are children of God and need to recognize the divine in each other. All religious people have a vital role to play by helping their members overcome the fear of "otherness" and accept diversity. We must pull off the masks of prejudice that separate us from one another and from God. Grace is absent when we ignore those who are being lynched, bashed, killed, shot, injured, rejected, separated, or abused. Grace is always present, however, when we hold hands, listen to each other, and honor our differences.

13

Death of a Priest

"I am free! I am free! I am going to die. No one will ever again tell me to stop smoking or having a martini before dinner!"

These were John Leffler's words in the hospital room when he found out that he had terminal cancer of the liver. I did not know how to react. He was eighty-six, and we had known each other for thirty-five years. He may have been ready to leave this world, but I was not ready to see him off.

The first time I met John Leffler, the Dean of St. Mark's Cathedral, I thought he was an old man. A rim of graying hair seemed to hold his bald pate in place, as he stood inside the entrance of the cathedral in his long, purple robe, shaking hands and talking with people as they filed out through the main doors. June and I had recently moved into our house just three blocks from St. Mark's, but we were not yet members. We attended that Sunday because June's sister-in-law had completed a consecration class to prepare for membership in the Episcopal Church, and, along with the others in her group, she was presented to the congregation during the service.

I stepped up to the Dean and introduced myself. He looked deeply into my eyes and said, "This will not be the last time I shall see you. You will be here again."

He was right. June and I soon became members. I soon learned that I was wrong—he was not so old then. He was only fifty-one, and he lived another three and one-half decades. During that time, John and I grew to know each other not just as priest and communicant, but as patient and doctor, and as intimate friends. June and I also came to know John's wife, Faith, a vibrant little woman with bobbed hair who had borne him three sons and remained his companion until she developed Alzheimer's disease late in life.

John Leffler, priest, father, husband, grandfather, Father Leffler, The Great Bald Ego. He was a great preacher, a master of the King's English. He had faults, like the rest of us; he was a man who would kneel and beat his chest, asking for forgiveness. He was a man of God who feared his sins might cause him to be rejected on the last day, a man of the flesh who was not above casting an eye (but nothing more) at a well-turned-out woman. I loved the man deeply, and he once said he thought of me as a son. There were times when I could not stand him. It is possible he could sometimes not stand me. To see him preaching from the pulpit or baptizing a baby was to recognize a priest of unquestionable authenticity. As he grew older, his white eyebrows and white mustache, the latter yellowed from cigarette smoking, made him seem all the more authoritative. You could tell he loved the church; he loved his position, and he loved standing at the front door of the cathedral in his vestments, glad-handing the parishioners as they departed. He loved all of them.

◆   ◆   ◆

As a young man, John played piano in a bar and had quite a following I am told. This must have been his rebellious phase, for he had been raised in the Methodist Church, known for its Bible-thumping preachers and teetotaling congregations who belted out the kinds of hymns small-town churchgoers sang in old Hollywood movies. His father was a Methodist minister, and that is what John initially became as well. However, one night he attended a midnight service at an Episcopal church in Rochester, New York, and something hit him. While kneeling to receive communion, he suddenly felt that the Episcopal Church, with its liturgy and other rituals, was where he belonged. In due time he shifted. At first blush it might seem curious that such a lively man would find his spiritual home within a denomination known then for its conservative forms and its sedate parishioners. The Episcopal Church has changed since then but John's ebullience endeared him to his flock and made him stand out among the priests I have known. He brought his musical abilities to Christmas parties often sitting at the piano playing carols by heart. He had a reasonably good singing voice, not brilliant and indeed a bit tremulous as he got older, but he knew his music.

John's ebullience helped him through his accident in 1967, and he survived the multiple fractures. His rehabilitation was complicated because he was born with a clubfoot that was never fully corrected as a child. This was his right foot, and now the accident had fractured his left leg so that he had no leg for steady support and it took much longer for him to walk again. Because his left shoulder was fractured, he could not use crutches. John was determined to recover as soon as possible, so he cooperated with the physical therapists with all the strength he had. He had never been an athlete of any sort, so it was hard for him. With the aid of a walker and someone to steady him, he gradually began to regain his sense of purpose and looked forward to returning to his church and his altar. He quickly resumed having his evening martini and he continued to smoke, despite the fact that smoking tends to decrease circulation in the legs; but no amount of persuasion would convince the good priest to quit.

John continued his rehabilitation activities after he was dismissed from the hospital. It was quite a sight to see the activity at his house. His dining room had been converted to hold a hospital bed with a crank at the foot to elevate his head or knees. A friend of his who was an expert on sports medicine came regularly to encourage and instruct him in his stretching and weight lifting exercises. The sports medicine trainer had arms and shoulders like a boxer, bulging biceps, a narrow waist, and a flat abdomen. In contrast, poor John looked like a plucked chicken with his skinny arms and legs and his clubfoot. He held a cigarette while he did his leg exercises. At times, I saw him naked, dependent, and small. I saw him also in times of great spiritual strength and other times of weakness and pain.

During the painful period following his accident, John never lost or questioned his faith. He prayed daily, read the scriptures, received communion, and looked forward to leading his flock again. A priest misses being at the altar as much as a surgeon misses the operating room.

John walked again, but it was agonizing. He limped and used a cane. While still confined to a wheelchair, John decided he could not wait any longer before returning to the cathedral. A Sunday was chosen, and the announcement went out that the Dean was ready to preach. Every seat was full. The congregation was seated. The choir, acolytes, lay readers, chalice bearers, and associate priests took their places. The grand Flentrop organ boomed and the choir began singing the Dean's favorite hymn, "Awake, Thou Spirit of the Watchmen." The Very Reverend John Compton Leffler rolled down the center aisle in a wheelchair, wearing a freshly starched clerical collar. His left leg, still in a cast, poked out in front of him as if pointing the way to the altar. The congregation applauded vigorously and wiped away tears. At the front, John turned to face them and led them in prayer. He preached that day about the pain that comes before joy, and the death that comes before resurrection. He thanked all of his friends who had nurtured him, prayed for him, and showed their love in so many ways. It was not Caesar returning triumphantly from battle, but a battered, old man in a wheelchair with a blanket over his lap. Yet, it was a triumphal return.

During John's tenure as Dean, I served on the vestry several times. I soon learned the Cathedral had been a military anti-aircraft training center during World War Two. Because of this, the large windows of the Cathedral were painted black. Soldiers lived in the concrete rooms beneath the nave. The walls of the area proudly display to this day the drawings and writings by the young soldiers. About ten years after the armistice, we finally had ten thousand dollars saved to pay to remove the paint. We finally had ridded our selves of semi darkness. It was worth shouting about.

Sometime after that, John and the vestry developed a project to add a building to the west side of the Cathedral for much needed new space. It is now called Bloedel Hall. John approached all the top-drawer people he knew, the powerful and the rich, to chair the fund raising committee. To his dismay, he had no takers. He was down to the bottom drawer and thought of me. I had no experience in such a project. I was hard at practicing medicine and not knowing what I was getting in to. I said I would do it. I learned a lot, and between John, the committee, and me we did the job. It was wonderful to befriend so many wonderful people who helped. Having a community is one of the most valued gifts bestowed upon a volunteer.

◆   ◆   ◆

Another twenty years passed before the day when John Leffler, in another hospital, shouted his freedom. I had retired and was no longer officially his doctor. I happened to be visiting him, however, when his current doctor came in to tell him that he would die. After they spoke for a while, the doctor said he was going away for several months. John turned to me and said, "Bob, I want you to be my doctor."

My retirement suddenly didn't matter; there was no question what I would do. If I had been planning a trip around the world, I would have canceled it.

By this time, Faith was in a nursing home with an advanced case of Alzheimer's disease. John was living alone in an apartment, and he went home to die. His three sons took excellent care of him. He received visits by his many friends and communion regularly kept his spirits high most of the time. He worried about leaving Faith behind; she was completely helpless, and John wished he could be with her when she died. He had visited her regularly in the nursing home. He held her hand and prayed with her. In the late stages of her illness, she didn't respond or show any sign that she recognized him, and he often cried as he left her.

John would not outlive his wife. His illness progressed rapidly. He grew more and more jaundiced, his lips were dry and cracked, and his tongue seemed too big for his mouth.

John took an active part in the planning for his funeral. He wanted it conducted by Carla Berkedal, a priest at St. Mark's. John thought of her as a daughter. He and she went over the details of the service at length—the music, who would be the eulogists, the seating arrangement, and so forth. "Don't forget to put in extra chairs," he said, with his customary immodesty. "There will be a lot of people."

On another day, John was breathing quietly as I sat at his bedside. The shade was drawn, and there was little light in the room. John's eyes were closed, and I wasn't sure he knew I was there. I was glad to have this moment alone with my old friend. I had the feeling it would be the last such moment, and I wanted to connect with him one more time. The next night, one of his sons woke me around midnight with a phone call asking me to come to John's apartment. His sons were there—B.G., Andrew, and Tim. John lay under a sheet and light blanket. His breathing was intermittent, and the pauses between breaths were getting longer. The tip of his nose, his earlobes, and his fingernails were purple from lack of oxygen. I took his wrist and felt an almost imperceptible pulse.

John and Jean Rolfe, friends of many years, joined us. Soon Carla arrived. She had not been in the room but a few minutes when John stopped breathing. Each of us leaned over and hugged him. We lit small, white candles, doused the lights, and held hands in a circle around his bed. Shadows from the candles danced on the walls as Carla read from the Service of the Dead in the *Book of Common Prayer*.

◆   ◆   ◆

The Great Bald Ego died. He had given me instructions what to say in a eulogy at his memorial service As I stood behind the lectern facing the congregation, I imagined John looking down and feeling pleased that all the extra chairs were filled. I remembered his grand entry in a wheelchair that day, long before, and I spoke the following words:

"When John first knew that he would die, when his room was quiet and the door was closed, he said to me, 'When I am gone,' and his lip quivered a little, 'tell my friends that it was their love for me that enabled me to know Christ. Some people say there is something special about me, but the only thing special is the gift of love from all my friends, and through them, the sustaining love of Christ. Yes, when I am gone, tell them that. Tell them I died like a Christian.'

"Some time before his death, he asked me to read to him an Easter sermon that he had written and included in his book, *Go Into the City*. I read the words he had written, about the death of Christ and how he rose that Easter Day. 'I do look for the resurrection of the dead,' John preached, 'and the life of the world to come. And I urge you to join me in that great search and great hope, without which life has no meaning and death is its only goal.'

"He listened as I read this, and then he turned to me with a twinkle in his eye and said, 'I think that's the best sermon I ever preached.'"

John had indeed asked me specifically to mention that he died like a Christian. He didn't elaborate on this, and I puzzled over it for a while before realizing that its meaning was clear in that Easter sermon of his. Like all of John's sermons, the message was simple, very human, and not at all abstruse. He always made his point, and he made it in a way that no one who paid attention could miss it.

His book carried the subtitle *Sermons for a Strenuous Age*. In keeping with that theme, one of the sermons included the following words: "It will do us little good to spend our time longing for the return of a day that has gone. For one thing, time doesn't turn backward, except in the imaginations of those pathetic people who cannot face present reality." I believe this is what he meant when he said to tell the congregation he died like a Christian.

There was a lesson for me in John Leffler's death. As I mourned the loss of him and thought about what his life had meant to me, I also began to be aware of a greater lesson, a deeper meaning for my own life. It was about facing reality, confronting the past in a realistic way, and accepting death. The way John accepted his own imminent death astonished me. He experienced a strong feeling of liberation. No longer did he fear and no longer did he have to live with the restrictions placed on his earthly life.

John gave me a deep, close friendship. He represented an image of what I believed a father should be. Someone who is always there for you; who is authoritative and discerning, yet also gentle and forgiving; someone who can be playful, who invites you to be one of the boys, and who will admit to you that he has his own faults. Friends tell me their fathers are not necessarily like this, that my image of a father is an idealized one. They say that most fathers have a hard time taking off their masks of fatherly authority and showing their sons the kind of vulnerability and tenderness John showed to me.

As I reflect on him now, I realize one thing was missing: I never talked to John about my father. It seems hard for me to believe it today, but despite how close I felt to John Leffler, I still kept my secret from him. It never occurred to me; I never thought about bringing John into that part of my life, and he never asked me anything that would have forced me to reveal or deny the truth. You might think that the subject would come up sometime amid such a strong friendship, but it did not. The need to keep my family secret was programmed into me. Not talking about my dad was automatic, involuntary, like breathing.

John's was a good death. His closest friends were with him, and we had spent many moments together in the days and weeks leading up to that final moment. John had time to reflect on his life prayerfully, and he looked forward to dying as a new adventure. He crossed the river into the hereafter in peace, not in shame or fear.

His death was a gift to me. I marveled at his courage and his unwavering faith as he accepted the inevitable. While I cannot say for sure that John's death made me start thinking about my own, it certainly set in motion a change in my outlook. I did not understand this change at the time, but the next major decision in my life had everything to do with death and dying. It had to do with faith, and how I saw myself living the rest of my life. Ultimately, it had to do with accepting the inevitability of my own death.

14

The Good Doctor Is Naked

"Barnes has a screw loose." This is what the medical director of Swedish Hospital told one of his colleagues, and the colleague passed it on to me. The director and I had started in medical practice at about the same time, and we knew each other well. He had once offered me a job as director of continuing medical education at Swedish, one of Seattle's largest and most respected hospitals.

It was 1989. I had enrolled in a course in Clinical Pastoral Education (CPE) to learn how to give spiritual guidance to patients, with special emphasis on ministering to the dying and their families. The medical director's attitude toward spiritual guidance was typical of many doctors. The hospital is a scientific setting, and some doctors believe that clergy get in the way except when the patient dies, at which time some doctors are more comfortable to step aside.

I once saw a cartoon depicting a hospital room with a troop of doctors and nurses responding to an emergency, administering oxygen, performing cardiopulmonary resuscitation, studying the electrocardiogram, injecting medications, while over in the doorway stands a chaplain waving a Bible but being ignored. He would only be getting in the way, as far as the others are concerned. Since then, many hospitals have spiritual help programs to all those who seek it, especially at the time of dying.

Getting in the way was certainly not what I had in mind. The medical director's comment hit me at a time when I was struggling with a major role change in my life, from doctor to spiritual counselor, and I was struggling to accept the change in my status within the hospital environment. Once again, I was visited by my old anxiety about who I was.

It all started when a friend of mine suggested that I might enjoy the CPE experience. The friend was a seminary student who had recently completed the course herself and she knew I was interested in spiritual matters. Indeed I was. Spiritual guidance, prayer, and meditation had played a major role in enabling me to overcome depression, and I was just pulling out of that long ordeal when I entered CPE.

The program's chief purpose was to train clergy, seminary students, and other church professionals, such as directors of religious education, and of course lay people, to learn pastoral care skills. Some of the enrollees trained for a year or more, but I decided to commit myself to three months of intensive training. The three-month agenda included lectures, seminars, and on-the-ward experience.

Why did I do it? Why should it make any sense to start counseling the terminally ill when you are already depressed? The simple answer is that I was retired and looking for something useful and meaningful to do. Pastoral care appealed to me because it was a spiritual activity. I believed the course would deepen my awareness of my inner self, and it might link me more closely to that mystery we call God. I hoped to carry that mystery to the bedside of patients who were dying and in need of assurance. I once had a brief experience with the original hospice program at St. Catherine's Hospital in London, and it left a deep impression on me.

The CPE program at Swedish Hospital sounded just right because it didn't carry any particular religious dogma. It was two decades since I had given up my private medical practice. I looked forward to being with people at the bedside as a friend, aware of body, mind, and soul. Indeed, I fancied myself as more than a rookie at the bedside because of my many years as a physician who could bring a medical perspective to CPE and serve as a resource for the program. As it turned out, I had a lot to learn, and the hardest thing of all was something that didn't occur to me when I applied to the program: I would have to let go of my role and self-image as a doctor, a role that carried with it power, authority, and the mask of infallibility. I would have to learn how to listen and not give orders; to humble myself and identify with the person lying in bed. CPE presented me with another challenge of personal transformation. It would not be easy.

◆   ◆   ◆

I took the first step by having lunch in the hospital cafeteria with the CPE program's director, Delmas Luedke, who was a Lutheran pastor. He was a tall, strong, attractive Texan dressed casually in an open shirt and gray trousers. He turned out to be a great listener, humble and comfortable to be with. He has become a good friend and counselor. The director told me no doctor had ever gone through training to become a clinical pastor and asked why I thought it was a good idea. I was surprised by the question, and answered that I assumed my experience as a doctor would be an asset. I always believed I had a good bedside manner and thought of myself as a sensitive listener. He surprised me by saying he was concerned that being a doctor might get in the way of the job I would be doing.

He listened carefully as I told him I could probably help him understand doctors better. I mentioned my experience at St. Catherine's and told him I believed hospice work was very important. He must have found me persuasive or maybe a new challenge because within a short time after the meeting, he wrote to tell me I had been admitted to the course.

Soon I found myself going back to school, at the age of seventy. It was a different kind of schooling, however. For one thing, I had only two classmates, Barbara P. and Bob Z. Barbara, who was in her mid-fifties, was director of Christian education at a large Presbyterian church. Bob Z. was an ordained Lutheran minister in his late forties who, at the time, was not serving a parish.

The course began with an orientation week that included an overnight retreat in a suburban location, and then it settled into an intensive daily schedule of classes and practical work in the hospital. It did not take me long to become aware that I *did not* know it all. In class, we covered such topics as pastoral authority and the patient's perspective. We discussed different types of illness and patient conditions; for example coronary disease, cancer, and AIDS, and how these conditions affect patients emotionally and spiritually. We also talked about how to communicate with patients who won't express their true feelings, their anger and their fear of death, and how important it is for the pastoral caregiver to persevere, gain the patient's confidence, and build trust. We discussed readings on all of these topics and more. The course of study was rigorous and intellectually stimulating, and there were times when I felt overwhelmed by the amount of material and the intensity of our sessions.

In addition, we jumped right in to practical work. Each of us was assigned to one or two hospital wards for visits with patients. I was assigned to an AIDS ward. One of our responsibilities for class was to document our patient calls in written reports called "verbatims," and we spent time each week discussing our verbatims with each other. Our director was a good teacher, with a strong spiritual sense and much personal humility; he taught us a great deal and showed patience when we were confused. I also learned much from my classmates Bob Z., who was intellectually sharp and detail-oriented, and Barbara, who was warm, compassionate, and accepting.

When I entered CPE, I assumed that the course would sharpen my skills at talking with patients and their families. There was more. The role of the pastoral caregiver is very different from that of the doctor. The pastoral caregiver cannot think of himself as a *fixer*, one who cures an illness or sets a fractured bone. There are no medical protocols, no standard procedures, no lab tests or stethoscope. It took me a while to come to grips with this. I felt a tension within myself over the new way I had to act, and this tension sometimes showed itself in the classroom as well. Our class conferences were always candid. We were there to help each other learn, and we did not hesitate to criticize each other in a kind and constructive way.

As course supervisor, the director ran a tight ship, and he or one of my classmates was always there to help me. We often had coffee during morning classes and conferences. Each of us had a hook on the wall to hang our cup. After finishing coffee, each of us was expected to wash the cup and hang it on the wall. It seemed that I tended to innocently leave my dirty cup on the floor. I had to remember I was no longer a doctor and had no nurses or assistants to clean up after me.

Two characteristics expected of a person who gives care to the dying or very sick are humility and listening. I needed a quiet mind, and I needed to develop an awareness of the presence of God, for He is the real healer, not I.

I had a way to go. There were skills I lacked. I also found out quickly that being an authority figure did not work. This keyed directly in to that matter of changing my self-image. I was in my natural habitat, a hospital, but was no longer in charge of anything. I could not do what all my professional instincts told me. Medical skills such as doing physical exams, or diagnosing the disease, or writing prescriptions obviously are of no value in being a pastoral care person. It was not my task to examine patients, prescribe treatment, evaluate their progress, or document medical observations in the patients' charts. Nurses and technicians did not jump at my bidding. Similar to visitors and family members, my presence was secondary to the medical staff. This was where I hit an unexpected roadblock. I ran up against situations in class and on the wards in which my lifetime role as a physician clashed with my new role.

For example, once I sat at the bedside of a dying patient, listening to him tell about his fear of death and his guilt over something he had done in his life, when his doctor breezed in and, without asking who I was, told me to leave the room while he examined the patient. I understood exactly where the doctor was coming from, but suddenly I felt sorry for the patient, who was in the middle of something that to him was more important at that moment than being examined by the doctor, something that had to do with his soul, not his deteriorating body. I felt personally humiliated by the busy doctor who was unaware of the work I was doing. As I left the room, it occurred to me that I would probably have done the same thing when I was practicing medicine.

Over time, I became aware that caring for the body and the soul are both important, each in its own time. To shift roles is not an easy journey.

As a CPE student, I wore a nametag. It was light blue with white lettering, and it read "Bob Barnes—Pastoral care." It made me uncomfortable. In my previous life, my tag read "Dr. Robert H. Barnes," or "Robert H. Barnes, M.D., Director of Hospital Medical Education," or "Robert H.

Barnes, M.D.—Captain, Medical Corps, U.S. Army." Even without my tag, nurses and other doctors in my previous life knew who I was and what I was there for. Now, however, I was embarrassed to wear my tag. When I arrived at the hospital in the morning, I carried it in my coat pocket. I didn't want to run into an old doctor friend who might say, "What is that tag you're wearing?" I kept a watch out for doctors I knew and avoided them whenever possible.

More than one experience with the hospital physicians confirmed my fears. These were doctors who didn't know me, and to them I was just another member of the clergy, getting in their way (even though I wasn't really a clergyman). Very often, they did not even acknowledge me when I smiled or nodded at them in the hospital corridors. In short, all too often the doctors treated me as a commoner within a universe where they were princes. Experiencing this treatment woke me up to the arrogance of those with whom I longed to identify, and it made me painfully conscious of my diminished status in the medical environment. I was the preacher in the doorway, waving the Bible and being ignored.

Becoming a lay minister to the sick had seemed like such a good idea, but once I tried putting it into practice, the change threw me off balance. I missed wearing the white coat, missed carrying the chart in my hand and the feel of the stethoscope hanging from my neck. Without those, I felt naked.

No doubt, the director knew what he was talking about when he expressed his concerns to me during that first meeting over lunch. I really had no clear idea then of what the job demanded. It seemed as though CPE was challenging me to stop seeing myself as a doctor and stop thinking like a doctor. The purpose of the training was to transform me from thinking like a physician to thinking like a *healer*—that is, a servant whose power came from God. I had never really lost my childhood image of being like Uncle Joe, carrying the black bag full of powerful and mysterious medicines that would not only heal the sick but make me into "somebody." Now I had to come up with a new vision of myself, who I am, what my assignment is on earth.

To put it another way, CPE training had to become a means of continuing the lesson I had begun to learn in therapy: My old self-image, which rested on status and skills, could not make me whole. What I needed most of all was to find my true self through humility, to shed that old self-image like an unneeded garment and appear naked before God and man. Only when I saw myself for what I am, without mask and costume, could I dress myself in the proper clothing of God's servant. My many years as a self-proclaimed Christian had not prepared for me this.

Could I do it?

◆   ◆   ◆

Doctors do not knock on the door before entering a patient's room—they just walk in. Usually, the patient is pleased. The doctor is there to relieve the patient's pain or hopefully dismiss him from the hospital. In serious cases, the one lying in bed may see the doctor as his only hope for survival. The doctor's visit is important, and if the doctor fails to come or is delayed because of an emergency, the patient may feel isolated or rejected.

The pastoral caregiver always knocks before entering. If the caregiver has seen the patient before, he or she may receive a warm welcome. If it's the first time, however, the patient may very well say, "Oh, I thought it was the doctor. What is it you say you are?"

The patient might say, "I'm not interested in spiritural things." He might give the pastoral caregiver a look that expresses skepticism, or disdain, or weariness. He may roll over in bed and turn his back to the caregiver. Some patients assume the pastoral caregiver is an evangelist who hopes to convert him to some religion. Some interpret the caregiver's visit as doomsday: I must be dying; why else would they be sending a chaplain in?

I had entered CPE training in the belief that I could do good for patients. I myself believed in the healing gifts of God, and I felt confident that I could help others. But it was hard, so hard. I felt confused by my role; I doubted my ability to be of help, worried about my nakedness.

Robert H. Barnes, M.D., would have known exactly whom he was and what he needed to do. Bob Barnes, Pastoral Care, stood outside the door to a patient's room and thought about running away from his task.

It was then that I had a dream, possibly a "Christ experience." In the dream, I am standing at the door of a patient's hospital room, about to make a pastoral care call. I glance up and down the corridor to make sure nobody is watching and then push at the door. It doesn't open. I do not panic; instead, I take a deep breath and lower my head in a prayer: "Dear Father, give me courage to do your work, and be present with me." Suddenly, a strong light seems to penetrate the door. I reach out again to push it open, but the door has vanished. I step into the room. The light is the warm radiance of sunset, red and gold, streaming through the window beyond the patient's bed. The room itself is dark and vague; the man in bed is a shadowy figure. Suddenly I become aware that I am naked. I feel cold, lonely, and exposed. I try to wrap my arms around myself. The patient gets up without saying a word and I now see him clearly, his flowing hair, his simple robe. He pulls the blanket off his bed and approaches me. He wraps the blanket around my body and hugs me. He is taller than I, and I must look slightly upward to meet the gaze of his deep-set eyes. He seems to be seeing deeply inside me, and he says, "I am with you always. It is through me that you shall know God." He returns to the bed and lies down again. I am speechless and tears are streaming down my cheeks, but I feel warm and loved. Outside, the sky has grown dark. My mind is quiet, my body at ease. I turn and walk toward the door, which is back in place. I pull it open and step out into the brightly lit hospital corridor. I am fully dressed, and the blanket is gone. No one else is on the ward and there is no activity at the nurses' desk down the corridor. A small Christmas tree stands there, its red and green and blue and yellow lights glowing with the joy of the season, the joy of new life. Never have I felt more at peace. I move on to the next door in the hallway with a sense of wonderful freedom and confidence. I am ready to make my next call.

◆   ◆   ◆

I had cleared a high hurdle and began now to grow into my new role at the hospital. I learned the routine and began to internalize it. In general, a pastoral care call goes something like this: You might say a silent prayer just before entering the room. You knock on the door, enter, and introduce yourself (if it's your first visit to the patient): "I'm Bob Barnes from the pastoral care office. I'm here to say hello and see how you're getting along." I sit down at the bedside and wait for the patient to speak. From there, the conversation develops in a kind of free-form fashion, depending on the patient's attitude and needs.

It takes a few visits to develop a relationship. Most patients are afraid of dying, and many are reluctant to confront the reality of it. Sometimes they don't seem to understand exactly what is happening, or they try to escape into denial. They need to accept the pastoral caregiver as a familiar, caring person; trust is crucial. I strove to become a friend, a listener, and I made it clear that I was not there to convert them or judge them. I wanted them to know I understood their fear or anger.

Often I met with the family outside the patient's room, and again I was a listener. On the AIDS ward, most of the patients were gay, of course, and it was common for a patient's family, partner, or friend to need help coming to terms with all sorts of issues related to the illness, its cause, and the likelihood of death. I tried to console them, and if they asked for prayer, I prayed with them. Sometimes the mother of a gay man would tell me the story of her son—how old he was when he discovered he was different from other boys, or how his father rejected the son because he was gay. When it became clear that death was approaching, I might answer their questions about arrangements for a funeral or memorial service.

I learned to do all of these things, and in particular I came to understand the importance of being a friend, not a fixer; the importance of not having my own agenda; the importance of *just being*, with a quiet mind and an open heart. The power of companionship, listening, prayer, and just silence—these were the tools and instruments of my new trade.

Still, it wasn't always easy for me to remember the boundaries of my task, and on one visit early in my CPE experience, I couldn't stop myself from reverting to my old role as a doctor. The patient, Oren, was a thirty-five-year-old man who was dying of AIDS. He lay in bed, covered only by a sheet and sweating from a high fever. His arms were blemished by black scabs from sores caused by the AIDS infection, and he flung them about as he turned from side to side. He was unconscious, but he seemed to be writhing in pain. His partner and his mother were there, trying unsuccessfully to give him comfort. They said to him, "We love you, Oren."

I introduced myself, and they begged me to help their loved one. Without a moment's thought, I helped them turn him on his back and pulled his sheet down. His abdomen was distended and he put his hand there from time to time, suggesting pain. It was tight and firm, like a four-month pregnancy. I percussed it and heard the dull sound of something solid low down. Ordinarily, the bowel gives a higher-pitched, hollow sound. I excused myself and hurried down the hall to the nurses' desk. At that point, I realized I was overstepping my authority, and so I spoke to Michele, the nurse on duty, in an apologetic tone. I told her I had examined the patient's abdomen and could tell something was dreadfully wrong. Unruffled, Michele filled me in on Oren's condition. He had a severe abdominal infection, and there was probably an abscess in his pelvic area. Everything had been done to control the infection, but his immune system was destroyed and they expected him to die. She said the family knew that, but like all families, they still hoped for a miracle and were anxious that he not suffer. He was receiving the maximum dosage of a painkiller, and Michele believed that he was not in pain, despite his thrashing around.

I returned to the room and sat down with the man's mother and partner. I reassured them that even though his body was twisting and turning, he was not suffering in his unconscious state. I told them what they had probably heard before, that every possible medical action had been taken, and I asked if they would like to pray with me for the one they loved. We held hands and gave thanks for his life, and we asked that he not suffer.

Oren died two days later. I spent a lot of time with his loved ones during those closing hours, and we came to feel close to each other. They asked if I would be the minister at a memorial service for him, and I said I would be honored. It took me a week to prepare for the service, which, in the Episcopal Church, is something a lay person ordinarily doesn't do, but I did my homework and carried it off, with my CPE class in attendance to give me moral support. We held the service at St. Mark's in a small chapel; it was full, and afterward some of the mourners addressed me as "Father." It was the first memorial service I conducted. There would be more, and I came to appreciate and value this new experience.

Changing my role in the hospital meant traveling a bumpy road, but I was learning to negotiate its twists and turns. The reason I had been assigned to the AIDS ward was that the CPE director hoped I would not be tempted to get involved with the medical care of the patients because I had no previous experience with AIDS, a disease that did not exist at the time I practiced.

Even so, I managed to overstep the boundary in the case of Oren. I worked hard at it and gradually became more comfortable with my non-medical role. For the most part, I was able to keep my former profession a secret from the patients. The nurses, incidentally, all knew I was a doctor doing pastoral care and treated me with patience and understanding, as Michele had.

Changing your role does not mean discarding your past. What I learned from my mistake with Oren is that personal transformation requires you not to forget who you are, but to act always in a way that is appropriate to your new purpose in life. For me, changing my role did not mean giving up my identity as a doctor. Somewhere along the way, I realized that I would never stop thinking of myself as a doctor—but that was all right: I could be both a doctor, albeit a non-practicing one, and a pastoral caregiver. I just needed to understand that my doctor's black bag stayed at home when I acted in the role of pastoral caregiver.

CPE represented a truly transformative experience for me. Like the earlier times in my life when I experienced a *kairos*, I reached a moment of truth during CPE—perhaps several, or even many moments of truth—that spun me around and pointed me in a new direction. I had been wrong to believe my experience as a doctor would make it easy for me to become a pastoral caregiver, and arrogant to think I could tell the director anything about doctors that he didn't already know. The friendly comeuppance I got from my CPE companions drove home to me the fact that I needed to readjust my self-image and learn humility.

Toward the end of the three-month program, the director told me I would never get over the feeling of being a second-class person until I felt comfortable doing God's work and unashamed to proclaim my mission. The challenge of CPE was to become more aware of myself as a spiritual creature, a child of God, and to recognize that that part of me was every bit as important as the part that was a doctor—maybe more so.

One Sunday evening I was on night duty in the hospital, visiting patients who were sleepless, discouraged, depressed, or frightened, when I ran into a surgeon whom I knew well. I was carrying the Episcopal *Book of Common Prayer,* a red leather-bound book with a gold cross on the front. The surgeon was surprised to see me and, noticing the book and my pastoral care nametag, he asked what I was doing. This time, I did not hesitate to tell him, and as I did so with enthusiasm, the surgeon became fascinated. We talked for about half an hour. He thought what I was doing was wonderful. He sometimes wished he were doing something different because he was exhausted, both physically and mentally, from working long hours. He had considered giving up surgery but could not think of anything else to do. At the end, he thanked me for listening to him and expressed the hope that we would talk again. It was the first time a doctor ever stopped me in a hospital and took time out from his busy schedule to tell me his story.

Not ten minutes later, I encountered a cardiologist waiting for the elevator. He was a vigorous man known for his teaching at the medical school and in the hospital training program. He, too, asked what I was doing and found it fascinating. He asked me to look in on a patient of his who had had heart surgery and seemed depressed. The cardiologist and I arranged to meet for lunch several days later, and he spilled his life story to me. Not long after that, he told the hospital's Chief of Staff about the Pastoral Care program and my participation in it. Astonishingly, the Chief of Staff was unaware of the program and, to my delight, he immediately expressed the desire to become acquainted with our work in the hospital.

I told my classmates about this chain of events, elated that I had drawn those two doctors out by listening to their stories and succeeded in spreading the gospel of pastoral care. My classmates and I agreed there was a lesson in this experience about who needs pastoral care: not only the patients, but doctors, nurses, and others on the hospital staff, too. From then on, I never hesitated to tell other doctors what I was doing, and as far as I know, nobody ever again said that Barnes had a screw loose.

◆   ◆   ◆

What are the healing gifts of God? The hands of the surgeon replacing a broken hip. The knowledge and wisdom of a physician when he or she diagnoses diabetes, shingles, or chronic fatigue syndrome. The alertness, skill, and discipline of a nurse in an intensive care unit. Miracle drugs and new therapies, the evolving science of biotechnology, the wonders of modern-day prosthetic devices. But also the gifts of love and human kindness, the support and caring presence of a sick person's family and friends, the touch of a hand, the mystery of silent prayer.

Doctors are good at what they do. Often an experienced physician can make a diagnosis by observing a patient as soon as he or she steps into the office. Pop-eyes: overactive thyroid. Curved, purplish fingernails: lung disease. A reddish discoloration in the palm of the hand: alcoholism. Sometimes the doctor needs to hear about a symptom or two: pain in the upper abdomen that goes away after eating suggests an ulcer; unusual thirst and frequent urination sounds like diabetes. Most of the time, of course, the diagnosis requires a careful examination involving blood tests, urinalysis, and procedures such as an MRI or CAT scan, an endoscopy, or exploratory surgery. All of these are routine for those skilled in performing them. What doctors are not so good at, however, is the other side of God's healing gift. Doctors tend to be shy about spirituality; they prefer to approach their jobs as the science of medicine rather than the art of healing, and many feel comfortable only when keeping an emotional distance from their patients.

Sometimes I dream of a program for training doctors how to be "naked" in front of patients—*naked,* that is, in the sense I have used the word in these pages. Each doctor would spend one or two weeks seeing patients without stethoscope, chart, white coat, or any other medical accoutrement, and he or she would approach each patient as a fellow human. Maybe doctors would learn something about the healing arts that they don't know.

Most doctors don't talk about healing except in the physical sense that a wound heals or an incision heals. They seldom talk about suffering; instead, they talk about *pain,* a physical symptom. Understanding the concepts of *healing* and *suffering* could make every doctor a better doctor. For a doctor to enter a patient's room, sit down, and say, "I know you're suffering and I'm here to help you; tell me about it"—this could be the opening to a new and much-improved doctor/patient relationship.

Medical skills, compassion, love, prayer, and the quiet communion of a friend or caregiver—all of these are God's healing gifts, and none of them is more important than any other. I was seventy years old when I learned how important it is to let the light of being human shine into the dark world of illness and despair. It is important for everybody—not just the patient who is sick or the distraught person who is at the end of his or her faith, but for the person who gives the care, too. My greatest wish for the future of medicine is that doctors learn more about the non-medical side of their patients' realities and become skilled at applying all of God's healing gifts.

15

Telling the Secret

At the age of seventy, I had one more vital thing to learn: the healing power of telling my own story. It is often said that telling your own story can be instructive for others and therapeutic for you. Not to tell your story is to deny yourself a life-affirming opportunity and to deny others the possibility of learning from your experiences. If you do not tell your story, you may eventually forget poignant details of your life. As Frederick Buechner wrote in *Telling Secrets* (Harper San Francisco, 1991), "to lose track of our stories is to be profoundly impoverished not only humanly but also spiritually."

If there is something in your personal story that you have kept secret because of shame or emotional pain, suppressing your story or attempting to forget the details will not heal the pain. I am living proof of that.

Some of the most vivid instances of telling personal stories that I have witnessed have unfolded at the University of Washington Medical School, where second-year medical students attend a three-day seminar on caring for patients with life-threatening illnesses. The seminar teaches the importance of pain control and raises hard questions about such issues as whether it is right to keep terminally ill patients alive through extraordinary measures (respiratory machines, intravenous feeding, and so on). Students are challenged to understand the grieving process of patients' families as well. The assumption of the seminar is that future doctors need to develop compassion for those about to die and learn how to treat them and their loved ones with real care and sensitivity.

During the first hour of the seminar a panel of students testify to experiences they have had. Of about one hundred second-year students, there are always a few who have lost a parent, a grandparent, or even a sister or brother.

One story I'll never forget is that of the young woman I'll call Marion. Marion was about twenty-four years old, with wavy hair cut just below the ear level and tortoise-shell eyeglasses that gave her a bookish appearance. She sat with three other panelists at a table in the pit-like front of the auditorium, looking up at her audience of fellow students and a handful of faculty members. Her lips trembled as she took the microphone, and she began to cry silently. She stammered an apology for being unable to control herself. In time, she got her story out. While at school one day the year before, she received a phone call bearing the news that her father had committed suicide. She rushed home to a small town in eastern Washington State, devastated. Her dad's body was already at the funeral home. She had been attached to him and had no idea he was depressed. His death upset her so much that she stayed home for a month.

Finally returning to medical school, Marion slept poorly and had difficulty concentrating. She fell behind in her work, and her immediate supervisor, a young resident physician, accused her of laziness; her father's death, he said, was no excuse and she needed to buckle down and get to work. Fortunately, a senior professor of medicine, to whom Marion's supervisor reported, was more sympathetic. He called Marion in to his office to hear her story. He was appalled at the resident's lack of understanding and required him to take an intensive course on grieving.

Marion wiped tears from her cheeks and finished her story by saying, "That's all." Her classmates had remained quiet through her story, but now they stood and clapped.

Other panelists told their stories—the young man whose sister died in an auto accident; the woman whose mother and father both died of illnesses within two months of each other. And there were more. Most of the students in the audience had never suffered the loss of someone close to them; as far as their experience went, death was something that happens to *other* people, in *other families*.

Equally moving were the stories told by members of a second panel composed of patients who were battling life-threatening diseases and knew they might not live much longer. There was a woman with cancer that had metastasized, and another with a brain tumor. They told of their experiences with illness, loss of energy, inability to work normally. They talked about how their illness affected their families. They told of their experiences, good and bad, with doctors, nurses, and hospital staffs.

The point of this story-telling exercise, which was of course grueling for the panelists, was to show the student audience that death happens to real people, people very much like them, and the grieving that follows the death of a loved one is a natural and inevitable process. Just as importantly, the exercise is meant to suggest that doctors need to be familiar with the dying process, not only in medical terms but also in human, emotional terms; and that doctors should be sensitive to grieving family members as well as to the dying patients themselves.

To me, of course, it was Marion's story that hit home most profoundly. I was in the audience the day she faced her classmates and told them of her terrible loss. I understood exactly how she felt and stood in awe of her courage. At her age, I could never have done what she did.

What about my story? The story about the little boy in the blue suit, Bobby Barnes, who lost his father to a violent, shameful death and grew up with a terrible secret? The man, Dr. Robert H. Barnes, who lived in fear that others would reject him if they knew the truth.

It took me almost a quarter of a century to reveal my secret to June. In a moment of total honesty, I opened myself to her and told her that my father had taken his own life when I was ten years old, and that I had never told her because I was afraid she would reject me. Then came a tremendous surprise: my father's suicide was not news to June. Just before we married, my mother had told June's mother. June's mother subsequently told June. June never mentioned it to me because she thought I did not know how my dad died. It didn't matter to June; she loved me for myself, and how my father died could not have caused her to love me any less.

What a moment of revelation! What a moment of supreme irony! It was an unveiling, an unmasking, for us both. I took off the mask that covered the secret of my father's death; June took off the mask that covered her knowledge.

Years later, I puzzled over my mother's motives in telling the family secret to June's mother. Was she trying to turn June's family against the marriage, or did she mean to gain their sympathy for her son? It does not matter now, it didn't matter then, and it certainly didn't matter at the time I told June. What mattered was that my fear and anxiety were relieved, at least as far as June was concerned; I didn't have to guard the truth from her any more, and she, too, no longer had to keep a secret from me. A cloud lifted, a dark cloud that had symbolized a lie between us. In that moment, our love for each other was solidified by the trust we no longer withheld from each other.

Trusting June enough to reveal my secret was one thing; telling others was another. If we define ourselves in life through an unending series of existential decisions, I had not yet succeeded in defining myself fully. For sure, the relief that I felt after telling June did not lead me to inner peace; the stone that I carried within me did not pass. One day it would, but not before I journeyed through the hell of depression and confronted myself again, and yet again.

It is hard to believe, but I never told my secret to the Sun Valley therapist who helped me so much. The subject of my father's death never came up. I did not raise the issue, and he never asked me anything that led me into it. Yet, I trusted and felt close to him. When I ask myself now why this crucial matter never arose with him, I think of two possible answers. First, I was obviously still afraid of rejection, afraid of revealing my secret—even to someone I trusted. This fear, I believe, was no longer a conscious fear for me; it was instinctive, and my behavior was instinctive as well. Just as I never thought of telling my dear friend John Leffler about my dad, it never occurred to me to tell anyone. I could share other intimate details of my life, but not that one. My self-protective shield was in place.

I may have taken a small step toward dealing with my father's suicide when I undertook a writing project sometime during the mid-1980s. I was still in therapy, when I became interested in the subject of suicide among teenagers. The topic was receiving much attention in the national media, and without thinking about why it fascinated me, I started to work on an article. The article was about how to prevent suicide among young people—how to recognize symptoms such as depression, low self-esteem, and desperation. I researched the topic in current newspapers and magazines, and I dug into numerous medical and psychiatric journals for whatever information I could find. I interviewed counselors on the staff of a crisis enter and talked with the counselor at a high school, where a student had recently committed suicide. I was moved by the stories of suicidal teens and believed I could write something that would help parents, counselors, and friends understand the problem and become aware of symptoms before more kids were driven to kill themselves. I intended to seek publication and hoped the article would be widely circulated.

I did not follow through. I completed the article—I still have a copy of it in my files, and it is a good article—but I never submitted it for publication. Why? I am not sure. Maybe the subject was still too close to me. Even though I was writing about others, I still could not bring myself to "go public" with the issue of suicide. I didn't know it then, but by writing about teen-age suicide, I was learning more about myself.

Perhaps I really wrote the article for myself. In any case, I now recognize in that article a clue about my state of mind at the time. What drove me to write the piece was my awareness that identifying a potential suicide victim is crucial to preventing the ultimate tragedy. I'm sure that, somewhere in the back of my mind, this thought was connected with my father's death. If only my mother had known, if only *we* had known, if only *someone* had known. If only someone had taken action. I did not consciously think these thoughts at the time I wrote the article, but they had been a part of my unarticulated feelings about my father for decades.

The article began with a kind of poem, or poetic monologue. The first two lines were:

I cry for help, I cry for help.
I send up smoke signals and hope to be heard.

As I read these lines today, I have to think they were not only the cry of the suicidal teenagers whose minds I was attempting to get into. They were also the cry of my father more than half a century earlier. They were the cry of the little boy in the blue suit.

◆   ◆   ◆

Clinical Pastoral Education taught me about the value of humility and transformed the way I saw myself. It did something else for me, too—something my soul had waited nearly six decades for.

One of the first things we did in the CPE course was to tell our life stories to each other. This, in fact, was the major item on the agenda of the overnight retreat at the beginning of CPE. We gathered in a Catholic retreat house in the country outside a Seattle suburb. The room where we met had a wooden floor with some area rugs, a few straight-backed chairs, and several large pillows suitable for floor sitting. I sat on a chair, and the others—Bob Z., Barbara P, and the director—took up positions on the floor pillows. They took their shoes off; I did not—doctors don't take their shoes off in front of other people. When he explained the exercise to us, I had mixed feelings. I was eager to tell my three colleagues about my life as a doctor, the evolution of my career, and the discoveries I had made through therapy. On the other hand, I had a sneaking suspicion they might ask me questions I didn't want to answer.

Bob and Barbara went before me. As they laid out their personal stories, I realized they were getting into aspects of their lives that they wouldn't tell just anyone. We had been asked to be honest and to tell what was important, and they did just that. I heard of marriages, divorce, depression, alcoholism. I heard about failures in their lives, a feeling of having taken a wrong turn, a sense of being on a long and difficult journey in search of spiritual satisfaction. In that quiet room with spare furnishings, something was happening that I had not expected. These people, total strangers to me, were expressing intimate and embarrassing secrets about themselves. I felt a bond growing among us such as I had never before experienced with friends or colleagues.

When my turn came, I took a deep breath and started with where I came from. I grew up a Presbyterian in Richmond, Virginia, attended

VMI, became a doctor, served in World War II. As I got deeper and deeper into my story, it became clear to me that I had to tell about my dad. I don't know where this feeling came from; it was a kind of revelation, or rather a sense of the inevitable. I stopped speaking and started to cry. No one spoke; no one asked me what was wrong. It took me a minute to pull myself back together.

"I feel compelled to tell you a secret that I've never told anybody," I said, finally. "I've always felt I'd be rejected if I told it, but I have to tell you now." I paused again, took another deep breath. "I lost my father when I was ten years old. It was during the depression. His company had fallen apart. He shot himself at home in the morning while I was at school."

I don't remember what I said next, or if I said anything at that point, but in an instant Barbara got off her pillow and gave me a firm, loving hug. Bob Z. and the director followed suit. I don't remember who specifically said the words, but they told me how sorry they were. They said I needed to understand that when people suffer devastating losses, it in no way diminishes them as humans or as children of God.

"You don't have to be ashamed," one of them said, "we accept you as you are; we love you for who you are."

They all meant it.

This was not the end of my exercise. I went on to tell about Mother, Uncle Joe and the turtle, and life in my own family as an adult and a father. When I told them about the death of Baby Sarah, they grilled me about my apparent lack of emotion over the tragedy. Through all the rest of it, I knew I had their friendship and support. They recognized me as a caregiver, like them; a seeker, like them. They understood the burden of my long-held secret, understood the stone I carried within me and the mask I wore, and through their acceptance of me, I understood that I was loved. I would not be rejected. When I finished, I was a wreck, exhausted and emotionally drained. But I knew I had passed another milestone in my life, taken another essential step toward realizing my wholeness. As I look back on it, taking that step was the most important thing I had ever done in my life-long quest for inner peace and contentment. The stone was gone. I felt light. I felt free. The mask was off.

I know now why we went through this exercise. The purpose was not only to get to know each other, but to get to know ourselves as human beings. The director wanted us to look inward, to accept and understand our own fragility. Such self-understanding is vital to establishing oneself as a spiritual healer. We must ourselves be vulnerable if we are to understand and care for others who are vulnerable. Those who are confronting death are stripped to their essentials; we, too, must be prepared to strip to our essentials and become naked.

It worked. This is not to say that I sailed through the rest of the CPE course. As I have indicated, CPE continued to challenge me and I did not complete the process of personal transformation from Robert H. Barnes, M.D., to Bob Barnes, Pastoral Counselor, in that one retreat day. To be honest, I didn't complete the process at all—at least not in those terms. I continued to be Robert H. Barnes, M.D., while *also* becoming Bob Barnes, Pastoral Counselor. After fifty years, I could not stop thinking like a doctor at least part of the time. I believe we all have many roles in life. This is healthy as long as we know ourselves and are joyful in what we do. All the changes I underwent in CPE would have been impossible without the experience of baring my soul that first day. That moment of nakedness enabled me to become fully aware of myself as a spiritual creature, assigned to do God's work.

When I think about what happened to me during that time, I sometimes think of words written by the sixteenth-century Spanish Carmelite known as John of the Cross: "I departed from my low manner of understanding, and my feeble way of loving, and my poor and limited method of finding satisfaction in God…I went out from my human operation and way of acting to God's operation and way of acting."

People who had known me for a long time noticed the change. June saw the difference. She remarked to me—and not only once—about how much calmer I became, how much more at peace with myself. She was right: I was and am.

Just how much about me had changed was confirmed sometime after my CPE experience, when I told the story of my dad to two old friends, Bob and Anne. They happened to be in Seattle, and June and I were having dinner with them at a restaurant near the airport just before their departing flight. My friendship with Bob went back to our childhood, and we were also classmates in college. In the course of the conversation, he asked about my mother and mentioned that he had never met my father. I said straight out, with no hesitation, that my dad took his own life when I was a boy. Despite my apparent ease at saying this, Bob's wife Anne read me like a book. She got up and hugged me. "Oh, a little ten-year-old boy, losing your father like that," she said.

Yes, the mask was off.

◆   ◆   ◆

I am blessed having a wife who is wise. One day, I don't know how many years ago, June gave me a gift she had made: a needlepoint piece bearing the words "THE IMPERFECT ARE LOVABLE." It was a touching gift that told me how deeply June understood me, and to this day, I keep it in a frame on my office wall.

Being imperfect is one of the defining qualities of being human. To be human is to have weaknesses. It is to make mistakes and misjudgments. To be human is to succeed and rejoice in one's successes, but it is also to fail and learn from one's failures.

To be human is to be susceptible to many desires: the desire to dominate, to rule and control others; to be powerful; even to be brutal. To be human is also to be kind, thoughtful, understanding, forgiving, and accepting. The person who recognizes his own weaknesses is more likely to forgive others.

To be human is to have secrets. Secrets are as natural to human beings as water is to a well. Not all secrets are harmful, and some are necessary. Others, however, are killers. From childhood on, we occasionally hear or see something we don't want to tell about. Very often, we do something we don't want others to know. I, for example, stole an apple from a fruit stand when I was a boy. I would have been mortified if anyone had found out.

The secret of the stolen apple was nothing compared with the secret of my dad's suicide. For me, my mother's warning not to tell anyone was so solemn that it was as if I had signed a contract in blood. If some boy at school had pinned me to the playground and threatened to kill me, I don't believe I would have revealed the secret.

"Don't talk, don't trust, don't feel is supposed to be the unwritten law of families that for one reason or another have gone out of whack," wrote Frederick Buechner in *Telling Secrets*. That was the credo of my family. Not even my sister, my grandparents, or my aunts and uncles ever encouraged me to talk about my dad's death. Nor did I bring it up with them

There is a price to pay for keeping a heavy secret deep inside, and I paid it in terms of feeling separate from others, frightened of intimacy, and afraid of being found out. My self-esteem suffered, and for many years, I was unsatisfied with who I was and driven to make myself something more.

For my mother, the price was enormous. Her immediate horror and grief at the violent death of my dad turned into a depression that lasted for the rest of her life. Her inability to demonstrate her love drove her children away. The mask she wore to cover her misery succeeded in the business world but failed to give her what she needed most: the comfort of a close family, the contentment that comes with accepting the fate God had given her, and the self-understanding that might have come from confronting her innermost feelings. Mother was a classic example of someone who suffers from the pain of a traumatic experience and cannot get beyond that experience.

Should my mother have told her story? I believe it would have helped her. This is not to say it would have been easy. I know she was dreadfully afraid of what people thought—and in Richmond, Virginia, at that time there were undoubtedly many people who considered suicide a blot on a family's reputation. Perhaps it was true that, publicly, she needed to keep her secret. She need not have kept it from people she trusted personally. She need not have impressed the secret onto her children in a way that frightened us so. She need not have tried to push the experience back into her subconscious, where the memory festered and made her eternally bitter. Late in her life, Mother told my sister that she wished she had seen a therapist at the time of Dad's death. I certainly wish she could have. At that time, however, psychotherapy was nowhere near as common as it is today; anyone who needed a psychiatrist was jeopardizing his or her reputation, for mental or emotional illness, like suicide, was labeled a mark of shame. I doubt that it occurred to Mother to seek therapy at the time when she most needed it.

It is hard for me to judge my mother. Nothing in her experience prepared her for the shock of my dad's death. No one in her family or community gave her the kind of advice she needed. If repressing her feelings was the wrong thing to do—and I have to believe it was—she did not do it out of mean-spiritedness, and she did not do it from lack of love. She just did not know how to do the right thing.

If it is hard for me to judge my mother, it is harder to judge everyone else in the world. Who am I to say that all must tell their stories? Must every individual who has suffered catastrophic pain share the experience with others?

I believe in the old cliché that there is a time and place for everything. If there is a time and place when it is appropriate for you to tell your story, you should do so. However, there are times and places when it is *not* appropriate to tell your story. For example, I do not believe you should sit down beside a complete stranger in an airplane and start rattling on about the intimate details of your life. There is no point in telling your story just to hear yourself talk. You need to tell your story in the right context. Tell it to a therapist; to your minister, rabbi, or priest; to your spouse or lover, to close friends. Tell your story only when you feel confident that your listener is open to what is in your heart. Tell it in a spirit of privacy and confidentiality, if that is important to you; by all means, tell it in an atmosphere of mutual sensitivity and care between you and your listener. Be willing to listen to the story of the person to whom you are telling yours.

You certainly don't have to tell your story to the whole world. Many people like to say they have only one good friend, one "best friend." If that is true of you, that one best friend is the person to whom you might want to tell your story. Maybe your best friend is your wife or husband; maybe it is a parent or one of your children. Maybe it's your college roommate, your business partner, or your golfing buddy. You may not need or wish to tell anyone else; at least you will have confided in someone, and the very act of doing so should help you know yourself better. Keep in mind the purpose of telling your story. You do not tell your story to impress others. You should not tell it to gain their sympathy (although that might be a by-product of your telling them). You do not mean to influence people's feelings toward you or to manipulate them into taking some action they might not otherwise take. You tell your story because you want to learn something about yourself—and because your experience might possibly teach others an important lesson.

I would like to add that it is all right for a doctor or therapist to tell his or her story, or some relevant part of it, to a patient if telling the story will help the patient. Doctors rarely talk with patients in such a personal way, but there are many times when a moment of personal revelation can benefit the healing process. For example, if a patient is in need of gall bladder surgery and the doctor himself has undergone the surgery, telling the patient about it might help calm any fears about the operation. Of course, it is not appropriate for a doctor to babble pointlessly about his or her own problems. Few doctors need to be told this.

Doctors need to be open to patients' stories. A good doctor is one who does not hesitate to listen to patients' stories. I realize today's health care systems place heavy demands on doctors and give them little time for their patients. This is a problem. The human touch is as important in caring for a patient today as it has always been. The time a doctor takes to listen compassionately to a patient's story can be as important in the healing process as the medicines that are prescribed.

It may not be necessary for some to tell their stories. My wife, June, is such a person. She had a happy childhood, growing up with love and a strong family. There is nothing in her childhood or youth that is eating away at her or that has ever stopped her from being whole. She has never hesitated to tell me about her past. But at the same time, it has never occurred to her that there is something she needs to get off her chest.

I do know that for me, being able to share my story finally released me from a cruel form of captivity. My personal story fits into a pattern that has been the research focus of Edward K. Rynearson, a Seattle psychiatrist. Dr. Rynearson's book, *Retelling Violent Death* (Brunner-Routledge, 2001), is based on his work with people traumatized by the death of a loved one through murder, suicide, or fatal accident. It is common, Dr. Rynearson says, for such survivors to shut out the memories they have of a violent death and avoid talking about it for a period of time, typically four to six months. Eventually, however, they need to deal with the trauma, to talk about it and confront their shock, horror, sense of loss, sadness, and anger. Those who do so are far more likely to get on with their lives in a healthy way than those who do not. Rynearson finds that the telling and retelling of these traumatic experiences take on discernible structures; they are *stories*. It is by telling their stories that the survivors of a loved one who died violently begin to work their way through their trauma.

Rynearson notes how hard it is for survivors of violent death to tell their stories. They are dreadful stories, stories that do not make sense, and there is nothing they can do to change the outcome. In most cases, the survivors are not present when their loved ones die. They have not seen the event and, thereafter, they can only imagine it. It is extremely hard for them to put their feelings into words, and they do not want to picture the moment of their loved one's death. Even so, they commonly have visions of it, whether while sleeping or awake. They are haunted by the images their minds produce and disturbed by the thought that they might have been able to intervene. Many have dreams in which they are present at the fatal moment, either watching in horror or trying to prevent the death.

I have tried to picture my father's death, and I have tried to imagine myself in my mother's shoes at the moment when she discovered him dying in that upstairs room. I do not know if she subsequently had recurring flashbacks to the scene, but she must have. Whatever she saw must have replayed itself in her mind, appeared to her in nightmares, and haunted her to the day of her own death in a nursing home more than sixty years later. Without someone to talk to, without someone to help her deal with those images, she had no chance of recovering from her trauma. I have often felt that my dad's suicide made me a true orphan. I lost not only my father, but also my mother.

For a long time, I had an image of myself hiding in a dark closet. My secret separated me from others; it made me unable to show myself for who I really was. As Buechner put it, "I not only have my secrets, I am my secrets. And you are your secrets. Our secrets are human secrets, and our trusting each other enough to share them with each other has much to do with the secret of what it is to be human."

The dark closet I hid in for so many years kept me from achieving wholeness as a human. And just as gay people talk about coming out of the closet to reveal to the world who they really are, I felt that when I finally told my deep, dark secret, I too, had come out of the closet as a human being.

PART IV
Naked at the River

16

Hand in Hand to the River's Edge

A Japanese-American woman named Yuki rang my doorbell on a sunny June day in 1997. She had smooth skin, except for some sagging under the chin and lines around her mouth that became part of a beautiful smile as I welcomed her. She looked younger than her seventy-two years and seemed bathed in an aura of peace. As she came inside, she spotted a collection of snuff bottles on the hall table, which my mother-in-law had given to June. Behind one of the tiny bottles, Yuki noticed another art piece—a small, ivory egg cracked open, with the head of a chick poking out. She said this delicate art form had a long tradition in Japan. As Yuki spoke, June came out from the kitchen, and the two of them talked about the collection for a few minutes. Yuki picked up the cracked egg with an elegant gentleness and admired it from all angles. She was so taken by the beauty of the egg—a symbol of life—that it was hard to believe she had come to discuss the arrangements for her own memorial service.

June left us, and we entered the living room. We sat in two armchairs, one on either side of the fireplace. Yuki held her feet together and rested her hands in her lap. She had on a simple cotton dress, and her black and gray hair was cut neatly in a Dutch bob. Behind her, I could see our large camellia bush blooming pink outside, with one branch brushing against the windowpane. I turned my attention wholly to Yuki and lit a candle on the table between us.

"Would you like us to start with a prayer?" I said.

She nodded quietly. "Oh, yes."

We bowed our heads and sat for a long moment in silence. The candle flickered and seemed to bless the space around us. We prayed, then, for the presence of the Holy Spirit and for our awareness of the great mystery in our presence. We prayed for each other and gave thanks for being together.

"I have no fear," she said. "I have lived a good life, and I am one with God."

Yuki had cancer of the esophagus, an advanced and incurable case. When she telephoned me a few days earlier to set up this appointment, she mentioned she had once heard me speak about my spiritual journey. I spoke then about how I had combined Christian and Zen Buddhist forms in conducting a memorial service for another Japanese-American woman. And she said, "Will you do the memorial service for me when I die? I want it to be a healing service for my family."

She did not want a minister or priest to conduct the service. "I spent forty years wandering in the wilderness of Christian fundamentalism," she said, "but slowly, over the last ten or twelve years, I have come into new spiritual surroundings that I find more comfortable." She still considered herself a Christian, but her Japanese ancestry pulled her toward Zen, and she found much peace in Buddhist teachings. The fact that she and I had that in common made her think of me for her memorial service. In a note to me later, she wrote, "I felt God somehow worked things out that you should be the one."

About combining Zen with Christianity she said, "It is like going from a two-dimensional life to many dimensions, with all the benefits of an abundant life, a greater appreciation of music and art, and, most of all, the ability to love everything and everybody."

Over the next several months, I got to know Yuki well. Her eclectic liking for Christianity and Zen reminded me of Frederick Franck, the renowned physician, sculptor, and thinker whom I once met. Dr. Franck compiled and translated *The Book of Angelus Silesius,* the writings of a seventeenth-century German Zen poet whose verses formed a bridge between the mysticism of the East and West. Yuki knew the book, read from it every day, and we discussed a number of its remarkable verses. One of them goes:

He who turns the senses
to the Light that is his center
hears what no ear can hear
sees where no light can enter

Yuki identified with this. "My senses are awake," she said. "I see more vividly than I did before the cancer. I hear and smell everything. When my family comes to see me, I feel such a sense of love and gratitude, and I don't need anything. I like to sit and just be, knowing God is with me."

At our first meeting, I could see no physical sign that Yuki had cancer. I admit that my doctor's instincts were on the alert: I caught myself looking at her fingernails and noting that the nail beds were pink, a sign that she was not anemic. She did not appear malnourished, and her cheeks were not sunken. I stopped myself from asking the questions that formed in my mind: *Are you having any pain? What happens when you try to swallow?* More than seven years had passed since I completed Clinical Pastoral Education, and I still thought like a doctor. But I knew not to stray off into that area. I was there as her friend and counselor, not her doctor. I would walk with her to the river separating the living from the dead, and I would do whatever she wanted me to as she prepared to cross that river.

I told Yuki again about the Christian/Zen service I had conducted, how the Japanese men in the congregation wore black suits, sat up straight, and did not smile. She laughed when I said the hymns were organ solos because no one sang.

Yuki lived her whole life in Seattle, except for several years during and after the Second World War. She spent the war in an internment camp for Japanese-Americans. She spoke of this tragic and humiliating experience matter-of-factly, with no anger in her voice. "Judgments and anger are not a part of my life," she said.

After the war, she contracted tuberculosis and spent two and one-half years in Firland Sanatorium. Then she worked at the University of Washington for thirty years before retiring. Soon bored with retirement, she took a part-time job with the City of Seattle in an office within walking distance of her home, and she was still working at that job when we met. She never married, and together with her sister Midori, she stayed home and they took care of their mother until she died.

She told me all of this about herself, and more. "How dull my life seems when I describe it," she said, "but I have no complaints. Really, I experience a rich, full life every day, and for that I feel joy and a deep thankfulness."

Some years have passed since Yuki died, and I think of her now in muted colors. I see her tan sandals, and the faded pink roses against the gray background of her dress. Her colors were quiet, like her spirit. Noise was foreign to her. She wasted no energy in body motions, and she moved softly, like a cat walking on a rug. Her handshake was a loving touch. Not once did I see anything in her actions, or hear anything in her words, that suggested anger or fear. I suppose this is why I remember Yuki so clearly.

By late September of that year, Yuki was clearly in decline. She was beginning to have difficulty swallowing, and occasionally she put her hand to her mouth and coughed. A hospice nurse visited her weekly and checked in on her by telephone more often. Yuki knew her worsening symptoms meant death was approaching, but she still showed no sign of fear or regret. As an exercise, she wrote for me several short pieces. In one of them, she described the spiritual life as the real life and the material life as a distraction from the real:

◆   ◆   ◆

Siddhartha saw the river hasten, made up of himself and his relatives and all the people he had ever seen...It seemed to him that whoever understood this river and its secrets would understand much more, many secrets, all secrets.

—Hermann Hesse, Siddhartha

◆   ◆   ◆

I make my way to the front of the Cathedral and find three clergymen in the vestry. Besides Father Northup, there is the Rev. Bruce Larson from University Presbyterian Church and Father Tom Dement of St. Dunstan's, an Episcopal church near an exclusive Seattle neighborhood known as The Highlands. Fred asks me to "get vested"—I will be carrying the cross. I put on a white cassock and step into an adjacent room to get the cross, a beautiful, jeweled cross. I have performed this role before and know exactly what to do.

The three clergy, the verger, and I return to the narthex through the underground passageway, from where we distantly hear a young woman singing to the accompaniment of a piano up front. As the singing ends, a navy color guard forms in the center aisle; a quiet command is spoken, and they march forward. The cathedral is silent now except for the cadence of the men's feet, leather slapping against the concrete floor. They stop up front and post the U.S. flag to the left of the altar; then they return down the chancel and take up position to the side. The mighty Flentrop organ booms out, and the congregation stands. I raise the cross, and we process down the center aisle. As we near the altar, an awful image passes through my mind, a navy jet hurtling downward, a young airman tossed out into the sky. In the front pew, Jomie's widow Pat stares straight ahead as if in a trance; her eyes are fixed on Jomie's hat, saber, and white gloves laid out on a table next to the altar. George and Judy, Jomie's parents, stand in a solemn silence.

Up front, I take my seat behind the altar and look out upon the sea of faces as the Rev. Mr. Larson reads familiar lines from the third chapter of Ecclesiastes: *To everything there is a season, and a time for every purpose under the heaven; A time to be born and a time to die...*My mind wanders: to Peter Garrett, who flew with Jomie and now sits in one of the front pews; to the young navy lieutenant who came all the way from Mississippi for the service; to June in another pew with two of our daughters, Tucker and Debbie, and Debbie's husband Buster, who has Huntington's Disease and is slowly dying. I think of my oldest daughter, Julie, who is in the air at this moment, a flight attendant with United Airlines. I remember myself long ago, proud to wear my army uniform, and I realize Jomie must have been about the age I was during World War II.

I snap back into the service when the navy hymn is sung. The third verse speaks appropriately, if a bit ironically, to Jomie's fate:

> *O spirit, whom the Father sent*
> *To spread abroad the firmament;*
> *O wind of heaven, by thy might*
> *Save all who dare the eagle's flight,*
> *And keep them by thy watchful care*
> *From every peril in the air.*

For an instant, my mind catches on the line about the eagle's flight, but that passes and I think how Christ died on the cross and lived again. I think about all the suffering in the world and the tragedies that make no sense. And then I remember what Christ said: "He who believes in me shall not die but have everlasting life."

The service ends. I pick up the cross and take my place in the procession. As we pass from the chancel through the crossing, I catch a glimpse of motion high overhead and glance upward toward the cathedral's beamed ceiling. In a flash, a great bald eagle swoops down and lights on the cross. He is heavy, and I struggle to keep the cross upright. As we reach the narthex, the creature's wings give a mighty flap and he flies through the door. I rush outside and my eyes follow him up into the sky. Two navy jets are passing overhead with a roar, and the eagle speeds to join them. The great bird draws parallel to the two jets and falls into tight formation with them. I blink, and there is no eagle—just three navy jets. From the window of one, Jomie smiles out and waves to me just before the three jets disappear into the heavy cloud cover.

17

Even Heroes Die

When I think of a hero, I usually picture a military leader—the hero in battle, the strong leader of men; the one you would readily follow into battle. As a Southerner, I grew up thinking of Robert E. Lee as a hero: Lee the General, Lee the gentleman sitting tall in the saddle on his horse, Traveler.

However, there are heroes who don't fight battles and don't win medals. A hero can be as humble as the widow of the New Testament story who gives her mite at the temple. A doctor can be a hero to the one whose life he or she saves. A man who serves his community can be a hero.

On my desk stands a photo of a hero, a man named John Stanford. He was a two-star General, an adviser to the Secretary of Defense, and an adviser to the Undersecretary of the Army. He reached his zenith in the U.S. Army in 1990–91, when he directed all transportation plans and programs for Operation Desert Storm, the Gulf War. It was in a radically different situation during the last stage of his life that John Stanford became a hero to me.

In 1995, John was chosen to serve as Superintendent of Public Schools in Seattle. In November 1998, he died of myelogenous leukemia at the age of 60. In the course of those three years, a whole city fell in love with him. His slogan about children was "Love 'em and lead 'em," and that's what he did. His programs were bold, his expectations high. He shouted to the hilltops about the responsibility we each bear for Seattle's children. I had lived in Seattle for five decades and, like everyone else, could not remember a single person, whether a political leader, a clergyman, a CEO, or a philanthropist, who had lifted us so high.

John Stanford was the kind of man I would follow into battle. Had he been a surgeon, I would have had no fear of being anesthetized and letting him care for me.

During the time I knew him, we became as close as brothers—he an African-American who grew up in Pennsylvania, I a white man who grew up in Virginia during the era of segregation. We were neighbors in Seattle, living on the same street, and we often saw each other in the mornings when he jogged and I walked my dog. One day he stopped to talk to me, and he mentioned the fact that I was involved in spiritual counseling. He stopped short of asking me to assume that role for him, and I never proposed it. Our conversations became more frequent, however, and we naturally, comfortably wandered into the realm of spiritual matters. We philosophized about living and dying. We laughed and cried together. I came to think of myself as his soul friend, and he trusted me enough to give me a glimpse of his soul.

◆   ◆   ◆

In my photo of John, he is a handsome, vigorous man with black, slightly graying hair parted on the left side. His eyebrows are curved long and neat over his brown eyes. In the background are the American flag and his two-star General's flag. He has broad, muscular shoulders like a boxer. He wears a narrow, black tie between the starched collars of a light green shirt. Over the upper left pocket of his army jacket are five rows of multi-colored ribbons, and above them, silver aviator wings. Below the brass buttons on each of the pockets are ribbons awarded for his work in the Pentagon. He gazes directly at me, smiling a friendly smile that reveals a gap between his teeth. I smile back at him, and I feel a twinge deep down.

John's instincts drove him to fight his disease with determination and hope. He fought together with an army of doctors, nurses, research scientists, physical therapists, and nutritionists who all brought out their weapons to kill his cancer. Within him, the battle of his immune system raged. His bone marrow, his antibodies, and his brain worked night and day to stay ahead of the death knell. The war involved attacks and counterattacks, as the army of medical scientists fought back the cancer and then tried to overcome the adverse effects of the treatment.

When John first entered the hospital, some people who had been working closely with him predicted that he would not only recover from leukemia but remodel the hospital management system as well. To their surprise, he didn't touch the management. He made every doctor, nurse, and hospital orderly feel as good as he made his school employees feel, and they loved him for it. Other leukemia patients dropped in to see him, and they would tell stories and share laughter. His wife Pat was a constant companion, staying in the room sometimes around the clock. John loved people around him.

He and Pat quickly learned the jargon—words like hematocrit, stem cells, lymphocytes, leucocytes, myelogenous, immune system, and the names of all the drugs used. He followed his blood counts as if they were hits and runs in baseball. He didn't want any secrets. To the best of his ability, he stayed in control.

In the early weeks of his illness, he was on the phone constantly. He called his office to keep up to date, give advice, and make decisions. He participated in a meeting of the entire school board by means of a conference call.

He couldn't stand inactivity and wanted out of the hospital. One night at about 1:00 a.m., he felt so claustrophobic that he took off on his own. He put on his bathrobe and slippers and walked down the hallway, pushing the stand holding his I.V. fluids. He waved to the nurses at their desk, but, expecting no trouble from him, they didn't see him get on the elevator. He rode down to the first floor and walked out of the hospital in the direction of his home, pushing the stand along. He walked for more than a mile before someone called the police, thinking it peculiar that a patient was out in the streets like this at night. John was caught. The police called an ambulance, but he refused to get into it until he called his wife because he wanted her to drive him back. The I.V. stand made that impossible, so he reluctantly got into the ambulance with Pat and returned to the hospital.

John once told me he had an image of cancer as a freight train rushing toward him at full speed, blowing its whistle and grinding its wheels on the rail. He formed his hands into two big fists and pushed them together. "I have my own freight train," he said, "roaring down the track toward the cancer. I will never, ever, give up."

◆   ◆   ◆

A Seattle columnist wrote that, while John believed in himself and the things he wanted to do, he never raised himself above others. "He didn't act like a big shot," the columnist wrote. "There's a difference between letting people know how good you are and trying to show people that you are better than they are."

Immediately after his arrival in Seattle, John leapt into the public eye. He couldn't meet everyone, of course, but sometimes it seemed as though he *knew* everyone. In no time, nearly every Seattleite had heard him speak, seen him on television, or read about him in the newspaper. He became known for having innovative ideas, such as forming partnerships with private corporations and individual philanthropists, and he moved quickly to realize them. People considered him tough, straightforward, and full of energy. He juggled many issues at the same time, and his attitude toward overcoming obstacles was: "Don't tell me why it can't be done, tell me how we will accomplish this." At the same time, he tended to be non-judgmental and scrupulously avoided putting others down. In a school district desperately in need of dynamic leadership, people asked each other, "Where did this guy come from?"

Fueled by his moving speech about America's children at the Democratic National Convention in 1996, there was talk of his being in line for a national leadership position, possibly Secretary of Education. A worried group of business leaders offered John a large bonus per year, in addition to his contractual compensation package, to keep him in Seattle. John turned it down.

♦   ♦   ♦

The day before John entered the hospital, I arranged for the Reverend Gerald Porter, an Episcopal priest, to serve communion to John and his family at their home. John was not sure he wanted to take communion. He identified himself as an Episcopalian, but he wasn't in the habit of attending church regularly. Now, facing cancer, he seemed troubled by the thought of receiving the bread and the wine, associating these elements with the Last Supper; John was not ready to die. Nevertheless, he agreed to the idea.

To reassure John, I accompanied the priest. When we arrived, John was asleep on a leather sofa. His head slumped down on his left shoulder, and his hands were clasped in his lap. John's two sons sat on chairs to his right, and his wife sat on the arm of the sofa, her left arm resting on the sofa back behind his head. I listened for the sound of his breathing but could barely hear it, although his chest was moving slightly. His feet were crossed just under the glass coffee table, and a magazine with the title *Penn State University* lay on the table, its cover carrying a picture of John in a dark suit, white shirt, and tie. In the lower-right corner was the caption "John Stanford Super in Seattle." Across the room, a fire crackled and gave off the woodsy smell of alder.

I sat down quietly on the sofa beside John, and the priest sat on the chair at the end of the coffee table. John's eyes opened, and he looked at each of us silently and without expression. Then he pushed himself into an upright position, rubbed his eyes, and said, "Welcome." All of us were quiet for a moment. I put my hand on his. His hand was warm, feverish, a little damp.

His two sons had on dark flannel pants and gray sweatshirts. They were tall, even sitting down, and their skin was lighter than their father's. Scott, the younger son, had a face and eyes like his mother's. Steve had the features of his father. Both were silent.

From a square black box, the priest pulled out a small silver chalice and placed it on the table. He picked six thin, white wafers out of a cylindrical silver container, and placed them in a row on the coffee table. Finally, he pulled out a small glass vessel, narrow at the top and ballooning out in the middle, containing a purplish-red wine. He removed the glass stopper and poured the wine into the silver cup. We could hear the deep purr of a commercial plane in the distance and the whir of rubber tires on wet pavement coming from the street in front of the house. Looking out the window on my left, I saw that the sky was a pale gray. A darker, bluish-gray cloud hung over Lake Union in the distance.

"John, this is not a last rite," the priest said to him, and we all chuckled. "This is your first rite toward healing. We want you to do as you have always done. Think positively and become aware of the power of healing already in you—the Holy Spirit."

◆   ◆   ◆

These are the pictures of John Stanford that I carry with me always: John the fighter, whose instincts drove him to battle against long odds; John the mover and shaker, a man of vision and compassion; John the vulnerable human being, who had to learn to accept his mortality.

I once challenged John to a mock boxing match in my living room. I was almost old enough to be his father, and my arms and body were shorter than his. I figured the only way I could touch him would be to come in close, get inside his arms and pound his abdomen with both fists. We squared off, arms and fists up, as we had both learned to do in the military. He calmly reached out with his right hand and held me by the top of my head. His arms were much longer than mine, and all I could do was flail my arms in empty space while he stood still with a big grin.

Another time, sitting in front of the fireplace, John complained of a sinus infection that gave him a headache and plugged his nose. He didn't like to take medicines—a reluctance he had to overcome for cancer treatments—and so I told him I could cure his sinus condition without medication. I excused myself and retreated to the kitchen to look for a medicine stick that a Suquamish Indian had carved. It was a Christmas present from my wife. I returned to the living room with the medicine stick, shaking it and chanting "Oh yo, yo, yo, yo..." John sat quietly and never changed his expression as I danced around and around his chair. Eventually I stopped, put one hand on his forehead close to his sinus, and solemnly declared him well. He paused for a moment, as if testing how he felt. Then he declared he was cured. We laughed and slapped each other.

Months later, when John was home on a weekend leave from the hospital, weakened by cancer treatments and surrounded by his family and a longtime friend, Fred, I repeated the ceremony. John's son Steve wore a Northwest Indian mask, Fred shook a rain stick, making it sound as if there were a downpour, and I wielded the medicine stick. Our antics amused John, who managed to forget for a moment just how serious his illness was.

"Friends expect a heroic fight from John Stanford." This was the headline in *The Seattle Times*, April 5, 1998. All of Seattle was pulling for him. Our culture expects a great deal from our heroes. In the case of John Stanford, we expected him to succeed in his role as a fighter: he would stand tall in battle; he would defeat the enemy of cancer.

We sometimes associate the battle against cancer with St. George, the warrior astride his horse, lance poised to kill the dragon; St. George the invulnerable, wearing a ton of armor, the beast ghastly to look upon with its tail switching and its deadly mouth ready to strike. St. George, with all his might and strength, slays the dragon. The king rewards him with a gold medal, a castle, and his daughter's hand in marriage.

A leukemia patient, however, is a sorry substitute for St. George. The leukemia patient faces the dragon without a horse and without a lance. Even if he had a horse, the patient would be too weak to mount him. If he had armor, his body could not support it. He might not even be able to lift the lance.

John went through rigorous training in two special military schools. He learned how to parachute from an aircraft, and he learned survival skills. Wouldn't it have been miraculous if that training had helped John change his bone marrow back to normal? I think of the headline, "Friends expect a heroic fight," and I shake my head sadly. What a burden to place on someone who hadn't the strength to get up from his chair or his bed without help. Attacking the enemy in combat is different from lying flat on a hospital bed with a gown open in the back and your body attached to tubes. How can a person who is seriously ill act heroically when deep down in his soul he fears death, and has no equipment or experience to offset that fear?

We have a hero-oriented culture. Our hero system expects perfectionism. It has little tolerance for the condition of the poor, the unemployed, the downtrodden—and, yes, the sick. It's a culture that rewards the surface image and lures many a person into a false journey, a quest for greatness that consists only in appearances.

My father was such a person. He had the illusion that if his business were a success, he would be a hero to his family and his friends. He would be accepted, looked up to. His business failed early in the Great Depression, and my father committed suicide. He felt he could not live up to the standards set by the culture—to be wealthy and powerful—and therefore his life was not worth preserving. My father was like Willy Loman, the archetypal character in Arthur Miller's great twentieth-century play, *Death of a Salesman,* who failed because his values were false. His suicide, like my father's, is the opposite of heroism.

I must confess that I, too, have been taken in by the siren song of the heroic image. Many years ago, I became a doctor believing the profession would bring me respect and admiration. When June, my bride-to-be, told me she loved me, I believed deep down that a good part of her love was because I was a doctor. Years later I confessed this to her, and she nearly fell on the floor laughing. She said, "Actually, it was your big brown eyes." I laugh now.

The standards our community sets, the values we all find so seductive, can lead as often to disillusionment as to heroism. That we should amass great wealth, achieve power, or have our names constantly splashed across the front page of the newspaper—these standards are misleading. To meet these standards, we are often required to play a role representing who we think we should be, or who society thinks we should be. We come to believe we will be accepted and loved only if we wear the masks associated with that role. But the masks can hide our true selves and even cause us to destroy the real man or woman under the mask—the man or woman who loves, who serves others, who is aware of the mystery of life, the everyday hero who moves through life with faith and humility.

There is another kind of heroism, quite apart from the version our community celebrates: a heroism that doesn't require superhuman feats, a heroism that admits the fact of mortality. This is the kind of heroism John Stanford achieved during his last weeks among us. It required him to see himself in a different light, to understand that his past had not entirely equipped him for his newest challenge. He could not arm himself to do battle with a normal enemy, for this time the enemy had weapons that John's arsenal could not overcome.

His new challenge was a challenge of the spirit. It was the challenge of *healing*, not in the sense of curing or fixing the physical body that was under siege, but in the sense of preparing the soul for the inevitability of physical death. John Stanford met this challenge, and the eminence he achieved as a leader blossomed into a true personal heroism.

◆   ◆   ◆

John wasn't quite ready for this challenge when he entered the hospital in April 1998, but he had taken the first step that day he took communion in his home. At the end of the service, after he and his family had drunk from the cup and eaten the bread, tears crept out of his eyes and down his cheeks. He thanked the priest, and me, a friend. He said he felt a kind of peace that would be with him when he started his treatment the next day.

What he really meant was that he felt ready to fight a new war, much as he had approached the challenge of fighting the Gulf War. This is what drove his attempt to keep running the school district from his hospital bed, what drove him, in frustration, to walk out of his ward in the middle of the night. He refused to see himself as a patient, refused to accept the likelihood that he would not win the last war of his life.

It was a fierce war. A month of powerful chemotherapy appeared to throw John's cancer into remission, but this improvement itself lasted only a month. Another month of chemotherapy produced a similarly short-lived benefit. The battle continued, but a stem-cell transplant involving cells donated by John's sister, Carolyn Stanford Adams, failed to turn the tide. A half-year had passed since the war began, and as the trees outside turned from green to gold, red, and brown, John Stanford saw the light.

First, however, his liver and kidneys reacted to the insults of all the drugs and intravenous treatments. His energy level dropped, and he spent the better part of two weeks in a heavily medicated state, aware of his surroundings but sleeping a great deal. He perked up the day before Election Day, 1998, just in time to receive a special visitor, Vice-President Al Gore. John was thrilled. He insisted on getting out of bed to greet this important caller. Together, they took a walk, making two full circles of the long hospital corridor, the ailing John Stanford supported by the strong Al Gore.

I was out of town when Gore came to Seattle, but I returned a couple days later and found John in Room 916 of Swedish Medical Center, under isolation. A lovely Asian-American nurse named Ping, wearing a yellow gown and gloves, let me in and pointed to a cart holding more such gowns and gloves. With John's immune system severely weakened, there could be no risk of visitors spreading bacteria. Struggling with the ties at the back of my neck and waist brought back memories of the days when I practiced medicine. After washing my hands, I slipped on a pair of latex gloves. Even before I stepped around the yellow curtain separating the patient from the entrance to the room, I heard John's strong voice, "Is that you, Bobby? Come in!"

Chemotherapy had robbed him of his hair, making his head now bald and slick, but he gave me a broad smile and stuck out his giant hand.

"Now, Bobby, come on, give me that strong grip," he said.

I squeezed as hard as I can, and we grinned at each other. I sat down in a rocker beside the bed and, with his permission, turned the volume down on the radio.

He asked me what I'd been up to. I told him I played golf in the Bishop's Open, explaining that it is an annual tournament sponsored by the Episcopal Church to raise money.

"Were they all Christians playing?" he asked.

"Well, that's what they call themselves," I said.

"How did you get in?" His eyes twinkled, and then we both laughed. "I've got an idea for a book," he said. *"The Devil at the Bishop's Open.* That's you, disguised as a Christian to put the evil touch on the unsuspecting golfers. I'm going to expose you."

We laughed again.

We turned, then, to more serious talk—fighting cancer. As we spoke, I saw that a change had come over him.

He leaned on one elbow, facing me, his face lit with energy. "You know, Bob," he said, "the last two weeks I've been sleeping most of the time. I didn't do anything, didn't even check my charts. And yet, all during that time, God held me in His hands like a baby. I was safe, cared for." John formed a big bowl with his two hands.

He talked about his arrival in Seattle, his enthusiastic reception, he a black man taking a demanding job in a majority white city, and he spoke about the support he found for his work.

"You know, Bob," he said, "I love every child in the schools, and I love my family. That's what I brought to this city. I brought leadership and love."

He talked about the power he had had as a two-star general, at one time responsible for an eighty-million-dollar budget in the Pentagon. He enjoyed rubbing shoulders with Presidents, Vice-Presidents, Secretaries of Defense.

He spoke about his strong will to survive. Yet, on this day his talk of survival carried a different tone. He talked again of the freight train and of his ability to stop it. He spoke also of his inner peace, in a way that he hadn't before.

There was something greater than being a hero astride a white horse, he said. "There is the spirit within. It's a gift more powerful than any vision of a hero." Through that spirit, he felt a love which opened the doors of a strength he'd never felt before, a strength that came from the support of his family and the community, a strength that joined forces with his own and made him unconquerable.

I looked around the room and saw the wall plastered with big, yellow daisies that had been drawn for him by schoolchildren and sent to him with love.

"It all boils down to being human," he said. "Here I am in a hospital gown that's open to expose my rear end. Sometimes I'm unable to get to the bathroom in time and I make a mess on the floor. Hardly the picture of a hero riding on a white horse."

He grinned at me.

Soon it was time for me to leave. On the way out, I took off my latex gloves and told him, through the yellow curtain, that I'd be back.

◆   ◆   ◆

I like to remember John Stanford as he appears in my desk photo, vigorous and gazing out at me. This is not how he looked the last time I saw him. The hospital room was a busy place when my wife, June, and I arrived. Two orderlies were cleaning the room. Steve and Scott were there, plus John's sisters Carolyn and Cecile. And, of course, Pat, who had been at his side almost continuously through the long struggle; Pat, herself a quiet hero. Pat reminded us to wash our hands and helped us with our yellow gowns and latex gloves. John's voice reached us from the other side of the curtain, much weaker than before.

"Is that you, June? Is that you, Bobby?"

John's family had been taking turns reading to him when he asked for June to read. She picked the best seller, *Under The Tuscan Sun.* My plan, not knowing he would die late that night, was to spend just a moment and leave June there to read. At his bedside, however, I could see that something was different. He was popeyed, and he seemed to be staring off into the distance. His eyeballs were yellow. He wore an oxygen mask over his nose and mouth and he was short of breath.

"Hi, Bobby," he said, with all the strength he could gather. "You know, we've got to get going on that book, *The Devil at The Bishop's Open.* "

I laughed and marveled; John's body was failing him, but his sense of humor was still strong.

Those were his last words to me.

His eyes slowly closed. He bounced back, alert but a little confused. June sat down to read, and I left the room. June told me later that while she was reading, his eyes never left hers; he seemed transfixed by the beautiful description of Tuscany.

Out in the hall, I stood and talked with his sister Cecile for more than an hour. We laughed about his being a stand-up comic. We recalled how he once claimed to have shot a 53 playing golf and quit the game because it was no challenge to him.

Late that night, after nine months of intensive medical treatment, John's body surrendered.

◆   ◆   ◆

For two weeks prior to John Stanford's death, the local newspapers had been discreetly quiet. On the morning after his death, both *The Seattle Times* and the *Seattle Post-Intelligencer* displayed his picture in color. Television clips showed him shaking hands with children on the playground. A writer planned a biography. Everyone had a story to tell, especially schoolchildren. Never had the community seen so many children express their love and admiration for a public school superintendent. They wrote letters and poems. They drew pictures of him and for him. For a short time, the troubles of President Clinton, at that time facing the possibility of impeachment, faded into the background as far as the attention of Seattleites was concerned.

John's dying left a deep sense of loss, but it also raised the hope that his legacy of loving the children and doing right by their education would live on through the donations of industry and private citizens. Before and after he died, million-dollar gifts were made for public education. John felt strongly that, like private schools, the public school system should build endowment funds to give all schools a level of excellence our children sorely need.

The family wanted a private memorial service, but it was impossible to keep it small. Eight hundred people poured into St. Mark's Cathedral—family, friends, neighbors, colleagues, and public officials. Bishop Vincent Warner of the Diocese of Olympia participated in the service. A number of people gave eulogies, including Washington Governor Gary Locke, Seattle Mayor Paul Schell, King County Executive Ron Sims, John's son Scott, and John's longtime friend, the Reverend Elbert Ransom, a Baptist minister from Washington, D.C. I, too, spoke at the services, beginning my eulogy with "I am here as a friend and neighbor of John Stanford." Beams of sunlight filtered through the big windows on the cathedral's south side. The music thundered as the congregation sang "A Mighty Fortress Is Our God." A school choir sang "I Believe I Can Fly."

That evening three to four thousand people—teachers, children, civic leaders and friends—gathered in a large auditorium at the University of Washington for another uplifting program celebrating John's extraordinary life. The family flew east the next day for the military burial at Arlington National Cemetery. June and I watched on television as a horse-drawn caisson carried John's flag-covered casket, followed by a beautiful horse with empty boots in the stirrups facing backwards, for the fallen soldier.

Time has passed now. John has joined the long list of friends who have moved on, and as I write, my mind sees two snapshots of him: one in his dress uniform with the medals, a full head of hair; the other in his hospital gown open down the back, his head bald. In both of them, he is smiling. I remember him fighting hard to stay alive, and finally letting go. I remember the notes he wrote to Pat, Steve, and Scott in the last few days of his life, telling them how much he loved them and wishing he had done more for them. And I remember Scott, his 28-year-old son, saying, "I didn't think there was a force strong enough to take him from this earth."

For me, John Stanford showed his greatest courage, his greatest heroism when he told me that God had held him in his hands and that he was ready to return to the peace that passes all understanding.

◆   ◆   ◆

How can we help a heroic person at that time of life when his concept of heroism is not enough to carry him into death? How can we help a person facing death who may not think of himself as heroic?

I have thought about this a lot. John Stanford's example is one that applies to anyone we love, to persons mighty and meek, famous and obscure.

Don't expect him to create a miracle for himself. Help him, on the other hand, to let go, to be at peace with himself. Give him friendship. Love and care for him—and tell him so. Hold his hand and listen to him. Give him hope, but not false hope. Sit quietly together. Accept the humility of those who are very ill, and be sensitive to their discomfort. Encourage their faith in themselves, and in those who care for them. Do not expect heroics in the conventional sense.

Above all, remember that healing is not the same as curing. Healing is rising above illness and death. To be healed is to know there is a greater power, a greater mystery to life, and when this event in life is over, your loved one will be wiser because he became acquainted with his own humanity, his vulnerability, his fragility.

Yes, don't burden your loved ones by requiring them to be heroes. Give them better than that. Give them love and hope and they will become heroes.

18

The Missing Father

At coffee hour after church some years ago, a young man came to me and introduced himself. The name Mark was familiar, but I could not immediately place it. He was in his forties and he had on a blue blazer, gray pants, and a nondescript tie. His hair was a dark brown with some flecks of gray, but it was his face at that moment that remains sharpest in my mind, a quiet face, a skin light enough to think he seldom exposed himself to the sun, a man who looked as if he might be carrying a heavy stone inside himself. He told me his father, Luke, had died thirty-some years earlier, when Mark was only thirteen, and asked if he could come and talk to me about him. I was his father's doctor at the time of his death. An image popped into my head: a man in his bed on the second floor of Doctors Hospital, a skeleton of a man weighing seventy pounds with a feeding tube in his mouth, a man of thirty-nine who looked like a Holocaust victim. I immediately felt a kinship with the son, knowing how terrible it is for a child to lose his father, and I readily agreed to meet with him.

I had first heard about Luke, the father, through his estranged wife Marge at a dinner party. I hadn't met Marge before. She was clearly disturbed and looking for help. We sat apart from the other guests as she told me her story. Some time previously, she and Luke had separated. He had moved into an apartment, but they had not been divorced. She took seriously her church's prohibition of divorce, and worried about the shame her marital problems might bring upon her family. Now Luke was dying.

More than a year earlier, she was alarmed when Luke did not answer his phone. She went to his apartment with a friend and found him unconscious on the floor. At first, they thought he had committed suicide, but they rushed him to the hospital still alive, and there it was discovered that

214

he had had a stroke, a massive hemorrhage at the base of the brain. His condition was grave, for at that time there was no effective treatment for stroke. He hung on to life, but he began to waste away and was in a pitiful condition by the time his wife met me. She was unhappy with his doctor and wanted to replace him with another. I agreed to see him.

My first glance at Luke told me that this was a young man dying. He was emaciated, but his skin was not wrinkled and there were no brown spots such as are common in old people. His teeth were white, not yellow, and there was no gray in his hair. He was not comatose. He was, however, completely paralyzed; the only part of his body that moved was his right eyelid. His left eye stayed shut. He could see through his right eye, he could hear, and he was alert enough to enjoy television. Gurgling and squeaking sounds issued from an opening in his throat, the result of a tracheotomy. He could not speak.

To communicate, we used a blackboard that had an alphabet painted on it at the top. I could ask him a question such as "Are you comfortable?" If he raised his eyelid, that meant yes. If he lowered it, that meant no. If he wanted to say something, I slowly wrote his words by asking him, letter by letter, if he wanted a consonant or a vowel and, by pointing to consonants or vowels, finding the letter by elimination.

Because I had not known him before, my image of him forever is a sad one: a small, gaunt man with his left eye perpetually closed, no facial expression, scrawny arms and hands resting motionless on the bed sheet. Inserted into this bird-like man were two tubes. One, a catheter, led from his penis to a jar on the floor; the liquid inside was brownish: the sign of bleeding or infection, or both. The other connected to his stomach via a bottle hung from a bedside stand, feeding him a nutritional liquid composed of milk, egg yolks, vitamins, and fats. The feeding bottle, which was changed two or three times every twenty-four hours, would soon become the center of discussions as his family and I considered what we could best do to help him.

Meanwhile, Luke continued to weaken. He developed a kidney infection, and despite the best efforts of his nurses, he began to suffer also from bedsores which no amount of turning and washing could prevent. Nor could the nurses' constant care eliminate the smell of fecal matter around him. His breath became almost unbearably foul because his tongue was dry and cracked in spite of daily swabbing. In short, his body was disintegrating.

Marge, who still cared very much for her husband, knew there was no hope and wanted to see an end to his suffering, but she was in an agonizing situation. Because she was separated from him, she didn't feel she had the right to ask that his feeding tube be removed. She never said it to me, but I believe she felt some guilt over their separation and may even have worried that it had precipitated the stroke. Other members of the family were opposed to removing the tubes because he was still aware of his surroundings; he could watch television and carry on those excruciatingly slow and simple conversations. None of them had the courage to ask Luke what he wanted.

I told Marge I would.

In those days, the term "physician-assisted suicide" was unknown, but it was quite common to let a person die by not doing anything beyond providing comfort. If a doctor believed it was useless to continue treating a patient who was clearly terminal and suffering, he could withdraw support quietly. The doctor might instruct the nurses to keep the patient comfortable, moisten the tongue and lips as needed, and use sedatives to induce as much sleep as possible—but to cease giving the patient nourishment. In some cases, the doctor might order extra morphine, even though he knew it could hasten death.

Luke's previous doctors would not consent to letting him go, and Marge asked me to step in because friends had told her she could trust my judgment. In fact, this was the first time I had ever been asked to make this kind of decision when other doctors refused to, and it made me cautious because there were no clear ethical guidelines. Informed consent was not widely used. I knew the hospital could come under criticism if we simply "pulled the plug." Because Luke was conscious and apparently of sound mind, it seemed to me crucial that he himself be consulted.

Alone with him, I asked, "Do you want to die?" Without hesitation, Luke used his eyelid to signal "yes." I then called in Marge and the head nurse, and repeated the question. Luke reaffirmed his answer.

Before the day was over, it seemed the entire hospital staff heard about it. Those who knew Luke, or knew about his case, were divided; some strongly opposed letting him die. They didn't want to give up; he was so young. One nurse even offered to take him home and care for him.

In my own mind, I had no problem with letting him die. He was miserable, and he had no place to go. It was only a matter of time before his heart would stop, no matter what we did, and it seemed to me that continuing to feed him meant prolonging his dying rather than extending his life. I arranged to meet with Marge and the rest of the family—their children and in-laws—together with a priest and the family's attorney. We all gathered in a small room. I told them my position: Stopping all treatment was not my decision to make; it was the patient's responsibility, and he made it clear he was ready to die. The attorney expressed the opinion that allowing Luke to die by stopping treatment and withholding nourishment was within the law. I had brought in another doctor who wrote a note on Luke's medical chart documenting my opinion that there was no hope. A Catholic priest reassured us that we were not murdering Luke; we were withdrawing artificial means of keeping him alive and letting nature take its course.

Thus it was decided. We agreed to remove Luke's feeding tube. We would keep him comfortable, and we would leave the catheter in to drain his bladder so his bed sheets would not have to be changed so often.

I had assumed that it was the nurses' duty to remove the feeding tube, but they wouldn't do it—they wanted me to pull the plug. I went into Luke's room alone, told him what we planned to do, and again got his consent. It was hard for me to remove the tube, and yet I proceeded. It was such a simple act, and I realized what it meant: I had come to this man, at this time, as the angel of death. I sat with Luke for a while; then we sedated him, and I held his hand while he went to sleep. I anticipated he might live three or four more days and would sleep most of the time.

I had not anticipated the effect on myself. I slept poorly, and when I awoke I immediately focused on Luke. The second day, I canceled my office appointments. I took walks and stopped in to see him several times. With one or two exceptions, the hospital staff and nurses let me know they supported my action, and they were particularly kind to Luke's family.

He died during the night while I was at home. The night nurse called, and I went to see him one last time. His time had come. He had no pain, no anxiety, and no fear, and his family was grateful that he died so peacefully. We all held hands around the bed as the priest blessed him. It was a good death.

◆   ◆   ◆

I don't know how long it took for my own dad to die, but I never saw him during the time he lay in the hospital. I have thought about this over and over throughout my adult life and I've tried to visualize him. Ten years after his death I was a first-year medical student, and the hospital in which he died was part of the medical school complex. It was an old, gray-stoned building, five stories high and occupying one-half of the city block. A new, taller, modern hospital was constructed while I was a student, and they were using the old building for administrative offices. But one day I walked over there with my dad on my mind. I climbed the wide stone steps to the front door, entered a dim hallway, and passed the first-floor offices with signs on the doors indicating Financial Office, Treasurer, and Chief of Nursing. Near the latticed iron elevator doors, I found the stairway and followed the steps to the dark corridor of the second floor. I pushed a door open. No bed. No bedside table. No I.V. equipment or nurse's cart. Just an empty space with walls of gray-white plaster, marred by cracks. A window looked out on a brick wall.

It made me unbearably sad to think he died in a place like this. There he lay, unconscious, probably with blood and mucus gurgling in his throat until he died.

I left the room and closed the door. It was an empty tomb. My dad had left it, like Christ; but unlike Christ, my dad never returned.

◆   ◆   ◆

I remembered vividly the controversy over letting Luke die when his son Mark made an appointment to see me those many years later, but I didn't remember a thing about Mark from that earlier time. To be truthful, I had some anxiety about meeting with him; I wondered how much he knew about his father's death and even worried that he might feel some resentment about my role. At the same time, I looked forward to seeing Mark because the more I thought about his father, the more I wanted to share what I had learned by being with Luke during his last days. I myself never had the opportunity to meet the doctor who was with my father during his death, and I figured that whatever Mark wanted to talk about, it was deep stuff.

He came to my home, and we sat down in the living room. I asked him, "What questions or thoughts do you have about your father?"

He said, "My mother told me you were a very spiritual person. It's the spiritual part that I want to talk to you about."

His answer surprised me, for it had not occurred to me that others saw a spiritual side to me back in the sixties; my memory of myself from that time is that of the doctor consumed by his work. I thought for a moment and said yes, I had been on a long spiritual journey. I asked him what in particular brought him to see me.

Mark spoke thoughtfully, reflectively, in a quiet voice. He told me about the months leading up to his father's death, about how it felt being unable to communicate effectively with him, and how isolated he was because none of his teenage friends understood what it was like to have a father who wore diapers and was being fed through a tube in his stomach. This confirmed the sense I had had that Mark and I shared something important, and I felt drawn to him.

His face lit up when he showed me a picture of himself holding his son, with his face pressed against the boy's forehead. The boy's shining eyes look straight into the camera and he holds his chubby left hand against his dad's chest. Mark is a sensitive father, and he knows how special it is for a small boy to have a loving dad. The photo shouts out their joy and makes me think, with sadness, about my own father. I don't remember him ever holding me and kissing me. I recall the thought I had when each of my daughters reached the age of ten—the age I was when my dad committed suicide. I thought how wonderful it was to be alive with them, and I prayed that I would never leave them.

Mark had become a teacher, and as we talked I could tell he took a close interest in his students, listened to them, loved them, and it dawned on me what a gift his father had bequeathed to him. Through the pain of losing his own father, his heart and soul had forever opened to the needs of children. A story he told me gives evidence to this, how he once wrote to a young girl whose father nearly died in a skiing accident. Mark praised the girl for giving support to her father, and he told her of his own father's illness when he was her age, and how his father's tragedy had made him a stronger person. He urged her to be courageous, and always to aim for her "personal best" in schoolwork, athletics, and her life in general, as a way of helping her dad recover from his injuries.

Mark continued to see me, and each time he took me a little deeper into his memories. He talked about feeling alone during the time of his father's sickness and how he felt "diminished" as a person. It was a word I have often used to describe my own self-image after my father's death—feeling small, confused, and *less of a person* than others around me. As a teenager, Mark struggled to be a football player and a gymnast. He worked at these sports excessively, and he did not feel diminished while playing football. I couldn't help remembering how I strove so hard to stay on the honor role and pushed myself to become the youngest Eagle Scout on record.

During the two or three years before his stroke, Luke was a very angry man who could lose control of his temper over trivial things. Sometimes, he physically abused Mark's mother and Mark didn't understand the cause of his father's anger, although he knew his dad drank too much. His older brother felt their father was a son of a bitch who got what he deserved, but Mark had a more benign attitude and sensed that his dad felt sorry for his behavior. He wished that he could have talked with his father after his stroke; he wanted to let his dad know that he loved him in spite of his anger. He couldn't bring himself to do it; he was only thirteen, and it was so difficult to talk to a paralyzed father whose only sounds were gurgles and squeaks, sounds that to Mark were spooky and shocking, coming from a father who had been such a powerful figure before.

What a strange, unfathomable experience for a boy to endure—his father wasting away slowly through weight loss and muscle atrophy; his right eyelid moving up and down to say yes or no; the tube inserted in his mouth and connected to a bottle on a stand to feed him. Mark stored all these things in his heart and never discussed them with anyone, not even his mother, like me.

Again, like me, Mark never consciously grieved over the loss of his father. We talked about it and agreed that this does not mean we had no feelings. We both experienced the sense of abandonment, confusion, and isolation, but we hid our feelings from others and tried to deny them to ourselves. Mark and I wondered if this might in fact be the way children grieve, through a myriad of secret, gut-wrenching memories that churn around on the inside. Such internalized pain and emptiness are compounded by outward silence. Mark and I had no one to share our pain with. There was no one to listen to us when we wanted to scream out, "What happened to my father? Where is he?" If that is what grieving is, then Mark and I can say that we grieved.

One day as we began a session in my upstairs office, Mark glanced out the window to the west where, far in the distance over Puget Sound, he saw a rock sticking out of the water like the top of a submarine. He said, "That rock is just offshore from where I grew up. It brings back memories." He described the family home as an old, wood-frame house bleached by the rain, wind, and salt air. It was on the porch of that house that he and his older sister had last seen their father before his stroke. He remembered how much quieter the house was after he moved out. It was a mixed blessing; no more temper tantrums, no more violence, just the empty space of a missing father.

These memories helped Mark as we discussed Thomas Moore's book, *Care of the Soul: A Guide for Cultivating Depth and Sacredness in Everyday*

Life (1992). Moore, a former monk and theologian who became a psycho-therapist, writes about the fact that so many families in our time are wounded by divorce, violence, and teen-age suicide. He says there are no perfect families and there probably never were. All families have their stress points, their bumps in the road, but families that are unable to mediate their conflicts dissolve into dysfunction because of guilt and inability to communicate. As a first step to healing, Moore stresses the importance of knowing the stories of your family and thinking of them as mythic. That is, you allow yourself to accept your parents, siblings, grandparents, and others as characters in an epic drama, each of them playing a role within that drama. In other words, you step back from your life to gain a true per-spective on it.

There were two things about Luke's life that Mark wanted to know. The first, why his father had become so violently angry, I could not tell him; the second, what his father was like facing death, I could tell him.

Mark had not been involved in the discussions about pulling the plug on his dad, and his eyes teared over when I told him the story: how I asked his father if he was ready to die, how he signaled a definite yes with his right eyelid, how he repeated the answer before Mark's mother and the nurse.

"What courage he had!" Mark exclaimed. "I'm proud of him and thankful to you for what you did."

In our subsequent conversations, Mark and I continued to talk about his dad, and we also talked a bit about his mother. I think I helped him sort out his feelings toward his mother and get a start on confronting her deteriorating health. It was hard for him to bear the thought that he might soon have to repeat what he went through while watching his dad die many years earlier. This time, he hoped to be better prepared. It seemed to me critically important that he talk frankly to his mother. I suggested that he tell her he loved her and ask her how she felt about herself. It was important that she know she could always count on the love and support of her family.

This conversation simultaneously uplifted me and saddened me. I thought what a great joy it would have been for me to have had a close relationship with my mother, how it would have helped us both so much if she could have expressed her deepest feelings and I, mine. I recalled my last visit with Mother, when she sat in the wheelchair and I told her, while rubbing her arms, that I loved her. Thank God I was able to do that, but how much better life would have been for both of us if we had been able to trust and share with each other from the day of Dad's death. Mark seemed to feel quite comfortable with the thought of sitting with his mother now and sharing love and intimacy. I told him what a gift that was for both of them. Mark and I gazed steadily at each other in silence for a minute, as if we were praying, and I envied him his opportunity.

◆   ◆   ◆

In her book *Necessary Losses* (1986), Judith Viorst describes how we all grow and change through the losses that are an inevitable part of our lives. If we can accept our losses as learning experiences, they can bring us a deeper perspective, a fuller wisdom, and a true maturity. We can turn our pain into gold and light. Our insights can create a new life for ourselves and others. This can happen—if we have faith and listen carefully to the lessons loss teaches us.

The pain of losing a parent can last for decades, but through the grace of God and one's own insight, such a tragedy can be transformed into a gift. Usually it takes time. Throughout most of my life, I could never have thought of my dad's suicide as a gift. Neither could the young Mark imagine that his father's death at the age of thirty-nine was a gift in disguise. Yet, thirty-five years later, Mark had come to believe that the experience changed his life in a positive way. Sixty years after my dad died, something similar became clear to me. My hidden gift was the awareness of what it means to lose a parent. In the course of my adult life, I received other gifts of insight. I learned how to face failure, learn from it and move on; how to have compassion for those who are depressed; how to seek help when in a deep, dark hole and return it when others have fallen in a hole. I learned about the joy of just being present and listening, as well as the ability to bond with those who are dying. In the late stages of my life, I have learned to find my natural, healing touch—and, just as importantly, I have come to be aware that it is God who holds my hand.

This is how God works His mysterious ways. This is how we grow. Suffering and pain can change a person for life, but we all possess the ability to transform our losses into gains. We can choose: Either we remain lost, or we grow in mind and spirit. Either we retreat within ourselves and wallow in our personal misery, or we turn outward to the wide world and save ourselves by engaging with others.

The right course may not be easy. I remember a time when a man who was dying visited me in my home. I was simply being his friend and listening to him as he confronted death. When he left, I suddenly felt overwhelmed, sad, and confused. I went into the kitchen, where June was washing dishes. I put my arms around her and cried deeply. I felt I didn't understand the deep mystery of life and questioned why I made myself available to those who sought help understanding the equally unknowable mystery of death. June listened to me, hugged me, said it was all right.

It was only a moment, and even though similar moments still occur, deep down within me, I know that the real meaning of life lies in loving others and serving them. I seem to have a gift for counseling those who are dying, and this has become my calling late in my own life. I cry because being present with the dying moves me. I don't know for sure, but maybe this feeling and my sensitivity to others are linked in a straight line to the death of my father and the misery of my mother. I do know that my dad's suicide figures somewhere in the equation, that his tragic and incomprehensible death have drawn me, at this late stage, to be present with those who are dying. What I wish is for all people to have a *good* death, without pain and not alone, in the words expressed by the Hospice organization, and, I would add, *having had the opportunity to tell their stories.*

I have no doubt that when I am on my own deathbed I will think of my dad, and I will think of all those with whom I have sat at the bedside as they lay dying. I will see them parading across my consciousness and into my soul. They will smile at me and encourage me, even though I may weep and ask, "Why?"

19

The Miracle of Reconciliation

Early one morning while I was still in private practice, my hospital rounds brought me into George's room to see how he was doing. Orange rays of sunlight poured through the window, giving warmth to the plainness of the light-green walls and white bedspread. A water glass, half full, stood on the bedside table beside the phone, along with George's eyeglasses with their thick lenses. George's head peeked out from the covers, and he appeared to be gazing up at the ceiling. The outline of his body under the white bedcover showed that he had been tucked in and made comfortable.

I put my hand on his face and said, "George," but I knew he was not going to answer.

His body was limp and still warm. He had apparently died shortly before I came in. I took a deep breath and hung my head for a moment, in a wordless prayer. Then, feeling the need to talk to George, I closed the door and stood at the end of his bed.

Diabetes had taken most of George's vision, and his eyes, sunken back in their sockets, appeared no different from how they had one day earlier. His face, now pale and covered by a gray stubble, looked peaceful. His bushy, black eyebrows stood out against his white forehead.

George, barely past fifty, had severe diabetes and multiple complications that ultimately weakened his heart. He taught school for many years, serving for a while as Dean of Annie Wright Seminary, an elite Episcopal girls' prep school in Tacoma, and most recently as a teacher at the highly respected Lakeside School in Seattle. He was known as an effective and popular teacher, as well as being something of a renaissance man, knowledgeable about history, literature, music, and other subjects.

"Say, George," I said, "I want to tell you how much I've enjoyed having you as a patient and a friend. I'll never forget the times you came to the office with the list your wife gave you, things to ask me about: 'Is there anything we can do about the pain in his feet at night? And what about the muscle cramp in his calves? He looks anemic to me, and his vision is getting worse—isn't there something we can do about that?'"

Some patients stick in a doctor's heart and mind, never to be forgotten. Every doctor has his favorites, and it is common for friendships to form between a doctor and a few of them. George was definitely one of those patients for me. He and I got to know each other well over the years. We occasionally had lunch together, and we talked about many things.

"George," I continued, "I loved hearing about your trip to Africa, not long ago, how enthusiastic you were when you returned. I remember how much you enjoyed teaching. And sailing. And your strong political opinions. I know you weren't much of a churchgoer, but you believed in a higher power and had great trust in the meaning of life."

George's death was expected. There were no I.V.s hooked to him, no fluids running into his veins, no machinery to keep him alive beyond his allotted time.

"George, you've been more than a patient. I've always cared for you as a friend and looked forward to your visits. Do you know, my secretary had to schedule extra time for your appointments because we talked so much."

I don't know how long I stood at the foot of George's bed, but at a certain point I noticed that the sunlight was more intense, no longer orange. The morning was wearing on and I had other patients to see. I was sad to see George go but comforted by the fact that he died at peace. It pleased me that I'd had these few minutes alone with him.

"Good-bye, George," I said.

I cast one more glance back at him from the doorway and walked off down the corridor. I pulled George's chart from the rack at the nurses' station and recorded his death on a progress sheet. It struck me suddenly as ironic that the "progress" sheet is where a doctor writes about death as well as recovery.

◆   ◆   ◆

Talking to the dead is not uncommon. We don't all talk to them in the literal sense of the word; each of us finds his own way to commune with our loved ones—father, mother, sister, friend. We reminisce, we relive moments of their lives, we remember things we wish we had done or said. We connect with them somehow, whether it's by standing over their graves quietly or holding them in our hearts.

Or maybe they express themselves in our behavior. June, for example, expresses something of her mother in the way she sets the dinner table, prepares tea, tends her garden. I see June's mother in her when she gives so generously to charities or reads to her grandchildren. Cultures that we think of as traditional or pre-modern believe that their ancestors are ever present in the life of the living, sometimes at a distance and sometimes close up. It's true—the dead are never gone.

My father and mother have never left my life. This was obvious through all the years I carried the stone of shame, through all the years that I tried to escape from my mother's misery. Sometimes today, I think about my dad; I wonder about the demons he was fighting. I think about that awful period of time after he pulled the trigger and before he died. I don't know how long it was, but I do know he was rushed to the hospital after my mother found him. Perhaps he was dead on arrival; more likely, it took several hours, perhaps many hours.

In combat, wounded soldiers may lie on the battlefield for hours, through the dark night, or in daylight while the battle rages above them and around them. They may lie in mud with flies buzzing about their faces. They groan, they bawl; they call out the names of loved ones or scream for a bunkmate whose body was blown to bits months earlier. If the soldier is lucky, he is eventually picked up off the ground and taken to a field hospital. If he recovers, there's a good chance he will revisit the moment he was hit over and over in nightmares, his brain flooded with the sounds and images of hell. If he dies, on the other hand, he has no chance to say good-bye. He cannot tell his sweetheart "I love you" one last time, or confess his sins to his priest. Sometimes on the blood-soaked field, stars will twinkle in the sky and the moon will rise slowly over the silhouette of a mountain and a soldier, sensing how near he is to death, will shout out, "Help me! Help me!"

What were those moments like for my dad? He did not die in combat—at least not in the literal sense; however, he did die in a battle: a battle with himself, a struggle that he lost to those darker forces within him. I assume he died lying on a firm hospital bed, made of iron and painted white. He lay there conscious or unconscious, seeing or not seeing, groaning or silent; like the shattered soldier, he faced the misery of detachment from all that gave life meaning. Whatever the scene, my mother must have walked into that room where he lay. Maybe my aunt did, too, and my grandparents, his own father and mother. Did he realize the suffering of those he was abandoning, did some sense of what he was doing to them reach him through his own pain? No doubt, my mother found the sight of Dad so terrible, the shock of what he had done so extreme, that she could never speak of it.

Dad's battle ended, but Mother's continued. It had begun with overwhelming horror. She must have heard the gunshot from somewhere else in the house. She might have hesitated for a moment, alarmed by the sound, and then dashed into the room where my father lay on the floor with blood rushing out of his mouth. The smell of gunpowder permeated the air, and the pistol lay near him. He was still conscious enough to tell my mother he loved her and that he was sorry. Mother rushed to the phone to call a doctor, and the next moments became a blur. The ambulance arrived, Dad was carried out on a stretcher, and somehow Mother got to the hospital, where in time others gathered as well. I don't know any of these details, for Mother never told me, so I am conjecturing. Did she run next door to the neighbor's house to call for help? Did she call his parents? She had to have called her sister in North Carolina, Uncle Joe's wife, because they came immediately. Did she touch my dad, try to give him whatever comfort was possible? Did she fall apart, get sick to her stomach, faint? Did she think about my sister and me at school, wondering what in the world she would tell us?

I'll never know exactly what happened; I can only imagine and specu-late. Even though she never said a single word to me about it, I have a feel-ing Mother relived those terrifying minutes repeatedly until the day she died, fifty-eight years later. This was the devastating trauma from which she never recovered. Like the soldier who sees his friend blown to smith-ereens, Mother saw her husband on that day, destroyed. He left her with-out having righted the wrongs, and he gave her no chance to paint the canvas clear again. There were no good-byes. As far as I know, she never visited his grave.

From that awful moment on, Mother covered her soul with costumes and masks: the mask of professionalism at work, the costume of misery at home. I visualize her soul, behind the mask, as a dark room stuffed with photographs too painful to think about. I wonder how hard it must have been for her to conceal her secrets, and I pray that she managed to keep a little door open to God's grace. There is evidence that she did; she was, after all, a lifelong church member.

It took me many years to put my own picture together, but I can under-stand something about my mother's misery now by reflecting on my expe-rience as an army psychiatrist. She was like a soldier who escapes serious physical wounds but is exposed to the agony and destruction of others. When they relive their experiences in nightmares and delusions, we called it shell-shock or, in the more modern terminology, PTSS—post-traumatic shock syndrome. The image of a violent death never goes away, and the lingering trauma changes the survivor forever, whether the triggering event takes place on the battlefield or in civilian life. You do not have to be in combat to feel you have been shot at, and you don't have to get hit by a physical object to fall into a trench and feel as though your soul is shut out from the light. If you lose a loved one through murder or suicide, it is much like seeing your friend shot to pieces by enemy fire. In a sense, when my dad shot himself in the head, he shattered my mother's brain along with his own.

Soldiers with PTSS need to open that door to the soul. In many cases, this will happen only under the effects of sedatives or hypnosis, but some-times it comes through the help of a clergyperson or counselor. So, too, with civilians who lose a loved one through violence. Both the soldier and the civilian need help and comfort; both need to tell their story when the time is right. Talking to a close friend can be healing. My mother never did this. She never sought help and kept her traumatic experience locked up inside her. In a way, I lost my mother because of this—lost her in the sense of having someone to commiserate with, share the intimate joys and tragedies of life with.

Mother had moments of joy and grace, but they did not last and she always returned to her misery. I remember some of those hopeful moments; for example, when she talked happily about her childhood in Cynthiana, Kentucky, how as a young girl she played the piano to the accompaniment of a snare drum while her friends danced to the music. I recall the time, in her late eighties, when she sat down and played the piano—something she hadn't done since my dad's death. She was visiting us in Seattle, and I persuaded her to play a few Christmas carols. At first, she only picked out the melody with one hand, but then it all came back, chords and harmony, and the spirit of the music. It reminded her of her early years, took her back to a place before her trauma, and she smiled. The door to her soul squeaked open, just a little.

Mother spent her last years in a high-quality nursing home, and I visited her on my trips to Washington, D.C. for conferences. I always stopped at the nurses' desk first and inquired about her. I looked at her chart to see what the doctor wrote about her and what he was prescribing.

The doctor saved her from pneumonia when she was ninety-three by treating her with penicillin, but she never recovered her strength or sense of well-being after that. I've often thought, what a shame the doctor didn't just let her die then. Pneumonia has always been called the friend of the elderly, giving a person an easy way to die. Instead, Mother languished for another four years. She lost most of her teeth and suffered little strokes that affected her speech and equilibrium. She was constantly angry, and when I stood at her bedside, she shouted that she wanted to get out of there.

The doctor, who had sat behind her in the Second Presbyterian Church for many years, wouldn't let her die. He ordered protein supplements, multi-vitamins, and extra calcium. I got so angry at him that I wrote a note on her chart asking him to stop trying to prolong a life that had no quality. Please, I wrote, let her go. He would not do it. I dismissed him and found another doctor who did his best to keep her comfortable while allowing nature to take its course.

Until very near the end of her life, an orderly came in every day and wheeled Mother down the long hallway to the large entry door. She insisted on being placed near the door, and she told everyone she was waiting for her son Bobby to come.

The last time I saw her, she was sitting in the wheelchair in her room. I stroked her arms and told her repeatedly that I loved her. She was unable to speak, but her mouth was open and she cried like a baby. By the time she died, her medical costs had almost drained the assets she had worked so hard to build. She was not buried in my dad's cemetery, but on the other side of town, next to the graves of her mother and father.

Years later, I stood at her graveside and told her I understood how lonely she had been. I told her I was proud of how she dedicated herself to her family, and I thanked her for enabling my sister and me to get a college education and have a profession. I regretted the fact that we all ended up living so far apart and wished we could have communicated better as mother and son. My soul felt at peace.

◆   ◆   ◆

...be transformed by the renewal of your mind, that you may discern what is the will of God, what is good and pleasing and perfect.
—Romans 12:2 (NAB)

There is no logical way to go about the process of reconciliation. It does not come from the head; it comes from deep in the heart and soul, the mysterious, sacred place, where love, acceptance, understanding, and compassion come from. This is what prayer is about. It is what surrender to a higher power is all about.

Jesus preached about the beginning of a new life and the death of the old. We can never go back and undo what has been done in our lives, but reconciliation with the past, with each other, and with ourselves is possible if each of us becomes aware of his own imperfections. Sometimes we don't find the motivation to turn ourselves around until we experience deep pain, but with God's help we can admit our faults, strip off our masks, and allow the image of God to shine through our faces. Our masks are the outer signs of fear within. To take the mask off is an act of courage. It is an act of God.

It took most of my life to reach the level of consciousness for which my soul yearned, and it might not have happened if I had not taken the course in clinical pastoral education, but finally it was such thoughts as these, about stripping off our masks and escaping our fears, that enabled me to stand at the graveside of my dad sixty-three years after his death and talk to him. Today I can still close my eyes and return to that moment. It is 1993, a sunny day in Virginia. The cemetery is called Hollywood, a name that goes back long before the city in California, and there is a great irony in the coincidence that the world's movie capital, which we mockingly call Tinseltown, has the same name as this venerable old cemetery where Jefferson Davis and twenty-six generals of the Confederate army lie. It strikes me as a further irony that my father, who was buried in shame because of his suicide, rests among those others whom Southerners to this day honor as heroes of the American Confederacy. The sun shines brilliantly down upon ancient oak trees, and a breeze causes the leaves to flutter, making the shadows dance against the green lawn.

I walk slowly from one grave to another. Behind and to the left of my father's grave is the grave of his younger brother Horace, who died of a ruptured appendix in his early twenties. I have seen his picture, a handsome young man with black hair, looking enough like me to be my brother. On his tombstone are the words

HORACE COLLINGSWORTH BARNES
SON OF ROBERT L. AND GERTRUDE BARNES
MARCH 18, 1893—DECEMBER 21, 1918
IN GOD'S CARE

To the right are the graves of my grandparents, and at the top of their stone in large letters is the name BARNES. Below that is engraved IN LOVING MEMORY and their names, and below that, GOD IS LOVE. It is on every grave all the way back to my great-great-grandfather. It strikes me that on my dad's grave there are no such words of love or family connectedness, and no mention of God. On my dad's grave are only his name and the dates of his birth and death:

ROBERT HARDY BARNES
APRIL 3, 1883—FEBRUARY 17, 1930

The obvious implication is that my dad's suicide separated him from his family.

The cemetery lies on a slope running down to the James River, and on this day, at this moment, it is quiet. The only other living person within my view is June, who wanders among the rows of grave markers nearby, exploring. It is now, with a sense that my father has been wronged after death, that I fix my eyes on his stone, on his name, and address him.

"Dad," I say, "you were unfairly separated from your family and your soul was rejected. All the members of our family have words of God's grace on their tombstones except you. At the time of your death, the souls of your sisters and your parents, as well as the soul of my mother, were blocked in grieving and confusion and disbelief. They failed to express on your tombstone what was in their hearts.

"Your five sisters have told me how much they loved you and what a wonderful brother you were. You were an honest and successful businessperson, a good father and husband. You and I had only ten years together, but I remember walking with you on the golf course. You let me carry one or two clubs, and I felt important. I remember, too, when you took me out to Byrd Park along with my sister, and we rolled down the hill from the water reservoir, laughing. I know you loved me—still love me—even if you never used that word.

"I confess that, like others in our family, I have been ashamed of what you did and carried the secret of it as a heavy stone. Now as I stand here feeling close to you and knowing that you hear my words, I am no longer ashamed of you. The secret is no more. I tell you, in the presence of all these lovely trees and the Confederate generals whom we honor, that I love you. I now have only a deep feeling of sorrow and sympathetic love for you. My own heavy stone has rolled away, and I feel the soft comfort of peace taking its place.

"I promise that I will have more words added to your tombstone, words that connect you to me and words that express the connection we all have to God's grace. I will now let you go, dear Father, knowing that you are loved by God. We are both free at last."

At this, I ran to find June and told her what had just happened. She saw the tears in my eyes and gave me a warm, loving hug.

Dad's youngest sister, Aunt Lucille, was still alive, a feisty little woman in her nineties. We showed her the graves, and she went with us to the engraver's shop across the street from Hollywood Cemetery, where she insisted on haggling with the man, an old fellow with callused hands gray from stone dust. Several months later, June and I returned, along with Aunt Lucille, to see the results. They were as we had requested. Today and forever, my dad's tombstone reads:

ROBERT HARDY BARNES
APRIL 3, 1883—FEBRUARY 17, 1930
BELOVED FATHER
OF
ROBERT HARDY BARNES, JR.
SALLY BARNES LINK
GRANT HIM GRACE

Now my image of Dad is different. No longer do I see him from over the rim of the casket, his waxy face in profile. Now I see him whole. His face is smiling, and his soul is alive. When I join him in death, I shall see him even more sharply. When he recognizes me, he will jump up and down for joy. He gives me a welcoming hug and tells me he loves me. We are one soul, united in the grace of reconciliation. Thanks Be to God.

Epilogue: Crossing the River—No Mask, No Shame, No Secret

...From earliest times, sages have insisted that to see reality one must die and be reborn.

—Ernest Becker, The Denial of Death

Out of the believer's heart shall flow rivers of living water.

—John 7: 35

The river to the other side will be dark. There will be rippling sounds as the boat crosses over. The oarsman is tall and lean, and you will not see his face clearly. You will sit in the middle of the boat. You will no longer be dying, no longer fearful. Your body will have disappeared, the body that had become *not you*. The pain will have stopped. You won't have to do anything. The oarsman knows what he is doing. He will protect you, and you will feel his love.

It will be peaceful sitting on the boat. You will see yourself from above as a fragile light reflected white in the water.

In the distance, through the dark night, a light beckons. The oarsman steers the boat in that direction. You will be surrounded by love, and you will not look back. You do not speak with the oarsman. You are one, as if you have known each other from ancient times.

When you reach the other side, your soul emerges from the white light and you become aware of a loving hand that reaches to help you. You leave the boat and enter a state of perfect peace: the peace, as it has been said, that passes all understanding.

◆   ◆   ◆

I am lying on my bed. My head is turned so I can see out the low window. Our maple trees have no leaves now, but the cedar and pine are as green as ever. Through the branches, I see down the slope into my neighbors' back yard. I have the sense of being in a tree house, and I can watch what is happening on the ground without being seen. There is a swing set in bright colors, pink and yellow and orange plastic, and I remember when the little girl sat in the swing and her dad pushed her. With the window open, I could hear her laughing. When she is my age, I will have been dead for…how many years? She will be an old woman.

There are more children. Across the street from the front of our townhouse is a Catholic school. I used to watch them as their mothers or dads brought them, and I thought about playing street hockey back in Richmond.

A siren sounds, not far away. We live near Children's Hospital, and nearly every day ambulances speed down Sand Point Way with a sick or injured child. I, an old man, am lying on my deathbed while a child suffers, too. I think of Courtney and Kerry, my granddaughters, who were born with respiratory distress syndrome. I think of my baby daughter Sarah, and I pinch my eyes shut. But Courtney and Kerry survived. Their lives were saved in the hospital when they were tiny. Maybe the child in the ambulance will be saved, too.

I open my eyes again and I am confused. Was I sleeping? For a minute, I do not recognize the room I am in, but then it becomes clearer. This is the townhouse. June and I moved here when we felt it was time to slow down. I think now about the house on East Blaine Street, where we lived for forty-nine years. There, my bedroom had a view down to Lake Union, with the Aurora Bridge and Queen Anne Hill in the background. If I close my eyes again, I see it. A seaplane climbs slowly off the lake, gaining altitude to clear the bridge. A sailboat and a motorboat head into the canal, passing far beneath the bridge. There were times when I wondered if the bridge, the canal, and the seaplanes would still be there after I was gone. In my room in the townhouse distant from Lake Union, I hear a familiar buzz outside. I cannot see it, but it is a small plane and it is flying toward Lake Union.

Where has everyone gone? Sometimes they are here, and they make such a fuss over me that I wish they would go away. But now, I am alone. I see the telephone pole outside. People must be talking to each other; their voices travel along the wire. Who is talking to whom? Nobody is talking to me.

My medication is good but I have some pain, and I am frightened. Who cares for the doctor when his body is tired and he feels alone? Will someone be with me when I go to the other side?

I put my hands together and think a prayer. Where is God? If only I had an intimate relationship with Him. If only I could see Him. Even the sense of His presence might dispel this loneliness, this fear, but I cannot summon it. I am about to leave a reality that I know—a reality I can touch, see, and smell. Is there another reality? I wish God were here to tell me.

Once I met a priest in Jerusalem who contracted hepatitis-C. He knew he was dying and he said, "I will soon find out if what I've been preaching all my life is true."

He meant resurrection. Did he find the life everlasting?

I take a breath and turn inward. Let all thoughts float down the river, like a beaver passing by. Silence sets in, a peaceful silence.

Images appear. Old images. The dream so vivid, of Christ hugging me in the hospital room, on the AIDS ward. Again, he rises from the bed, and his dark eyes look into mine. Again, I back out the door and glance down the corridor to where the little Christmas tree sits on the nurses' desk, lights aglow. I turn and knock on a door. In the room is a patient with black scabs on his arms. His eyeballs are sunken, his face is pale, and he burns with fever. I touch his scabs with both of my hands. He is dying, like me. My loneliness drifts away, like a morning fog in the valley when the sun rises over the mountain.

Now I am sitting at John Leffler's bedside, and he is smiling. "I am free at last! No one can take away my martinis or cigarettes."

He closes his eyes. His lips are dry and cracked. But suddenly he sits up and says, "Bob, tell them I died like a Christian."

He slumps back onto the pillow.

"I will, John."

I see myself standing at the lectern, giving a eulogy. My voice resonates in the vast space, flies through the air, and settles down at the bank of a river. John is there, and he is holding my hand. We feel the Presence.

◆   ◆   ◆

In my room is a collage that I created by superimposing photographs onto squares cut from a large abstract painting. A photo of me as a toddler, in a sailor suit. My harmonica, representing the fool in me—I used to play it while wearing a funny hat. A mink bow tie, given to me by the furrier from whom I bought June a mink coat when we were young. The Bishop's Cross, a medal presented to me by the Diocese. And my dad's pocket watch. I still have the actual watch, with the initials "RHB" engraved on the back.

These objects in the photos are my treasures. My art instructor, Margaret, had asked me to collect five valuable things that I couldn't live without.

"Okay, now give them to me," she said.

"Will you give them back?" I said.

"Forget them. We're going to paint," she said.

The objective was for me to get rid of the things I was most attached to, in order to free my creative energies. It worked. Margaret took my things and helped me paint. Later, she brought my treasures back into the studio. They became part of what I was working on. When I finished the collage, Margaret returned my treasures to me; in the meantime, I had learned to let them go.

◆   ◆   ◆

Bishop Lewis, whom we called a saint, lies on his left side. His eyes are shut, and there is a blanket pulled up below his chin. I see him today as I saw him dying decades ago, and he is still smiling.

I understand now what he tried to teach me then, when I was not ready to learn. In those last days he did not preach to me, he only gave me a book titled *By Means of Death*. Much later, I read it. It is about the meaning of Christ's death, and now I realize it is about mine, too, about how death gives life its value. Bill Lewis wanted me to know he was letting go of the journey we call life, letting go of the things he had accumulated, and letting go of his anxieties. He let it all go willingly. To let go of our earthly life is to achieve oneness with God.

The Bishop smiles at me; he knows I'm getting it. He radiates courage, and it becomes a part of me forever. I give thanks for his life and for God's gift to me through him.

I see what has been happening. The Holy Spirit has come to me. I have seen again the image of Jesus, and I have communed with those I once accompanied to the river's edge. My questions have been answered. I know who cares for the doctor when his body is tired. God is telling me I have never been alone.

Outside, it is the time of the year when nature seems to be resting. I think about our old place on East Blaine Street and picture the garden where June spent so many days. I picture the deck on the garage roof, overlooking the garden. It is *this* time of year, the time when nature hides its great beauty. In the middle of the deck is the black iron furniture, and the chaise longue rests in one corner. There are flower boxes on three sides. They are empty except for dead, brown stems left over from the summer. The umbrella over the table has been taken down and stored in the basement. Did I do that, or did June? I wonder if I will be here when buds appear on the styrax trees, and when the warmer weather brings tulips, azaleas, and honeysuckle. Red, yellow, purple, rust.

In my mind, I hear a word: *resurrection.* Yes, I am dying, but I remember the garden's summer beauty. The garden will flower again. Whether I will flower again is not for me to say. Only time will tell. Until then, it is a mystery

John and Pat Stanford are sitting on the deck. How can that be? John is dead. His two sisters are there. His closest friend from Philadelphia is there, and his two sons, Steve and Scott. And June and I. I am not in my body but somewhere above, looking down at us. I blink, and we are all in a hospital room. John, John, my dear friend. Why are you lying in that bed jaundiced, passing in and out of consciousness? His lips twitch, and his brown eyes open wide. "Bob," he says, "we've got to get busy on that book, *The Devil at the Bishop's Open.*" I take his hand.

All is clear to me now. John and I held hands as he crossed the river. He will be there when it is my turn. I have the thought that God, through his love, will assign John to be my ferryman. I may not recognize him in the shadows, but his giant hand will help me board. He will again help me off the boat, and as we come out of the darkness, I will see that beautiful smile once more.

◆   ◆   ◆

At the river's edge, my family gathers. June, Julie, Bob, and Andrew. Debbie, Buster, Courtney, and Kerry. Tucker and her daughter, Sara. My sister, Sally. Our Kerry blue terrier, Tory. I sit close to the river, facing it. June comes forward. She stands in front of me for a moment and then sits down gracefully, her back to the river. She extends both hands toward me, palms up. I reach out and hold her hands from below. I feel her wedding ring.

Together, we say, "It was good, wasn't it."

She kisses me and says, "I love you."

June moves aside and each of the others comes forward, kisses me, and repeats, "I love you."

Tory is the last. She wags her tail and barks. I hold my hands out, and Tory licks them. Tucker leads her away. Tory squats to pee on the ground, and we all laugh.

The ferryman has waited patiently. I stand up, and June helps me board.

"Someday, we shall cross the river and join you," she says.

We smile, and the boat pushes off from the shore into the shadows. A light shines in the distance, ahead of us. The little boy in the blue suit begins to see the face of his father. The living face, not the face in the coffin.

About the Author

Robert Hardy Barnes grew up in Richmond, Virginia, during the Great Depression and was graduated from the Virginia Military Institute in 1940. He received the Doctor of Medicine degree from the Medical College of Virginia and served as a military psychiatrist during World War II. After residencies at the Virginia Mason Hospital in Seattle and the Joslin Clinic in Boston, Dr. Barnes moved permanently to Seattle, where he and his wife June have lived for more than 50 years.

Dr. Barnes's success as a specialist in internal medicine earned him an appointment as Clinical Associate Professor of Medicine at the University of Washington's renowned School of Medicine. He changed careers in midlife, however, to open a pioneering health-care consultancy business. Five decades after his father's suicide, Bob suffered a serious depression; pulling out of it, he decided to become a pastoral counselor. This latest stage in his professional development has opened his eyes and led him through a profound process of self-discovery. Bob's hard-earned wisdom qualifies him to write with authority and passion about reconciling with the past, living in the present, and facing the future with grace and confidence.

0-595-31575-5

CPSIA information can be obtained
at www.ICGtesting.com
Printed in the USA
FSHW02n1249241018
53258FS

9 780595 315758